INFORMAL LEARNING AT WORK

Informal Learning at Work reflects the growing interest in changing the way the workplace encourages and enhances learning and professional development. Due to societal, economic, and technological developments, organisations face the pressure of growing knowledge-intensity and the need for innovations. As a result, employees are expected to adapt to new situations and constantly update their skillsets within an increasingly challenging environment.

This book brings together cross-disciplinary perspectives from leading international researchers, drawing on a range of theoretical and empirical studies.

Extensively researched and expertly edited, this new addition to the EARLI *New Perspectives on Learning and Instruction* series outlines the starting points for future research, and highlights the benefits and implications for those aiming to foster informal learning at work, covering areas such as:

- professional judgement
- improving the structure of work tasks
- facilitating innovative work behaviour
- the place of informal learning within teaching.

Informal Learning at Work presents original quantitative and qualitative studies as well as integrative analyses of worldwide research and is an invaluable introduction to this highly topical subject.

Gerhard Messmann is Assistant Professor at the Chair for Vocational Education and Training and Learning in Organisations at the Institute of Educational Science, University of Regensburg, Germany.

Mien Segers is Professor of Corporate Learning at the Department of Educational Research and Development, Maastricht University, The Netherlands.

Filip Dochy is Professor of Research on Learning & Development and Corporate Training at the Center for Professional Learning & Development, Corporate Training and Lifelong Learning, KU Leuven, Belgium.

New Perspectives on Learning and Instruction
Editor in Chief – Mien Segers (Maastricht University – The Netherlands)
Assistant Editor – Isabel Raemdonck (Université catholique de Louvain – Belgium)

Editorial Board members
David Gijbels (University of Antwerp – Belgium)
Sanna Järvelä (University of Oulu – Finland)
Margareta Limon (Autonoma University of Madrid – Spain)
Karen Littleton (The Open University – UK)
Wolff-Michael Roth (University of Victoria – Canada)

Advisory Board Members
Costas Constantinou (University of Cyprus – Cyprus)
Veléria Csépe (Hungarian Academy of Sciences – Hungary)
Sibel Erduran (University of Bristol – UK)
Sylvia Rojas-Drummond (UNAM – Mexico)
Martin Valcke (Ghent University – Belgium)
Lieven Verschaffel (Katholieke Universiteit Leuven – Belgium)
Kate Wall (Newcastle University – UK)
Marold Wosnitza (Murdoch University – Australia)

New Perspectives on Learning and Instruction is published by Routledge in conjunction with EARLI (European Association for Research on Learning and Instruction). This series publishes cutting-edge international research focusing on all aspects of learning and instruction in both traditional and non-traditional educational settings. Titles published within the series take a broad and innovative approach to topical areas of research, are written by leading international researchers and are aimed at a research and post-graduate student audience.

Also available:

Interpersonal Regulation of Learning and Motivation
Edited by Simone Volet and Marja Vauras

Affective Learning Together
Michael Baker, Jerry Andriessen and Sanna Järvelä

Learning Patterns in Higher Education
Edited by David Gijbels, Vincent Donche, John T. E. Richardson and Jan D. Vermunt

Multi-dimensional Transitions of International Students to Higher Education
Edited by Divya Jindal-Snape and Bart Rienties

Informal Learning at Work: Triggers, Antecedents, and Consequences
Edited by Gerhard Messmann, Mien Segers, and Filip Dochy

For a full list of titles, please visit: https://www.routledge.com/New-Perspectives-on-Learning-and-Instruction/book-series/EARLI

INFORMAL LEARNING AT WORK

Triggers, Antecedents, and Consequences

Edited by
Gerhard Messmann,
Mien Segers, and Filip Dochy

LONDON AND NEW YORK

First published 2018
by Routledge
2 Park Square, Milton Park, Abingdon, Oxon OX14 4RN

and by Routledge
711 Third Avenue, New York, NY 10017

Routledge is an imprint of the Taylor & Francis Group, an informa business

© 2018 selection and editorial matter, Gerhard Messmann,
Mien Segers, Filip Dochy; individual chapters, the contributors

The right of Gerhard Messmann, Mien Segers, and Filip Dochy to be identified as the authors of the editorial material, and of the authors for their individual chapters, has been asserted in accordance with sections 77 and 78 of the Copyright, Designs and Patents Act 1988.

All rights reserved. No part of this book may be reprinted or reproduced or utilised in any form or by any electronic, mechanical, or other means, now known or hereafter invented, including photocopying and recording, or in any information storage or retrieval system, without permission in writing from the publishers.

Trademark notice: Product or corporate names may be trademarks or registered trademarks, and are used only for identification and explanation without intent to infringe.

British Library Cataloguing in Publication Data
A catalogue record for this book is available from the British Library

Library of Congress Cataloging in Publication Data
A catalog record for this book has been applied for

ISBN: 978-1-138-21659-4 (hbk)
ISBN: 978-1-138-21660-0 (pbk)
ISBN: 978-1-315-44196-2 (ebk)

Typeset in Bembo
by Keystroke, Neville Lodge, Tettenhall, Wolverhampton

CONTENTS

List of illustrations   *vii*
List of contributors   *ix*
Preface   *xiii*
Acknowledgements   *xv*

1   **Emergence, theoretical foundation, and conceptualisation of informal learning at work**   1
    Mien Segers, Gerhard Messmann, and Filip Dochy

2   **Antecedents of informal workplace learning: a theoretical study**   12
    Eva Kyndt, Natalie Govaerts, Kelly Smet, and Filip Dochy

3   **Effects of complexity of work tasks on informal learning at work in the IT domain**   40
    Katrin Hirschmann and Regina H. Mulder

4   **Deliberate practice as a lever for professional judgement: lessons from informal workplace learning**   63
    Therese Grohnert, Roger Meuwissen, and Wim H. Gijselaers

5   **Informal learning at work as a facilitator of employees' innovative work behaviour**   80
    Maike Gerken, Gerhard Messmann, Dominik E. Froehlich, Simon A. J. Beausaert, Regina H. Mulder, and Mien Segers

6 **Vital but neglected: the informal learning of new teachers in Scotland** 100
Rachel Shanks

7 **The potential and paradox of informal learning** 134
David Boud and Donna Rooney

8 **Informal learning at work: what do we know more and understand better?** 153
Herman Baert

Index *188*

ILLUSTRATIONS

Figures

1.1	Formal and informal learning defined on five continua	7
3.1	Less complex work task vignette	52
3.2	Complex work task vignette	52
4.1	The relationship between information search and judgement accuracy	72
4.2	The relationship between information search and judgement accuracy by the interaction between task experience and deliberate practice	74
5.1	Standardised estimates for effects of learning from others and background characteristics on innovative work behaviour	89
5.2	Standardised estimates for effects of innovation-specific reflection on innovative work behaviour	92
6.1	Age of respondents by gender (questionnaire one, year one)	108
6.2	Age of respondents by gender (questionnaire two, year one)	109
6.3	Active and passive participants	122
6.4	Antecedents, triggers, and consequences of new teachers' informal learning at work	124
8.1	The sliding scale of informal and formal learning	160
8.2	Influencing factors for learning at work	164
8.3	Process factors of learning at work	173
8.4	Working and learning: embedded activities	174
8.5	Context factors that influence learning at work	175
8.6	Learning at work: a theoretical framework – revisited	178

Tables

2.1	Factors that inhibit or promote informal learning	17
3.1	Extent of agreement with the question "what would you do" to solve the described trigger for informal learning at work (mean, standard deviation, and Mann-Whitney-U-Test)	55
4.1	Descriptives	71
4.2	Correlations	72
5.1	Descriptive statistics and correlations for learning from others and innovative work behaviour	88
5.2	Multiple hierarchical regression analysis	89
5.3	Descriptive statistics and correlations for reflection and innovative work behaviour	92
6.1	Visual model for mixed methods sequential explanatory design	104
6.2	How have you been learning to be a teacher in your induction year? (questionnaire two, year one)	109
6.3	Three most useful experiences (questionnaire one, year two)	111
6.4	Percentages of respondents rating specific activities as very important (questionnaire two, year two)	112
7.1	Identification of practices that generate learning informally	141
8.1	Learning conditions: categories and items	167
8.2	Context factors and variables that influence informal learning at work	168
8.3	Possible outcomes or consequences of informal workplace learning	170
8.4	Factors and variables with an impact on learning at work – revisited	176

Appendices

2.1	Literature search	32
2.2	Critical appraisal of qualitative research	33
2.3	Critical appraisal of quantitative research	34
2.4	Overview of the categories, subthemes and codes of barriers and facilitators of informal learning	35
6.1	Coding glossary	128

CONTRIBUTORS

Herman Baert, Center for Professional Learning & Development, Corporate Training and Lifelong Learning, KU Leuven, Belgium.

Herman Baert has a PhD in educational sciences. He is Emeritus Professor of the University of Leuven (Belgium) at the Center for Research on Professional Learning & Development, Corporate Training and Lifelong Learning. His fields of research and expertise are policies and strategies of lifelong learning and human resources development in formal and informal contexts.

Simon A. J. Beausaert, Department of Educational Research and Development, School of Business and Economics, Maastricht University, the Netherlands.

Dr Simon Beausaert is Associate Professor in the field of workplace learning at Maastricht University, the Netherlands. His current research focuses on supporting (in)formal learning and assessment for learning in the workplace, and their relation with employees' professional development, employability and innovative working behaviour.

David Boud, Centre For Research In Assessment And Digital Learning, Deakin University, Geelong, Australia; Faculty of Arts and Social Sciences, University of Technology Sydney, Australia; and Institute for Work Based Learning, Middlesex University, London, United Kingdom.

David Boud is Professor and Director of the Centre for Research in Assessment and Digital Learning, Deakin University, Melbourne. He is also Professor Emeritus in the Faculty of Arts and Social Sciences, University of Technology Sydney and Research Professor in the Institute for Work Based Learning, Middlesex University, London.

Filip Dochy, Center for Professional Learning & Development, Corporate Training and Lifelong Learning, KU Leuven, Belgium.

Filip Dochy is Full Professor of Research on Learning & Development and Corporate Training at the Center for Professional Learning & Development, Corporate Training and Lifelong Learning (KU Leuven – University of Leuven, Belgium). His research focuses on L&D, team learning, and high-impact learning that lasts (HILL). He is a Past President of EARLI, the European Association for Research on Learning & Instruction (www.earli.org). He is also Founding Editor of the *Educational Research Review* and *Frontline Learning Research*. He is currently the Editor of *Frontline Learning Research* and he is a member of the European Academy of Science.

Dominik E. Froehlich, Department of Education, University of Vienna, Austria.

Dominik E. Froehlich is a postdoctoral researcher at the University of Vienna. His research focuses on themes such as methodology in education and learning research – especially social network analysis and mixed methods – and learning in the workplace, age and work, innovation, and employability.

Maike Gerken, Witten Institute for Family Business, Faculty of Management and Economics, University of Witten/Herdecke, Germany.

Maike Gerken is a post-doctoral researcher in the field of learning and organisation in Family Firms. She received her PhD in informal learning, employability, and innovation at the workplace at Maastricht University. Her current research interests focus on resource management and learning processes for strategic decision making in family businesses.

Wim H. Gijselaers, Department of Educational Research and Development, School of Business and Economics, Maastricht University, the Netherlands.

Wim H. Gijselaers is Full Professor of Educational Research in the Department of Educational Research and Development at the School of Business and Economics of Maastricht University; email w.gijselaers@maastrichtuniversity.nl. His research focuses on professional development, sharing expertise within teams, and expertise development in business. He received his PhD in Education from Maastricht University. Currently, he is chief editor of the Springer book series 'Innovation and Change in Professional Education'.

Natalie Govaerts, Center for Professional Learning & Development, Corporate Training and Lifelong Learning, KU Leuven, Belgium.

Natalie Govaerts is a PhD Candidate at the Center for Research on Professional Learning & Development, Corporate Training and Lifelong Learning (KU Leuven – University of Leuven, Belgium). Her PhD research focuses on the role of the supervisor in facilitating employees' transfer of training to the workplace. Her other research interests include informal workplace learning, learning intentions, and learning patterns in the workplace.

Therese Grohnert, Department of Educational Research and Development, School of Business and Economics, Maastricht University, the Netherlands.

Therese Grohnert is a post-doctoral researcher at the Department of Educational Research and Development at Maastricht University, School of Business and Economics; email t.grohnert@maastrichtuniversity.nl. Her research interests include judgement and decision making – especially overconfidence, workplace learning – especially from errors, and expertise development.

Katrin Hirschmann, Quality Management and Coordination of Studies and Teaching, University of Regensburg, Germany.

Dr Katrin Hirschmann was formerly researcher at the Institute for Educational Science at the University of Regensburg and works now in the field of quality management at the University of Regensburg, Germany. Her research focused on informal learning at work and triggers of informal learning at work.

Eva Kyndt, Center for Professional Learning & Development, Corporate Training and Lifelong Learning, KU Leuven, Belgium.

Eva Kyndt, PhD is Assistant Professor (tenure track) at the Center for Research on Professional Learning & Development, Corporate Training and Lifelong Learning (KU Leuven – University of Leuven, Belgium). Her research focuses on workplace learning, approaches to learning, learning climate and the transition from education to work. She is past coordinator of SIG 4 Higher Education (2011–15) and current coordinator of SIG 14 Learning and Professional Development (2017–21) of the European Association for Research on Learning and Instruction (EARLI).

Gerhard Messmann, Institute of Educational Science, University of Regensburg, Germany.

Dr Gerhard Messmann is Assistant Professor at the Institute of Educational Science at the University of Regensburg, Germany. His research interests include innovative work behaviour, informal learning at work, and instructional design.

Roger Meuwissen, Accounting & Information Management, School of Business and Economics, Maastricht University, the Netherlands.

Roger Meuwissen is Full Professor of Control and Auditing at Maastricht University School of Business and Economics; email r.meuwissen@maastricht university.nl. He is the author of several articles in academic journals and co-author of several textbooks on Internal Control and Accounting Information Systems. Currently, he is also a member of the editorial board of *Accounting Education* and director of the Maastricht Accounting, Auditing & Information Management Research Center (MARC).

Regina H. Mulder, Institute of Educational Science, University of Regensburg, Germany.

Regina H. Mulder is Full Professor of Pedagogy/Educational Science at the University of Regensburg. Her research interests include a variety of topics in vocational education and training (VET) and on learning in organisations, such as evaluation of training, teachers' and trainers' professionalism, innovative work behaviour, informal learning at work, feedback, learning from errors, and team learning.

Donna Rooney, Adult Learning and Applied Linguistics, University of Technology Sydney Australia.

Donna Rooney is a researcher/lecturer at the University of Technology Sydney. Her research focuses on adult learning in a variety of settings: communities, organisations, workplaces, and higher education institutes. She makes use of a number of conceptual resources including practice and other sociomaterial theories.

Mien Segers, Department of Educational Research and Development, School of Business and Economics, Maastricht University, the Netherlands.

Mien Segers is Professor of Corporate Learning at the Department of Educational Research and Development, Maastricht University. Her research addresses tools and conditions to support learning in school settings as well as in the workplace, with a special focus on the role of assessment for enhancing development.

Rachel Shanks, School of Education, University of Aberdeen, Scotland.

Rachel Shanks is a Senior Lecturer at the University of Aberdeen. She has been a law lecturer, employment rights adviser, trade union lifelong-learning project co-ordinator and adult educator. Her research focuses on community learning, professional learning, and the use of educational technology. She is co-editor of the journal *Education in the North*.

Kelly Smet, Center for Professional Learning & Development, Corporate Training and Lifelong Learning, KU Leuven, Belgium.

Kelly Smet is a PhD candidate at the Center for Research on Professional Learning & Development, Corporate Training and Lifelong Learning (KU Leuven – University of Leuven, Belgium). In her PhD research, she focuses on the work context as a possible antecedent, and perceived employability as a possible outcome, of work-related learning.

PREFACE

Due to societal, economic, and technological developments, organisations are confronted with increasing knowledge-intensity and need for innovations. As a consequence, they expect their employees to flexibly adapt to new situations and tasks and develop the necessary competences. Besides formal training, growing attention has therefore been devoted to informal learning at work, that is, all activities carried out in order to facilitate the accomplishment of one's work tasks. The book aims at reflecting this interest in informal learning at work by integrating the work of scholars who have been studying learning processes of professionals intensively and who provide current investigations which approach the topic from different angles and with different methodologies.

The book provides empirical evidence concerning research questions about (1) triggers of informal learning such as specific characteristics of tasks, about (2) relevant antecedents of informal learning such as characteristics of employees and of the work environment, and about (3) beneficial consequences of informal learning such as proper decision-making processes and innovative task accomplishment.

Providing state-of-the-art research on informal learning, the book therefore outlines starting points for future research and draws implications for practitioners in all kinds of organisations concerning ways of fostering informal learning at work.

ACKNOWLEDGEMENTS

We would like to thank all our colleagues who supported us in the peer-review process of this book and whose invaluable comments and suggestions significantly contributed to the quality of the book.

1

EMERGENCE, THEORETICAL FOUNDATION, AND CONCEPTUALISATION OF INFORMAL LEARNING AT WORK

Mien Segers,[1] Gerhard Messmann,[2] and Filip Dochy[3]

For many decades the topic of Learning and Development of professionals has been on the agenda of chief learning officers, learning consultants, professional trainers, managers, and staff members of human resource (HR) and human resource development (HRD) departments as well as scholars in the academic community. To an increasing extent, Learning and Development is defined and implemented as a valuable resource for organisational and employee success. The rise of interests in Learning and Development is linked to work and organisational developments in Western countries, in particular to the transition from an industrial to a post-industrial society. Its conceptualisation in terms of why, what, how, and for whom has been evolving correspondingly.

In rural society with limited school attendance and the phenomenon that most of the working-class population had to learn their job by doing, a well-developed system of apprenticeship offered important learning opportunities. Later on, this system of workplace learning – and the experiential knowledge about this system that was available – lost its status and was overruled by the upcoming formal school system. In industrial society, the core reason for providing Learning and Development was to ensure that employees possess the knowledge and skills they need for carrying out their daily work tasks. However, as organisations were confronted with increasing knowledge-intensity and need for innovations due to societal, economic, and technological developments, the work tasks became more and more complex. Consequently, organisations expected their employees to develop the necessary knowledge and skills for flexibly adapting to and anticipating the rapidly changing

1 Maastricht University, The Netherlands
2 University of Regensburg, Germany
3 KU Leuven, Belgium

requirements of complex work situations and tasks. This was achieved through proper and systematic implementation of employee Training and Development programmes. The need for Training and Development was determined by the employee's knowledge and skills deficiency or obsolescence with respect to the work tasks to be conducted. These work tasks were defined as specifically as possible (see the 'scientific organisation and management' ideology), and therefore, a narrow conception of skills training was the mainstream approach and Skinner's theory of learning as drill offered a rationale.

The transition to a post-industrial society was characterised by a high value on knowledge as the source of innovation and competitive advantage. Organisations had to deal with knowledge and technological advancements at an even faster speed than before, as well as with increasing global competitiveness. Certainly, these more complex processes and products required another concept of learning than the previous skills training. With respect to the ongoing changes organisations are facing, Roffe argued:

> They [the changes] are discontinuous and not part of a pattern; it is the little, unnoticed changes that make the biggest differences to our lives and the change in the way we work will make the biggest difference to the way we live; and discontinuous change requires discontinuous "upside-down" thinking to deal with it.
>
> *1999: 224*

In this context of discontinuous change, employees are described as the organisations' main asset: they help the organisation to accomplish successive growth and make it possible that current and forthcoming changes are turned into opportunities for realising a competitive advantage. In the same vein, new concepts with respect to work organisation have become popular, such as functional flexibility, stressing the importance of employees who can fulfil different tasks, roles, and functions to meet ongoing changes in their daily work (Van Den Berg & Van Der Velde, 2005).

The new landscape described above has been slowly influencing organisations' human resource management (HRM) systems. Based on a literature review, Soderquist, Papalexandris, Ioannou, and Prastacos (2010) argue that current "HRM processes need to be centred on the flexible and dynamic deployment of employees' competences, rather than on task-related and pre-defined sets of qualifications, as traditionally has been the case" (p. 326). Today, the key question refers to the competences that superior performers possess in order to successfully execute a range of activities (e.g., in projects, inter-functional teams, or problem-solving task forces): "In this context, competences differ from KSAOs (Knowledge, Skills, Abilities, and Other characteristics) in that they shift the level of analysis from the job and its associated tasks, to the person and what he or she is capable of" (p. 327).

The transition from job-based HRM systems to competence-based HRM systems has been reinforcing the re-conceptualisation of Learning and Development in organisations. It is argued that Leaning and Development practices should encompass a wider variety of learning opportunities for employees than traditional Training and Development programmes (e.g., Manuti, Pastore, Scardigno, Giancaspro, & Morciano, 2015). In this respect, the concepts of workplace learning and work-related learning became popular again, but in a different context than before in the rural society. For Manuti et al. (2015), workplace learning refers to "the process that engages individuals in training programmes, education and development courses as well as experiential learning for the purpose of acquiring and/or implementing competences necessary to meet organisational demands" (p. 134). A similar definition is proposed by Kyndt and Baert who define work-related learning as

> ... the engagement in formal and informal learning activities both on and off the job, whereby employees and groups of employees acquire and/or improve competences (integrated knowledge, skills, and attitudes) that change individuals' present and future professional achievement (and eventually also their career) and organisational performance.
>
> *2013, p. 275*

Theoretical foundations of learning for and at work

The trend towards broadening the scope of employee development from a focus on training to an increasing consideration of the workplace as a resource for work-related learning is reflected in the learning theories that have been developed or adopted to address learning for and at work since the 1970s until today (Dochy, Gijbels, Segers, & Van den Bossche, 2011).

Foundational theories of learning for and at work

During the 1970s and 1980s, in order to explain learning behaviours and processes of adults/professionals, pivotal scholars such as Kolb, Mezirow, and Schön developed learning theories which became prominent in the workplace learning literature. Kolb's (1984) experiential learning theory (which was first presented in 1975 and further developed in the 1990s) describes experience as a main source of learning and outlines multiple interdependent sources and paths of making and processing experiences. In a similar vein, Mezirow's (1990) transformational learning theory (which was first articulated in 1978 and further developed in the 1990s) focuses on meaning making, and addresses experience and corresponding critical reflection as core learning processes. Likewise, Schön (1983) emphasises the importance of reflection by introducing reflection-in-action. Portraying the reflective practitioner, he describes the rather intuitive behaviour of professionals when they adjust their actions immediately as they happen. In addition, building on Kolb's theory, Boud and Walker (1990) stress reflection as one of the key processes in learning from experience. Moreover, in the 1990s, Lave and Wenger (1991) provided a socio-cultural perspective on learning. Their situated learning theory depicts learning as an integral and inseparable part of social practice taking place in the real world.

In addition to the domain of adult and workplace learning, other strands of research provide theoretical perspectives on workplace learning, for example cognitive theories of information processing. In his theory of the Adaptive Control of Thought, Anderson (1982) presents a stage model relating to the development of professional performance through the acquisition, compilation, and tuning of knowledge and skills. Also focusing on professional performance, the theory of case-based reasoning by Kolodner (1992) describes how individuals can adjust and improve their levels of knowledge and performance through a cyclical process of retrieving, reusing, revising, and retaining experiences with similar situations and tasks. Another example is the theory of deliberate practice developed in the domain of expertise development. Ericsson, Krampe, and Tesch-Römer (1993) provide an account which describes how people become professionals through deliberate practice, involving a concerted programme of excessive practice and guidance.

In addition to the aforementioned theories addressing individual professional learning, some theories focus on learning at the level of teams and organisations. A well-established example is the theory of expansive learning by Engeström (1987) which describes learning as a series of cycles, involving questioning existing standards of practice, analysing contradictions in practice, and modelling a vision for a zone of proximal development of practice. In addition, learning is defined as examining and implementing this new model of practice in organisational life in order to attain High Impact Learning that lasts (HILL) (Dochy & Segers, 2017). Likewise, in their theory of organisational learning, Argyris and Schön (1996) present two contrasting ways of coping with errors through reflection. That is, learning either includes the detection and correction of errors within the range of existing routines (i.e., single-loop learning), or it contains an additional evaluation (and potential re-definition) of underlying values, norms, and goals (i.e., double-loop learning).

Commonalities and complementarities among theories of learning for and at work

The outlined theories have many commonalities and/or are complementary regarding the phenomena they are able to explain. Firstly, all theories share the view that learning for and at work does not happen in isolation but is embedded within the context of daily work practice. This includes, on the one hand, an inextricable relation to the engagement in work tasks and, on the other hand, the relation to other persons with whom information is shared, problems are discussed, and solutions are created.

Secondly, with the exception of the outlined cognitive theories (i.e., Anderson, Kolodner), all theories more or less explicitly contain both concrete physical activities and cognitive activities (often termed "reflection"). While physical activities can be any learning activities that lead to new information or new experiences, cognitive activities refer to all mental operations through which individuals process information and experiences and, thus, actually learn in the sense of altering mental representations.

Thirdly, concerning complementarity, theories which take an activity perspective on learning (e.g., Kolb) lack an explication of the cognitive processes that take place when individuals reflect on new information or new experiences. This gap can be closed by theories which take a cognitive perspective on learning (e.g., Anderson). That is, these theories explicitly address the mental operations that take place when individuals reflect on existing information and experiences in order to facilitate the accomplishment of a current task or, subsequently, when they reflect on new information and experiences that result from their engagement in this current task.

Fourthly, a combined view of the theories shows the broad range of behaviours that immediately or indirectly refer to reflection. Different terms that are used in the theories to refer to reflection include critical reflection, reflective observation, reflection-in-action, single/double-loop-learning, or case-based reasoning. The theories thus inform about the variety of purposes for which reflection is used at work. These purposes of reflection may relate to aspects such as looking back versus looking ahead, examining products versus processes, or questioning something deeply versus at the surface.

Fifthly, the combination of the different theories also shows that learning for and at work is a cyclical process with different physical and corresponding mental or cognitive steps towards knowledge and performance development. This conjunction of physical and cognitive activities and, thus, of making and processing information and experiences is exemplified in learning behaviours such as critical questioning of practice, or detecting and analysing errors.

Sixthly, the theories are furthermore complementary in the sense that they do cover learning at different levels. That is, some theories focus on learning that takes place at the individual level (i.e., Anderson; Boud & Walker; Ericsson et al., Kolb, Kolodner, Mezirow, Schön), while other theories focus on learning at group and/or organisational level (i.e., Argyris & Schön; Engeström; Lave & Wenger).

Finally, one could state that the outlined theories are also complementary in the types of learning outcomes they address. Some theories tackle beliefs, meanings, and perspectives (including becoming more critical, reflective, and open; see Boud & Walker, Mezirow, Kolb). Others refer to knowledge and skills or competences as learning outcomes. A third group of theories is more concerned with the development of learning organisations, including the creation of new knowledge, the identification of new problems, and the development of innovative solutions for existing problems (i.e., Argyris & Schön, Engeström).

Although most of the above mentioned theories originated from the 1970s, '80s, and '90s, in research as well as in practice, activities encompassed in work-related learning have been mainly related to formal training. This is illustrated by the vast amount of research dedicated to the topic of transfer of training. Since the first review study on transfer of training by Baldwin and Ford (1988), more than thirty review studies have been published. However, as a consequence of the changing internal and external environment of organisations as described above, a growing number of scholarly as well as popular articles have stressed that people learn for work not only through formal education but by doing the job itself. Co-operating and interacting with colleagues, working with clients, coping with challenging and unfamiliar tasks, reflecting on and evaluating one's work experiences, and extra-work contexts make the daily work a rich learning environment (Dochy & Segers, 2017; Tynjälä, 2008). In this respect, the concept of informal learning has been stressed since the turn of the century and further developed beyond earlier uses as learning by doing and on-the-job training.

Defining informal learning at work

In the early 1990s, based on the aforementioned theoretical foundations, Marsick and Watkins (Marsick & Watkins, 1990; Watkins & Marsick, 1992) developed a model of informal learning. The core idea was that people learn from their experiences when they face a novel challenge. Given that their current understanding is not sufficient to deal with the challenge in an effective way, they have to look for alternative ways of interpreting and analysing the situation. In turn, they are in need of novel responses. A critical reflection on the results of using these novel responses in work practice leads to new insights that can be used when addressing novel problems in the future.

In summary, the model proposes a cyclical process with experience and reflection (i.e., double-loop learning) as key concepts. Moreover, in their revised model, Marsick, Volpe, and Watkins (1999) stressed the importance of the context. The context is the lens through which the learner interprets and frames the challenges observed, and chooses the novel responses, as well as evaluates the results of the actions taken. At the same time, the context can be seen as a macro-level trigger for interpreting events as critical incidents that evoke the learning process. The early work of Marsick and colleagues has inspired many scholars to define the concept of informal learning. In the next section, we will thus elaborate on the conceptualisation of informal learning by comparing it to formal learning.

Continua of formal and informal learning for and at work

Since its first introduction, many authors have proposed definitions or key features of informal learning (e.g., Froehlich, Beausaert, & Segers, 2015; Kyndt & Baert, 2013; Marsick &Watkins, 2001; Mulder, 2013; Noe, Tews, & Marand 2013). These definitions have in common that they define informal learning by comparing it to formal learning. Moreover, they position both formal learning and informal learning as different types of work-related learning on a continuum. In a similar vein, we summarise the key features of (formal and) informal learning on five continua (Figure 1.1).

The first continuum refers to the degree of structure in terms of planning and organisation of the learning content, support by others, time, and objectives. Informal learning activities are characterised by a lower degree of structure than formal learning activities (Kyndt & Baert, 2013). Informal learning implies that the learner engages in learning contents s/he needs in order to solve an issue at hand (e.g., a problem or question s/he faces).

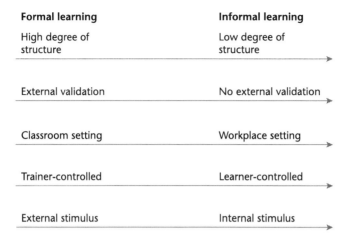

FIGURE 1.1 Formal and informal learning defined on five continua

The second continuum reflects the difference between formal and informal learning in terms of validation (Noe, Tews, & Marand, 2013). While formal training programmes lead to a certificate, this is not the case for informal learning activities. During the past years, validation of informal learning has become a key concern in EU lifelong-learning policies. The acknowledgement that learning takes place in a variety of settings – including outside of classrooms – has led to a plea for making visible "the entire scope of knowledge and experience held by an individual, irrespective of the context where the learning originally took place" (Colardyn & Bjornavold, 2004, p. 69). However, by organising a validation process, part of the informal learning process – more precisely the assessment of the outcomes of the informal learning activities – becomes formalised.

The third continuum refers to the physical place where learning takes place. While informal learning takes place in the workplace, integrated into daily work life, formal learning takes place in face-to-face or virtual classrooms.

The fourth continuum represents the locus of control of learning with more learner control in informal than in formal learning activities. That is, much more than in formal learning, in informal learning the when, what, how, and why to learn primarily depend on the learner's choice and motivation (Noe et al., 2013).

The fifth continuum refers to the stimulus for learning which significantly differs between formal and informal learning. While in formal learning the stimulus for learning is mainly external, that is, set by an instructor or a curriculum, in informal learning, learning is primarily triggered by an internal stimulus that signals dissatisfaction with the current ways of acting or thinking (Marsick & Watkins, 2001; Noe et al., 2013).

By describing the key features of formal and informal learning on these five continua, we acknowledge that many learning activities can be described as partly formal and partly informal. An example is described by Tynjälä (2008) who refers to Poell & van der Krogt's (2006) model of learning projects. With learning projects, participants intend to learn and improve work at the same time. The learning projects are organised by a group of employees and originate from a work-related problem. Employees participate in a set of activities which are centred on the work-related problem and which take place in different kinds of learning situations, that can be both on-the-job and off-the-job, self-organised and facilitator/instructor-directed, action-based and reflection-based, group-focused and individual-oriented, externally and internally inspired, as well as pre-structured and open-ended.

Although formal and informal learning are described as different ends of continua, they can be complementary. That is, formal training programmes can be accompanied by informal learning activities (e.g., discussions during breaks) and informal learning activities may lead to the need of participating in formal training programmes (e.g., when feedback seeking leads to the identification of gaps in skills which may be most efficiently addressed by participating in a formal skills training).

Types of informal learning at work

In addition to the above-mentioned continua helping to describe work-related learning activities as being more or less formal or informal, different authors have identified different types of informal learning which result from different characteristics of the learning activities and the setting at hand.

Firstly, with respect the intention to learn, Eraut (2004) distinguishes between deliberate, reactive, and implicit informal learning activities based on the level of consciousness and goal-directedness of learning. Implicit learning is a totally unconscious learning process in which the learner recognises neither that s/he has been learning nor what s/he has been learning. While informal learning hardly ever is fully implicit, it is also quite likely that explicit forms of informal learning have some implicit aspects. Reactive learning refers to learning activities that are near-spontaneous, such as reflection on past experiences, noting facts, asking questions, and observing the effects of actions. It involves a more conscious and intentional effort to learn. Deliberate informal learning means that there is a clear work-based goal that leads to learning activities. Learning in the sense of individual professional development is a probable by-product of these activities. Deliberate learning involves activities that are part of daily work such as discussing and reviewing past actions and experiences, engaging in decision making, and problem solving.

Secondly, according to several authors (Mulder, 2013; Noe et al., 2013), informal learning includes cognitive activities and observable behaviour. Mulder (2013) argues that in addition to cognitive activities, physical activities, such as searching the Internet, are part of informal learning. In accordance with Marsick et al.'s (1999) conceptualisation of informal learning, physical and cognitive activities form the sides of action-reflection-action cycles that are characteristic of most theoretical accounts of learning for and at work. Moreover, given that reflection is argued to be a core informal learning activity, the cognitive component of informal learning contains meta-cognitive activities which are important to monitor and plan actions.

Thirdly, a distinction is made between individual informal learning activities and informal learning in social interaction (e.g., Kyndt & Baert, 2013; Mulder, 2013).

According to Noe et al. (2013), individual informal learning includes learning from oneself and learning from non-interpersonal sources while informal learning in social interaction includes learning from others. Learning from oneself refers to reflection and experimenting with new ways of thinking and acting. Learning from non-interpersonal sources implies retrieving information from written material (e.g., via the Internet). And learning from others involves interaction with peers, supervisors, and relevant others in the learner's network by seeking information, help, or feedback or by exchanging ideas and discussing problems at hand.

Triggers, antecedents, and consequences of informal learning at work

The increasing interest in informal learning by scholars and practitioners has led to a series of questions relating to the emergence of informal learning, to means of fostering it, and to potential benefits at individual, group, and organisational level. First of all, questions are raised with respect to the *triggers* of informal learning embedded in work situations and tasks, such as the level of complexity of work tasks, which increase employees' perception of pressure and challenge and which motivate them to engage in work-related learning activities. Closely related to this issue, the role of *antecedents* of informal learning at work has to be questioned. Various factors, including organisational and job characteristics, the social work environment, and employees' personal dispositions and perceptions, facilitate and enhance the initiation of informal learning activities. Moreover, scholars and practitioners have tried to answer the issue of the individual and organisational *consequences*, such as better decision making and innovative accomplishment of tasks, which emerge as a result of employees' engagement in informal learning at work.

With this book, we bring together those researchers who have tried to find answers to the aforementioned questions, based on solid empirical evidence.

Two chapters address the question of triggers of informal learning. Starting from a conceptualisation of informal learning, Kyndt, Govaerts, Smet, and Dochy (Chapter 2) summarise recent research studies in order to identify barriers to and facilitators of informal learning. The authors describe thirteen themes brought together in three broad categories: personal characteristics, work environment factors, and job characteristics. Building on the same conceptual framework of informal learning, Hirschmann and Mulder (Chapter 3) take a closer look at one specific trigger of informal learning, that is, the complexity of work tasks.

With respect to the issue of consequences of informal learning, Grohnert, Meuwissen, and Gijselaers (Chapter 4) explore the importance of informal learning at work for enabling professionals to make high-quality judgements. They investigate whether deliberate practice, within the context of informal learning at work, leverages the effect of experience on professionals' judgement quality. They explicitly address task experience, learning climate, valuable feedback, and engagement in reflection as moderators of the relationship between informal learning and judgement quality. Gerken, Messmann, Froehlich, Beausaert, Mulder, and Segers (Chapter 5) focus on the consequences of informal learning activities for employees' innovative work behaviour in organisations. In two studies, they address the complementarity of individual and socially interactive informal learning by investigating the role of reflection as well as of seeking feedback, help, and information as determinants of innovative work behaviour.

Shanks's chapter (Chapter 6) addresses triggers as well as consequences of informal learning in the context of new teachers, taking Lave and Wenger's (1991) theory of situated learning in communities of practice as theoretical framework. Informal learning is analysed and discussed in terms of what led to it, what went beforehand and what happened as a consequence of this learning.

Next, Boud and Rooney (Chapter 7) seek to position the discussion of informal learning as a part of everyday working life. They present the reflection on a lengthy series of research studies conducted in Australia over the past decade. It uses a practice theory perspective to show how learning can be understood as a key feature of working and how it is implicated in the normal ebb and flow of work practices. They elucidate some of the tensions that such a view generates and points to the paradox of how promoting informal learning can effectively inhibit it.

Finally, a review and integration of the single contributions is conducted to further elaborate and empirically underpin and/or reframe a tentative model of informal learning (Chapter 8). In doing so, the book closes with an integrative view on triggers, antecedents, and consequences of informal learning at work which illustrates the state of the art of theoretical and empirical insights into informal learning at work.

References

Anderson, J. R. (1982). Acquisition of cognitive skill. *Psychological Review, 89*(4), 369–406. doi:10.1037/0033-295X.89.4.369

Argyris, C., & Schön, D. (1996) *Organizational learning II: Theory, method and practice*. Reading, MA: Addison-Wesley.

Baldwin, T. T., & Ford, J. K. (1988). Transfer of training: A review and directions for future research. *Personnel Psychology, 41*(1), 63–105. doi:10.1111/j.1744-6570.1988.tb00632.x

Boud, D., & Walker, D. (1990). Making the most of experience. *Studies in Continuing Education, 12*(2), 61–80.

Colardyn, D., & Bjornavold, J. (2004). Validation of formal, non-formal and informal learning: Policy and practices in EU member states. *European Journal of Education, 39*(1), 69–89. doi:10.1111/j.0141-8211.2004.00167.x

Dochy, F., & Segers, M. (2017). *Creating impact through future learning: The High Impact Learning that Lasts (HILL®)-model*. London: Routledge.

Dochy, F., Gijbels, D., Segers, M., & Van den Bossche, P. (Eds.) (2011). *Theories of learning for the workplace. Building blocks for training and professional development programs*. New York, NY: Routledge.

Engeström, Y. (1987). *Learning by expanding: An activity theoretical approach to developmental research*. Helsinki: Orienta-Konsultit.

Eraut, M. (2004). Informal learning in the workplace. *Studies in Continuing Education, 26*(2), 173–247. doi:10.1080/158037042000225245

Ericsson, K. A., Krampe, R. T., & Tesch-Römer, C. (1993). The role of deliberate practice in the acquisition of expert performance. *Psychological Review, 100*(3), 363–406. doi:10.1037/0033-295X.100.3.363

Froehlich, D. E., Beausaert, S. A. J., & Segers, M. S. R. (2015). Age, employability, and the role of learning activities and their motivational antecedents: A conceptual model. *International Journal of Human Resource Management, 26*(16), 2087–2101. doi:10.1080/09585192.2014.971846

Kolb, D. A. (1984). *Experiential learning*. Englewood Cliffs, NJ: Prentice-Hall.

Kolodner, J. L. (1992). An introduction to case-based reasoning. *Artificial Intelligence Review, 6*(3), 3–34. doi:10.1007/BF00155578

Kyndt, E., & Baert, H. (2013). Antecedents of employees' involvement in work-related learning: A systematic review. *Review of Educational Research, 83*(2), 273–313. doi:10.3102/0034654313478021

Lave, J., & Wenger, E. (1991). *Situated learning: Legitimate peripheral participation*. Cambridge: Cambridge University Press.

Manuti, A., Pastore, S., Scardigno, A. F., Giancaspro, M. L., & Morciano, D. (2015). Formal and informal learning in the workplace: A research review. *International Journal of Training and Development, 19*(1), 1–17. doi:10.1111/ijtd.12044

Marsick, V. J, & Watkins, K. E. (1990). *Informal and incidental learning in the workplace*. London: Routledge.

Marsick, V. J., & Watkins, K. E. (2001). Informal and incidental learning. *New Directions for Adult Continuing Education, 89*, 25–34. doi:10.1002/ace.5

Marsick, V. J., Volpe, M., & Watkins, K. E. (1999). Theory and practice of informal learning in the knowledge era. In V. J. Marsick & M. Volpe (Eds.), *Informal learning on the job* (pp. 80–95). Baton Rouge, LA: Academy of Human Resource Development.

Mezirow, J. (1990) *Fostering critical reflection in adulthood. A guide to transformative and emancipatory learning*. San Francisco, CA: Jossey-Bass.

Mulder, R. (2013). Exploring feedback incidents, their characteristics and the informal learning activities that emanate from them. *European Journal of Training and Development, 37*(1) 49–71. doi:10.1108/03090591311293284

Noe, R. A., Tews, M. J., & Marand, A. D. (2013). Individual differences and informal learning in the workplace. *Journal of Vocational Behavior, 83*(3), 327–335. doi:10.1016/j.jvb.2013.06.009

Poell, R. F., & van der Krogt, F. J. (2006). Learning at the workplace reviewed: Theory confronted with empirical research. In J. N. Streumer (Ed.), *Work-related learning* (pp. 71–94). Dordrecht: Springer.

Roffe, I. (1999). Innovation and creativity in organisations: A review of the implications for training and development. *Journal of European Industrial Training, 23*(4), 224–241. doi: 10.1108/03090599910272103

Schön, D. (1983). *The reflective practitioner. How professionals think in action*. New York, NY: Basic Books.

Soderquist, K. E., Papalexandris, A., Ioannou, G., & Prastacos, G. (2010). From task-based to competency-based: A typology and process supporting a critical HRM transition. *Personnel Review, 39*(3), 325–346. doi:10.1108/00483481011030520

Tynjälä, P. (2008). Perspectives into learning at the workplace. *Educational Research Review, 3*(2), 130–154. doi:10.1016/j.edurev.2007.12.001

Van Den Berg, P. T., & Van Der Velde, M. E. (2005). Relationships of functional flexibility with individual and work factors. *Journal of Business and Psychology, 20*(1), 111–129. doi: 10.1007/s10869-005-6994-9

Watkins, K. E. & Marsick, V. J. (1992). Towards a theory of informal and incidental learning in organizations. *International Journal of Lifelong Education, 11*(4), 287–300. doi:10.1080/0260137920110403

2

ANTECEDENTS OF INFORMAL WORKPLACE LEARNING

A theoretical study

Eva Kyndt, Natalie Govaerts, Kelly Smet, and Filip Dochy[1]

Informal learning has become a prominent concept in today's society. First of all, the labour market makes an effort to assess and promote informal learning, as it seems that informal learning is a key to corporate competitiveness, as well as employment, adaptability and employability (Skule, 2004). Secondly, national and international policies are emphasising the importance of assessing and validating informal learning (Colardyn & Bjornavold, 2004; European Commission, 2007). Finally, scientific research on this topic has experienced an enormous growth within the last decade. To meet the full potential of the benefits of informal learning, it is crucial to investigate informal learning in further detail.

Informal workplace learning can be defined as spontaneous, unplanned learning that occurs at any time in work contexts that are not explicitly created to evoke learning. During the last ten years many studies have already been performed investigating the nature (Eraut, 2004; Marsick & Volpe, 1999), forms (Eraut, 2004; Lohman, 2000), effects (Enos, Kehrhahn, & Bell, 2003; Van der Heijden, Boon, Van der Klink, & Meijs, 2009), assessment (Skule, 2004), and validation (European Commission, 2007; Svetlik, 2009) of informal learning. Despite these endeavours, there is a lack of overarching theoretical frameworks combining the results of the individual studies. Moreover, little is known about how informal learning can be supported, encouraged, and developed (Marsick & Volpe, 1999). By analysing the current literature using the term 'informal learning', this study will answer the research question: which antecedents of informal learning have been identified by prior empirical research?

1 KU Leuven, Belgium

Theoretical background

The roots of informal learning can be traced back to Dewey (1938, in Marsick, 2006). Although he did not speak of informal learning, his theories concerning learning from experience and the role of reflection have some interfaces with the concept. It was Knowles who first introduced the term 'informal learning' in his work entitled 'Informal adult education' in 1950 (Ellinger, 2005). Since then, research on informal learning has grown.

Defining informal learning

When it comes to understanding informal learning, Marsick and Watkins can be viewed as pioneers (Marsick & Watkins, 1990; Watkins & Marsick, 1992). The definition they provide of informal learning is repeatedly referred to in the existing literature. They view informal learning as resulting from experience, taking place outside formal educational settings in a planned or unplanned manner, happening mostly unconsciously and finally, the activities are not specifically aimed at learning (Watkins & Marsick, 1992). Marsick and Volpe (1999) examined informal learning in further detail and came up with six characteristics of informal learning: (1) it is integrated with work and daily routines, (2) triggered by a jolt that can be internally or externally situated, (3) is not a highly conscious activity, (4) is haphazard and influenced by change, (5) is an inductive process of reflection and action, and (6) is linked to the learning of others.

When comparing several recent definitions of informal learning, different characteristics of informal learning come to the fore. First, all definitions unanimously state that this type of learning could take place, during *any daily life activity at any time and place*. Focusing on the workplace, this means that every work activity contains a potential learning opportunity. Second, almost every definition claims to view informal learning as something *unstructured* in terms of learning objectives (European Commission, 2001; Kyndt, Dochy, & Nijs, 2009), criteria (Livingstone, 2001), certification (European Commission, 2001) and subject or material (Baser & Buntat, 2010). However, Lohman (2006) asserts that informal learning can be "either planned or unplanned and structured or unstructured". A third element characterising informal learning is its *spontaneous* character, meaning that the activity is not deliberately planned on beforehand (Baert et al., 2011; Kyndt et al., 2009; Marsick, 2003). However, not all authors elaborate on what is meant by spontaneous. For some authors, spontaneous refers to the fact that an activity was planned to occur at a specific moment in time, while for other authors, it refers to the intention to learn. Some claim that informal learning is primarily *unintended* (Baert, et al., 2011; Eraut, 2004), though others state that informal learning can be both intentional and non-intentional from the learning perspective (Berg & Chyung, 2008; Doornbos, 2004; European Commission, 2001; Marsick, 2003; Van der Heijden et al., 2009). It is important to note here that while informal learning is considered largely unintentional from a learning perspective, activities are often undertaken with an intention to solve problems or tackle challenges. Fifth, several definitions state that it occurs rather unconsciously or not highly consciously, leading to the fact that individuals often only realise later on that they learned something (Baert et al., 2011; Kyndt et al., 2009; Marsick, 2003; Marsick & Volpe, 1999; Van der Heijden et al., 2009). In addition, informal learning is *initiated by the worker* (Lohman, 2006). Finally, when considering whether or not informal learning is intentional, there seem to be some differences among the authors.

In recognition of the above definitions and analysis, it can be inferred that informal workplace learning is spontaneous, foremost without an intention to learn, and that it can occur at any time in work contexts that are not explicitly created to evoke learning. Informal workplace learning occurs while executing work tasks in which learning and work processes are interwoven. It concerns a process of sustainable change of the existing knowledge, skills, and attitudes with the purpose to improve the execution and progress of the work.

Why invest in informal learning?

Learning at work is beneficial in multiple ways. Four reasons for promoting learning in the workplace are given by Billett (1995). First, the workplace can provide learning opportunities to compensate for the skill development that is not provided by formal educational settings. Next, formal education is struggling to keep up with the changing work context that is getting more and more specific and complex. In contrast, the workplace can indeed meet these demands. Third, it is a cost-effective option. For instance, there are no enrolment fees, learning is intertwined with work and consequently there are no replacement costs or transportation costs involved. Finally, informal learning takes place within an authentic setting. This is an important consideration, since "the socio-cultural context will ease the development and transfer of knowledge" (Billett, 1995, p. 21).

It is important to notice that both the individual and the context in which the individual is situated deserve attention: "While the organisation of work sets the context and conditions for learning, it continues to be the reciprocal interaction between the individual and the workplace that determines learning" (Tynjälä, 2008, p.141). Billett (2001a) states that the workplace must be designed in a way that people are invited and stimulated to learn. Doornbos (2004) adds that the individual's initiative is pivotal: people do not just learn from these workplace opportunities. Depending on previous experiences, they will or will not take up these opportunities – if and how they learn is determined by this.

In order to create a work environment that will promote learning, attention needs to be given to both the enabling as well as the inhibiting factors. The inhibiting factors are defined as barriers that impede informal learning. These barriers can arise before learning has started, can interrupt the learning process or terminate the learning process before a (learning) result has been obtained (Hicks, Bagg, Doyle, & Young, 2007). The facilitating factors are defined as factors that promote learning. They motivate people to learn and sustain or enhance learning (Hicks et al., 2007).

Methodology

Meta-synthesis

By conducting a meta-synthesis, "a review of qualitative studies is undertaken alongside a review of quantitative studies and the results of these two syntheses are combined" (Centre for Reviews and Dissemination, 2009, p. 269). An individual study should be seen as just one piece of a puzzle (Aveyard, 2010). By performing a literature review, these pieces are brought together in order to see the bigger picture. Hence, it provides insight into relations within and between studies and creates a greater depth of understanding.

Both qualitative and quantitative studies are considered because both research methods address distinctive features of informal learning (Sawchuk, 2008). By including both, the pitfall of foreclosing this study to one method – and thus not completely grasping informal learning – was avoided.

Literature search strategy

During the first phase, online databases and search engines were searched in order to find relevant studies. The included electronic databases were: Education Resources Information Center (ERIC), Web of Science (WoS), Business Source Premier, EconLit, psycINFO, LIBISnet, IngentaConnect, and ScienceDirect. In addition, the following search engines were used: Google Scholar and Scirus. In order to avoid publication bias, unpublished research was also included. Therefore, Google Advanced and the website www.nall.ca were consulted. All of these databases, search engines, and websites were navigated by using the following key words: "*informal learning*" and "*informal workplace learning*". During the second phase, references of the selected studies were back-traced in order to find more relevant research studies that could meet our criteria for inclusion.

Inclusion criteria

Given the fact that the current study aimed at synthesising empirical research focusing on the antecedents of informal learning at the workplace, the following inclusion criteria were used to select the studies:

- The target population consisted of employees working at every level within the organisation in any country.
- Only empirical studies were included.
- The interest was on the factors that influence informal learning in the workplace. Studies investigating the effects of informal learning were not included.
- Studies lacking information about the study design (such as the sampling strategy, sampling size, use of reliable and valid methods) were excluded due to the fact that it was impossible to critically assess the quality of the study.
- Only studies written in English or Dutch were included as a good understanding of the paper by the researchers was necessary in order to draw valid conclusions.

An initial search of the literature resulted in 4,509 hits, of which 34 studies met the criteria for inclusion. Eighteen studies were qualitative, fifteen quantitative, and there was one mixed method study. Appendix 2.1 illustrates the selection process in more detail.

Critical appraisal

In the next step, each study was critically appraised (Appendix 2.2 and 2.3). The appraisal was performed by one researcher; however, specific doubts were discussed with another researcher. To assess the basic quality of the primary studies, critical appraisal tools were applied. To assess the qualitative and mixed-method research studies, the Critical Appraisal Skills Programme (CASP, 2013) was used while the checklist of the National Institute for Health and Clinical Excellence (NICE, 2009) was used for the quantitative studies. The main criteria for the quality appraisal were: (1) a well-focused research question, (2) an appropriate research design, (3) an appropriate data collection and analysis method, and (4) a clear description of the findings of the research (Aveyard, 2010; NICE, 2009). Each study was given a rating: low-, medium-, or high-quality (for details on the specific criteria and cut-offs, see Appendix 2.2 and 2.3). Studies were not excluded if they were of low quality, but given lesser weight when answering the research question; if a low-quality study contradicted other studies, the findings of the other studies were proposed as the conclusion. In addition, if only low-quality studies identified a factor, these results were not considered as a main finding of this meta-synthesis.

Analysis of the studies

The method of analysis was based upon the guidelines of Aveyard (2010). First, every study was read and re-read. Subsequently, every individual study was thoroughly examined and important paragraphs were coded using the content analysis method. The inductive coding process led to more than a hundred different codes (see Appendix 2.4). In the course of the data-analysis, the codes could be subsumed under thirteen themes. Consecutively, this led to the development of three main categories: factors at the individual level, job characteristics, and work environment factors. A category brings together factors that can be situated at the same level, in the same area of an individual's life. Factors at the individual level are tied to the individual him- or herself and can be different even if individuals hold the same type of job or work within the same organisation. Job characteristics entail factors that are similar for individuals holding the same job or function within the organisation; different jobs within the same organisation might possess different characteristics. Finally, factors situated at the level of the work environment are comparable for employees from the same organisation. Subsequently, each of the thirteen themes – factors that are similar in terms of conceptualisation (e.g., interaction opportunities comprising informal contacts and networking opportunities) – was analysed for its precise positive or negative influence on informal workplace learning.

Results

In what follows, the results of the content analysis will be presented in line with the categories and thirteen themes that were identified and introduced above (see Appendix 2.4 for an overview). While many factors have been identified, not all factors showed conclusive results, Table 2.1 presents the factors with the most consistent findings.

TABLE 2.1 Factors that inhibit or promote informal learning

	Barriers	*Facilitators*
Personal characteristics		
Tenure	A long tenure	A short tenure
Age	Older people will collaborate less	Older people will engage in more individual informal learning activities
Hierarchical position	Managers lack the availability of coaches or experts	Managers get more support and reward for learning
Personality	/	Having an outgoing or nurturing personality
Work environment		
Time	Lack of time	
Opportunities to interact	Formally establishing conversations that are already happening informally Lacking interaction opportunities	Having a lot of opportunities to interact
Change	Too much change too fast	Up to a certain level, change promotes informal learning
Colleagues	Being far away from colleagues' work areas	Being close to others' work areas
Computer technology	When it replaces face-to-face interactions	Availability of email communication and possibilities to search the Internet
Information technology	Long distance from libraries	/
Networks	/	Exchanging knowledge with colleagues, experts, customers . . .
Social support		
Colleagues	/	Trusting relationships Receiving collegial support
Supervisor	Managers who do not provide learning support Or give little feedback	Managers that are learning committed and role model learning

(continued)

TABLE 2.1 Factors that inhibit or promote informal learning *(continued)*

	Barriers	Facilitators
Culture	Unsupportive organisational culture	Value learning Support learning
Job characteristics		
Job demands	Too high workloads decrease time to interact with others	/
Job control	/	Having the control to autonomously organise one's work
Job variety	/	Having variety in one's work
Job challenges	Being under-challenged or over-challenged	Having challenging tasks

Personal characteristics

According to Kwakman (2003), the engagement in informal learning can mainly be explained by personal factors. In her research, work environment and task factors did have an effect, but they were rather small in comparison to personal factors. Accordingly, the research of Van Woerkom, Nijhof, and Nieuwenhuis (2002) showed that in the prediction of critical reflective behaviour the individual features were most important.

General individual characteristics

Research unanimously indicates that a longer *tenure* is detrimental to the amount of informal learning (Coetzer, 2007; Doornbos, Simons, & Denessen, 2008; Van der Heijden et al., 2009). The work environment and supervisors' support for learning are viewed less favourable for employees with a long tenure (Coetzer, 2007) and they are less coached than people with a temporary contract (Kyndt et al., 2009).

The influence of *age* was investigated in ten studies. Three studies found that older people learned less: their work was reported as less challenging (Tikkanen, 2002) and they perceived their work environment and supervisor's support for learning less favourable (Coetzer, 2007). Likewise, Livingstone and Stowe (2007) identified a decline in participation but emphasised that overall they continued to participate actively. However, Skule (2004) found the opposite: older people engaged significantly more in informal learning. Van Woerkom et al. (2002) found no effect of age on critical reflective working behaviour. Other research suggests that the influence of age depends on the informal learning activity at hand. Reading professional literature and searching the Internet increased with age (Berg & Chyung, 2008; Richter, Kunter, Klusmann, Lüdtke, & Baumert, 2011), while collaboration decreased (Richter et al., 2011). Moreover, mentoring and coaching were provided more to young people (Kyndt et al., 2009; Livingstone & Raykov,

2008). In addition, younger employees participated significantly more in networking activities within the organisation (Van der Heijden et al., 2009). As people grow older or work longer within the same organisation, a decrease in diversity of experience can occur (= *experience concentration*). The research of Van Woerkom et al. (2002) studied the effect of experience concentration on reflective behaviour and discovered that less reflection occurred when employees had a high level of experience concentration.

The distribution of informal learning opportunities among employees with a different *sex* showed that males have more interactions with supervisors, read more professional literature, learn more individually and lastly have more chances to acquire information and knowledge, and to receive feedback (Kyndt et al., 2009; Richter et al., 2011; Van der Heijden et al., 2009). Females reported having more opportunities to learn different tasks and received more encouragement to learn (Coetzer, 2007). Yet, when sex is put in a regression analysis together with job and organisational factors, it seems that it no longer has a significant effect (Skule, 2004). No significant differences were found either in the research studies of Berg and Chyung (2008), Van Woerkom et al. (2002) and Doornbos et al. (2008).

Richter et al. (2011) investigated the impact of *marital status* on teacher collaboration and reading professional literature and found no effects. However, the study of Van der Heijden et al. (2009) found a significant difference indicating that the learning value of the job was higher for married people. Whether people are a *member of a trade union* does not seem to matter. But union members appear to be more willing to learn in order to keep up with new developments in the field (Livingstone & Raykov, 2008). A low *level of English-language proficiency* seems to be detrimental for informal learning (Coetzer, 2006b): employees are inhibited in their communication and this consequently impedes informal learning.

A total of five studies investigated the *educational background* of employees. One study found that the presence of learning conditions for informal learning is different for various educational levels (Kyndt, et al., 2009). People with a master's degree significantly score higher on the learning condition "feedback and knowledge acquisition", "acquisition of information", and "the availability of communication tools". Conversely, for the other two learning conditions, "being coached" and "coaching others", employees with a low educational level score higher. Other studies show no effect (Berg & Chyung, 2008; Van der Heijden et al., 2008) or a very low but significant effect of education on informal learning (Skule, 2004). Lastly, the study of Coetzer (2007) suggests that employees with a high educational background perceive the work environment and supervisors' level of support less favourable for informal learning.

Personality

Besides these general personal characteristics, more psychological characteristics were investigated. Berg and Chyung (2008) discovered that personality was in the top three factors that were most influential for the engagement in informal learning. Lohman

(2005, 2006, 2009) performed studies with teachers, HRD and IT-professionals and uncovered that an outgoing personality – expressed as the gratification to interact – promoted participation. For teachers and HRD-professionals, a nurturing personality – expressed as the enjoyment of supporting others and being a team player – also enhanced their engagement. Moreover, being open-minded, honest, curious, and having a teamwork ethic are positively related to engagement in informal learning (Hicks et al., 2007; Lohman, 2009). Similarly, employees with a high level of work engagement read more professional literature and collaborate more (Richter et al., 2011). Finally, how employees cope with change limited learning in one study (Sambrook & Stewart, 2000), but did not prove to be impeding learning in another research study (Van Woerkom et al., 2002).

Attitudes concerning learning

Employees' attitudes towards learning were also investigated and proved to be significant triggers for informal learning. For instance, employees who love to learn (Lohman, 2005, 2006, 2009; Skule, 2004), are interested in the field and the development of the field (Berg & Chyung, 2008; Lohman, 2005, 2006, 2009; Tikkanen, 2002), want to remain up-to-date in the field (Hicks et al., 2007), or want to continuously improve their competences (Lohman, 2005, 2006), and are more engaged in informal learning. Next, when employees lack motivation to learn, this inhibits their informal learning engagement (Sambrook & Stewart, 2000). Finally, when employees are seeing the value or relevance of learning (Doornbos et al., 2008), they are more involved in informal learning.

Proactivity

Research suggests that people do not passively undergo the learning conditions created within the workplace. Employees can be characterised as proactive (Ashton, 2004; Ha, 2008; Hoekstra, Korthagen, Brekelmans, Beijaard, & Imants, 2009). Dependent on how they perceive the learning conditions and act accordingly or create learning opportunities themselves, proactivity is important for their engagement in informal learning. Similarly, other research studies also found that showing initiative promoted informal learning engagement (Lohman, 2005, 2006, 2009; Skule, 2004).

Self-efficacy

In most studies, self-efficacy was found to positively influence engagement in informal learning (Berg & Chyung, 2008; Kwakman, 2001, 2003; Lohman, 2005, 2006, 2009; Van Woerkom et al., 2002). Yet the study of Doornbos et al. (2008) showed that people learned less together with or from peers when their perceived level of competence is high. Moreover, the confidence that people have in their capacities enhanced informal learning (Eraut, 2007; Sambrook & Stewart, 2000).

Other

Finally, two additional factors tied to the individual were identified. Because only one study examined these factors, we categorised these under the header of "other" rather than creating a separate category. According to Berg and Chyung (2008) employees perceive that *job satisfaction* promotes informal learning. Kwakman (2003) investigated how *feasibility* of collaborative activities affected three types of professional learning activities and found that it was negatively related with individual and instructional activities, but positively related to collaborative activities. Next, feasibility of innovative activities was positively related to individual and instructional activities, but negatively related to collaborative activities (Kwakman, 2003).

Work environment factors

Organisational features

How the *size of organisation* influences informal learning seems to lead to inconsistent results. While Skule (2004) discovered size did not affect the amount of informal learning, Van Woerkom et al. (2002) stated that a larger organisation leads to more critical reflective behaviour. Kyndt et al. (2009) found that size had differential influence upon the various learning conditions. Employees in small organisations had more chances to learn informally because they were positively related to some learning conditions, but for other learning conditions, their chances to learn in an informal way decreased.

Concerning the *type of organisation*, Skule (2004) found no effects. Kyndt et al. (2009) on the other hand found that employees in government, profit, or non-profit organisations differed in their chances for informal learning. The learning conditions "feedback and knowledge acquisition" and "coaching others" occurred mostly in non-profit organisations. Whereas employees from non-profit organisations report less that they act as a coach, they do report that they receive more coaching, for example, by an external coach. Finally, employees working for the government had the most opportunities to acquire information.

The *organisational structure* can also impact informal learning. For instance, Ashton (2004) found that a hierarchically structured organisation restricts the distribution of knowledge and access to knowledge. A flexible organisational structure on the other hand facilitated informal learning.

According to Ashton (2004) the *payment system* of an organisation can influence informal learning. Within the organisation he studied, salary was contingent on how the employee was performing in comparison with his colleagues. This induced competition among the employees and detained them from sharing information, which consequently reduced informal learning.

Reward system

How the organisation *rewards* learning, can increase informal learning participation. Skule's research study (2004) indicated that people who receive more rewards for proficiency have significantly more jobs with high informal learning opportunities. However, employees claim that the rewards they receive are too low. Especially, more monetary rewards and recognition would be appreciated, since lacking those diminished their motivation to engage in future informal learning activities (Ashton, 2004; Coetzer, 2006a; Hicks et al., 2007; Lohman, 2000; Nawab, 2011). Yet, these results are in sheer contrast with findings from quantitative research indicating that a lack of monetary rewards and recognition do not seem to hinder employees much from engaging in informal learning activities (Berg & Chyung, 2008; Lohman, 2005, 2006, 2009).

Interaction opportunities

People learn a lot from interactions. Nawab's study (2011) indicated that *lacking structures for interactions* were inhibiting informal learning. A work schedule in which teachers have joint non-teaching time would stimulate informal learning (Jurasaite-Harbison, 2009; Lohman, 2000; Nawab, 2011).

Informal contacts can change into learning activities because people can discuss their ideas, share knowledge, or ask for help (Hicks et al., 2007; Mitchell & Livingstone, 2002; Nawab, 2011; Tikkanen, 2002). However, one must be careful to formalise them as this might create some kind of obligation to share knowledge and discuss certain issues, and some people withhold themselves from doing that – especially when management is attending these activities (Boud, Rooney, & Solomon, 2009; Nawab, 2011). Likewise, teachers perceived the cancellation of workshops and replacing them with ready-made schemes of work detrimental for learning (Nawab, 2011). Teachers used these workshops to discuss certain topics and receive advice from other teachers. But these informal learning opportunities vanished altogether with the disappearance of the workshops.

Participating in networks can increase informal learning. When employees become members of a network, they make contact with peers, experts, customers, vendors, and other people within and outside the organisation and it is within these networks that problems can be discussed and knowledge exchange can occur (Doornbos et al., 2008; Ellinger, 2005; Ha, 2008; Skule, 2004).

Getting the opportunity to cooperate within a *project-team* also triggered informal learning as people got the chance to collaborate, discuss viewpoints, and solve a challenging task (Ashton, 2004; Ha, 2008).

Finally, the research study of Lohman (2000) saw that a large environmental inhibitor to informal learning were *other people who were reluctant to participate* in informal learning as it restrained talking, collaborating, and observation possibilities. Likewise, Ellinger (2005) found that a meeting in itself can stimulate learning, but if its members hold some kind of old-guard cynicism, or act territorial when it comes to sharing knowledge, this can definitely get in the way of informal learning.

Learning resources

Within the work environment, access to learning resources should be made available as these enhance learning. First of all, *colleagues* are an important resource for learning, since a large proportion of informal learning occurs through interactions. According to ten studies, it is important that colleagues' work areas are nearby, since work isolation is a strong inhibitor of social interactions and thus participation in informal learning (Berg & Chyung, 2008; Ha, 2008; Hicks et al., 2007; Jurasaite-Harbison, 2009; Lohman, 2000, 2005, 2006, 2009; Noble & Hassell, 2008; Reardon, 2004). For instance, the exchange of knowledge and ideas is absent, other viewpoints do not challenge employees' perceptions, and feedback, observation and collaboration opportunities are reduced when colleagues are not nearby (Eraut, 2007; Ha, 2008; Jurasaite-Harbison, 2009; Lohman, 2000, 2006; Noble & Hassell, 2008; Reardon; 2004). Especially, the architectural structure of organisations and employees' attitudes characterised by a refusal to share knowledge made it difficult for people to make contact and learn from each other (Ellinger, 2005; Ellinger & Cseh, 2007; Ha, 2008; Jurasaite-Harbison, 2009).

Second, *lacking access to experts* is also detrimental to informal learning (Lohman, 2005). People had the impression that they were not guided enough by experts in their field (Noble & Hassell, 2008). Moreover, according to Hicks et al. (2007), the difficulty of finding a mentor and the lack of expert others who could offer their help are two large inhibitors to informal learning. This is unfortunate, since research findings suggest that having a mentor increases learning opportunities as they can provide observation possibilities, guidance, advice, and support (Ellinger, 2005; Mitchell & Livingstone, 2002). Next, having extensive professional contacts also enhanced informal learning and critical reflective behaviour (Skule, 2004; Van Woerkom et al., 2002). Employees who did not have the opportunity to consult experts argued that this was impeding their learning, but they found a solution by developing a network outside the organisation to gather knowledge (Reardon, 2004).

Third, the *accessibility of managers* was perceived to be an important factor conducive for learning too (Coetzer, 2006b). An open door policy provided employees with opportunities to ask for help and advice. Moreover, managers who were willing to delegate responsibilities enriched employees' informal learning (Ashton, 2004).

Gaining access to *information* was also important (Ellinger, 2005; Tikkanen, 2002), for example, a long distance from libraries impedes employees' informal learning (Lohman, 2000; Noble & Hassell, 2008). Likewise, Ashton (2004) acknowledged the importance of information accessibility, as this resides in a form of collective memory. But, as he emphasises, most knowledge occurred in human interactions and therefore access to information alone is not sufficient.

A fifth learning resource of importance is *computer technology* as it makes communication via mail possible and people can do research on the Internet (Berg & Chyung, 2008; Ellinger, 2005; Lohman, 2000). Other research adds that as long as technology does not replace face-to-face interactions or distracts people; it can promote informal learning (Ashton, 2004; Boud et al., 2009; Ellinger, 2005). Although having access to computers increased employees' informal learning, a lack of access is not perceived to be an inhibitor (Lohman, 2005, 2006; Hicks et al., 2007).

In one research, the lack of computer access was even positively correlated with more informal learning activities (Lohman, 2009). So it can be stated that if computer technology is accessible, employees will use it and consequently learn, but when it is absent, they seem to compensate for this by turning to other learning resources.

In two research studies, *a lack of one's own workspace and personal computer* appeared to be detrimental to informal learning because it detained reflection and reading opportunities (Lohman, 2009; Noble & Hassell, 2008). Due to the *lack of funds*, there was no money to hire substitute teachers who could cover for teachers who wanted to observe others. This was found to be a large inhibitor, according to Lohman (2005, 2006).

Finally, Sambrook and Stewart (2000) stated that *HRD resources* were also of importance. When there was a lack of sufficient HRD resources (such as budgets for learning and development of new HRD initiatives), this was perceived to be impeding learning, while the presence of these HRD resources enhanced learning. Although all these resources may exist, this does not unconditionally lead to more informal learning. Mitchell and Livingstone (2002) argued that is crucial that employees *know of their existence* and have the time to use these tools.

Finally, *participation in formal learning* and its relationship with informal learning was studied in one research study. Livingstone and Stowe (2007) found that even when employees did not participate in formal training, their participation in informal learning remained high. However, a continuing lack of participation in formal training decreased engagement in informal learning.

Social support

Social support was found to be an important factor that can facilitate informal learning. It appears that this support depends on who the provider is: a colleague, a supervisor, or the organizational culture. Tikkanen's research (2002) found that *collegial support* increases people's informal learning: employees found it easier to talk to people and ask for help to solve problems. These informal learning opportunities most likely occurred when there was a foundation of trust and openness within that relationship (Ashton, 2004; Jurasaite-Harbison, 2009). Moreover, employees dare to experiment within these relations, because they know they will not be punished for making mistakes (Ashton, 2004). However, quantitative research results (Kwakman, 2001, 2003; Ouweneel, Taris, Van Zolingen, & Schreurs, 2009) showed that although collegial support had a significant positive effect on informal learning and teachers' instructional activities, these effects should be nuanced because the explained variance was relatively weak in all of them.

The relationship between *supervisor* support and learning was investigated in five quantitative research studies. Three of them found no significant effect (Kwakman, 2001, 2003; Doornbos et al., 2008), one appeared to have very little explained variance (Ouweneel et al., 2009), but a fifth study discovered that it was a strong predictor of the amount of informal learning (Skule, 2004). Moreover, Skule's research (2004) also identified that superior feedback triggered informal learning.

Qualitative research findings give further insight into how managers can facilitate informal learning. Sambrook and Stewart (2000) found that managers could inhibit as well as facilitate workplace learning. Whether or not managers provided support for learning was crucial in this case. In another research study conducted by Eraut (2007), supervisors' support and feedback were very important enhancers to informal workplace learning. Evidence from an ethnographic study within three different school cultures (Jurasaite-Harbison, 2009) found that the kind of leadership that was exercised had an influence upon the informal learning possibilities within that school context. When supervisors did not value learning, this negatively impacted their subordinates learning. On the other hand, managers that did value learning made efforts to make sure their staff learned, for instance, by creating a work schedule that allowed time to interact or by including them in organisational decision making. Likewise, Ellinger (2005) found that it is important that managers adopt a learning-committed orientation, as this seems to promote informal learning opportunities. More concretely, they mustn't only offer learning opportunities; they should also role-model learning, supporting it, and emphasising its importance to others. These efforts will not only make it easier for employees to learn informally, they will also make employees more inclined to facilitate the learning of others (Ellinger & Cseh, 2007). Research findings also suggest that the beliefs, skills, and knowledge of managers concerning learning at work had an impact on the quality of the provided support (Ashton, 2004; Sambrook & Stewart, 2000). Other informal learning triggers stemming from the supervisor were activities such as making efforts to promote dialogue within the organisation and otherwise giving employees access to learning facilitators (Coetzer, 2006b). Finally, in two research studies, employees noted that the supervisor's support was perceived as low and that they were not doing enough to foster their subordinates' learning. For instance, they provided little feedback or goals, and their support was limited to solving work-related problems (Coetzer, 2006a; Noble & Hassell, 2008).

Every organisation possesses their own specific culture that is constituted of organisational values, norms, and beliefs, and consequently defines how employees behave and interact with each other. According to nine studies, employees' learning benefits a lot from *a culture that promotes and supports learning* in the workplace (Hicks et al., 2007). Lohman (2005, 2009) interrogated teachers, IT-professionals and HRD-professionals and discovered that an unsupportive organisational culture appeared to be an important environmental inhibitor. HRD-professionals reported that they talked less with others and engaged less in trial-and-error learning, while teachers found that an unsupportive learning culture impedes them from observation and collaboration with others. One of the research questions of Kwakman's study (2003) concerned the impact of cultural support on teachers' learning activities. Results indicated that engagement in professional learning activities differed significantly based on the amount of cultural support. Likewise, the results of Eraut's longitudinal study (2007), which focused on accountants, nurses, and engineers within their early years of employment, confirmed that a positive learning culture contributed to their informal learning. Ellinger's study (2005), carried out to expose environmental inhibitors within a manufacturing firm, also identified the importance of a culture that is committed to and supports learning. Furthermore, this kind of culture made it easier for employees to act as learning facilitators of others' learning (Ellinger & Cseh, 2007). One study examined learning-oriented organisations (Sambrook & Stewart, 2000) and found similar results: the absence of a learning culture impedes learning, while the presence of one was perceived to be an important facilitator. Finally, the study of Van Woerkom et al. (2002) uncovered a relation between the learning culture of an organisation and its effect on reflection and asking for feedback. In contradiction to the above-stated research findings, two studies found opposite results. Berg and Chyung (2008) studied the relation between learning organisation culture and individual informal learning engagement. Their research findings show that informal learning cannot be predicted based on the organisational learning culture. They assume that these surprising results were obtained because individual informal learning is just one of the components of a learning culture. When it is investigated in the absence of the other components, it is not a strong enough component to show a relationship with the organisational learning culture (Berg & Chyung, 2008).

Macro-environment

The macro-environment entails antecedents that are tied to (national) policies, cultures, or larger groups of people, and as such transcends the specific private or job situation of the individual. One research study was executed in Pakistan, and results suggested that the non-western culture had a significant impact on the informal learning opportunities of teachers (Nawab, 2011). Employees were only allowed to talk with people of the same gender, and disagreeing with a senior or more experienced worker was viewed as inappropriate. These cultural norms led to less informal learning because people hesitated to disagree with others and could not openly share their knowledge with everyone (Nawab, 2011).

Job characteristics

Allocation of work

Although one study claimed that having managerial or service responsibilities did not affect collaboration or reading professional literature (Richter et al., 2011), the *hierarchical position* of an employee within the organisation was found to promote the uptake of informal learning in three studies. For instance, Coetzer (2007) detected that managers experienced their work environment more positively: they had more challenging tasks and received more rewards for learning. These results are affirmed in a case study by Ashton (2004). He discovered that the hierarchical structure of the organisation made it more possible for managers to engage in learning than for subordinates. They received more support and rewards for learning, participated more in networks, and even gained more access to knowledge than juniors. Moreover, they had more task variation and opportunities to experiment and act autonomously (Hicks et al., 2007). However, managers found it more difficult to locate coaches and expert others than did subordinates (Hicks et al., 2007; Kyndt et al., 2009).

Whether people worked *full- or part-time* also influenced their engagement in informal learning. Research conducted by Van der Heijden et al. (2009) states that the learning value of the job and networking behaviour with people outside the organisation was lower for part-time workers. Regardless of the number of working hours, Van Woerkom et al. (2002) found that the participation in informal learning remained high. Only those with a part-time job who were chronically excluded from formal learning opportunities decreased their engagement.

Structuring of work

The *amount of change* people experience within their jobs relates to their participation. Up to a certain level, change can promote informal learning opportunities, but when there is too much change going on too fast, people argue that this impedes engagement in informal learning or leads to less thorough learning (Ellinger, 2005; Ellinger & Cseh, 2007; Mitchell & Livingstone, 2002; Noble & Hassell, 2008; Reardon, 2004; Tikkanen, 2002). Only one quantitative study points out that a fast pace of change contributes to more informal learning (Skule, 2004). Perhaps the differential results can be explained by the fact that Skule did not investigate a non-linear relationship between exposure to change and informal learning.

The empirical evidence upon the following six job factors confirms that the structuring of work can either inhibit or facilitate informal learning. Within the job, a *lack of time* is the most frequently mentioned inhibitor. A total of thirteen studies mentioned that, because of a high workload, people don't have enough time to participate in informal learning activities (Ellinger, 2005; Ellinger & Cseh, 2007; Jurasaite-Harbison, 2009; Sambrook & Stewart, 2000; Hicks et al., 2007; Mitchell & Livingstone, 2002; Lohman, 2000, 2005, 2006, 2009; Nawab, 2011; Noble & Hassell, 2008; Tikkanen, 2002). More specifically, this restricts people from interacting with others, sharing ideas, observing colleagues, and reading journals (Jurasaite-Harbison, 2009; Lohman, 2000, 2005).

On the contrary, there exists evidence that *job demands* can influence informal learning positively (Ouweneel et al., 2009; Skule, 2004; Van Woerkom et al., 2002). Doornbos et al. (2008) detected that high workloads were related to more learning together, from colleagues, outsiders, and newcomers, as well as learning on an individual basis. Likewise, Kwakman (2001, 2003) uncovered that teachers with a high workload and/or high emotional demands, engaged more in collaborative and instructional activities.

Third, *job control* was mainly investigated by researching the level of autonomy or the decision-making power of employees. Regarding the level of autonomy, research is in disagreement. For police officers and teachers, the amount of task autonomy does not seem to significantly influence informal work-related learning

(Doornbos et al., 2008; Kwakman, 2001, 2003). In relation to other learning facilitators, having autonomy is less likely to be one for accountants (Hicks et al., 2007). However, Coetzer (2006a) found that lacking autonomy was related to less learning opportunities and Ouweneel et al. (2009) discovered that a high amount of autonomy was related to more informal learning.

Next to autonomy, *participation in organisational decision making* was also investigated. It seems that democratic and shared leadership within an organisation allows people to have some control and this promotes informal learning (Jurasaite-Harbison, 2009; Livingstone & Raykov, 2008; Skule, 2004). Moreover, it affects task extension activities (Kwakman, 2001) and critical reflection (Van Woerkom et al., 2002). When people lack participation, their engagement in informal learning also decreases (Lohman, 2000). However, there was one study claiming participation is not affecting informal learning engagement (Kwakman, 2003). Livingstone and Raykov (2008) nuanced their findings indicating that in general informal learning is present in almost any job and therefore the effects of workers' power were limited.

The fourth job factor deals with *job variety*. In two studies, it was found that employees perceive that informal learning occurred because of opportunities to engage in a wide range of workplace activities (Coetzer, 2006a, 2006b; Hicks et al., 2007; Kwakman, 2001, 2003). A longitudinal research study conducted with engineers, accountants, and nurses in their early career development confirmed that participating in various tasks enhances their learning (Eraut, 2007). Likewise, young engineers found this helped them to develop competence (Tikkanen, 2002). It was peculiar that one study did not find a significant relation (Doornbos et al., 2008). None of the six identified types of informal work-related learning seemed to be related to task variation. However, this study seems to be the exception. All the other studies seem to suggest that job variety contributes to the engagement in informal learning.

A total of five studies examined *job challenge*. They all seem to confirm that this factor can act as a source for informal learning (Coetzer, 2006a; Ellinger & Cseh, 2007; Ha, 2008). Especially, the encounter with novel situations, the confrontation with problems, and the introduction of new products and projects can challenge people and act as a trigger for informal learning (Ha, 2008; Tikkanen, 2002). Whereas a lack of challenge can suppress learning, being over-challenged can also be negative, according to Eraut (2007).

Last but not least, *opportunities to experiment* promote informal learning (Ha, 2008). However, in comparison with other learning facilitators, opportunities to experiment were least likely to facilitate learning (Hicks et al., 2007).

The research on the *interaction between job demands and job control* hypothesises that to meet job demands, a high level of job control is necessary. Ouweneel et al. (2009) found no interaction effects between job control and job demands. However, another study confirmed that when people experience high demands, the amount of job control matters (Kwakman, 2001). When job control is high, more professional learning will take place, whereas at low levels, they will decrease. However, these factors only play a modest role in explaining professional learning and other factors must be taken into account. In sum, the factors for which consistent results were found are presented in Table 2.1. They are presented according to their inhibiting or facilitating influences on informal learning.

Discussion

In line with Eraut's work (2004), the current study identified a wealth of antecedents of informal learning. However, as mentioned in the introduction to this study, a clear overarching theoretical framework *organising* and *explaining* antecedents of learning is lacking. Moreover, empirical studies are often unclear about which aspect of learning they are actually investigating; the term "learning" is often used interchangeably for antecedents, activities, or outcomes (Kyndt & Baert, 2013; Kyndt, Gijbels, Grosemans, & Donche, 2016). The current study contributes to the literature by clearly identifying and discussing antecedents of informal learning and not confusing them with activities or outcomes. In addition, the inductive analysis of this study revealed that these antecedents can be situated on three levels – the individual level, the level of the job/task and the level of the work environment – and as such provides a way of *organising* the antecedents based on empirical research.

With regard to *explaining* why certain factors can be considered an antecedent of informal learning, insights from this and other theoretical studies point towards the "conservation of resources theory" (Hobfoll, 1989) as an inspiration. The model of conservation of resources is a widely used model in the area of occupational health psychology and explains behaviour during stressful circumstances: "The model's basic tenet is that people strive to retain, protect, and build resources and that what is threatening them is the potential or actual loss of these valued resources" (Hobfoll, 1989, p. 516). The current study – identifying personal and workplace conditions (both job/task and work-environment factors) – confirms Billett's theoretical argument (2001b) that in order to promote workplace learning, one has to consider personal characteristics next to workplace conditions. Not only are the workplace opportunities crucial; it is also important to consider how and to what extent the individual decides to participate in these workplace opportunities. Moreover, the categorisation, derived from the coding process, affirms the statement of Kwakman (2003) that work environment factors, and personal and task factors influence learning. This finding is in line with the basic conceptualisation of resources by Hobfoll (1989): resources entail personal characteristics, conditions, energies, and objects that are valued by the individual. Individuals may employ the resources they possess to use or activate resources that are available within their context. Hobfoll (1989) notes that the contextual conditions are only resources when they are identified and valued by the individual. Thus the individual's perception and active contribution in the process is central in determining whether a contextual condition is a resource or not. Resources and learning alike result from the interaction between the person and the environment. With regard to explaining learning, the idea of "resources caravans" seems particularly interesting as this theory states that individuals with many resources can maintain and extend their resources by investing these resources to form stronger "resource caravans" (e.g., De Cuyper, Mauno, Mäkikangas, Kinnunen, & De Witte, 2012). As such, three basic insights from the theory of conservation of resources are interesting when examining informal learning: (1) resources are used to maintain and build more resources, (2) resources entail both personal characteristics and contextual factors, and (3) in both types of resources, the individual plays an active role as the contextual conditions need to be recognized, valued, and pursued by the individual. Future research can build on both these insights as well as the organisation of antecedents identified in this theoretical study.

Strengths and limitations

A first strength of this theoretical study was that qualitative as well as quantitative research studies were included. Results showed that both streams made an important contribution. However, the incorporation of both qualitative and quantitative research studies also holds a limitation for this study, because this brought along some difficulties and challenges. First, there was no method explaining how these study types can be combined. By focusing on the occurrence of the antecedent rather than the strength of the relationship, this integration was simplified. In addition, both quantitative and qualitative findings were given an equal weight in the interpretation. Second, the decision was made to critically appraise all studies. Sometimes studies were given a lower quality rating due to the difficulties in retrieving information about certain characteristics of the studies, such as the recruitment strategy and the quality of the relationship between the researcher and the participants. The fact that there is no evidence on the strength of the influences of certain factors on informal learning could also be viewed as a limitation. However, this was not the aim of the current review. The focus of this study was to develop a rich and coherent representation of the possible barriers and facilitators and this goal was attained.

The current study also acknowledges that the sole use of the search terms "informal learning" and "informal workplace learning", is a limitation of this study. While the main interest of this study was to examine studies that used these specific terms and as such the use of these terms aligned with the goal of the study, a lot of conceptual confusion and discussion exists in the area of learning within organisations (cf. the Introduction of the current volume). Many terms are used interchangeably, other terms such as "workplace learning" and "on-the-job learning" could (in part) refer to the same phenomenon. In this respect, a clear need, that goes beyond the scope of this study, for an extensive and critical discussion of the different conceptualisations of learning exists. Given the conceptual confusion, this study focused on the term "informal (workplace) learning" which is neither free from debate nor critique, but is still the most commonly used term for studying this type of learning process at work and, as such, is a good starting point for untangling the many scattered research results. Finally, as with many review studies, this study is not free from selection bias, although attempts were made to reduce this by searching in many databases and reference lists, and including unpublished literature.

However, with the exception of two studies, every included article was published. Moreover – with one exception – all studies were executed in western countries.

Conclusion

Despite its limitations, the current study provides two important building blocks for the future development of an overarching theoretical framework for organising and explaining the antecedents of informal workplace learning. This theoretical study clearly identifies antecedents of workplace learning and organizes them on three levels: the personal level, the job/task level, and the work-environment level. In addition, in line with the conservation of resources theory (Hobfoll, 1989) and prior theoretical studies (Billett, 2001b; Eraut, 2004; Kwakman, 2003), findings from the synthesised empirical studies show that the interaction between the person and the environment is essential when explaining informal workplace learning. However, the current study and insights from the conservation of resources theory indicate that contextual antecedents, at both the level of the job and the work environment, are only antecedents for learning when they are recognised and valued by the individual. As such, the initiative and active contribution of the individual seems to be conditional for the potential influence contextual antecedents may have. Future empirical research is needed to examine if this hypothesis holds.

Appendix 2.1 Literature search

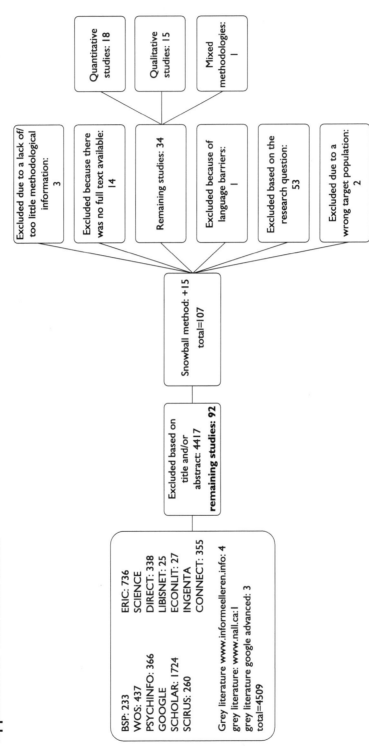

Appendix 2.2 Critical appraisal of qualitative research

Criteria for appraising Qualitative research	Ashton, 2004	Boud, Rooney, & Solomon, 2009	Coetzer, 2006b	Ellinger & Cseh, 2007	Ellinger, 2005	Eraut, 2007	Ha, 2008	Hoekstra, Korthagen, Brekelmans, Beijaard, & Imants, 2009	Jurasaite-Harbison, 2009	Lohman, 2000	Mitchell & Livingstone, 2002	Nawab, 2011	Noble & Hassell, 2008	Reardon, 2004	Sambrook & Steward, 2000	Tikkanen, 2002
Was there a clear statement of the aims of the research?	Y	Y	Y	Y	Y	Y	Y	Y	Y	Y	Y	Y	Y	Y	Y	Y
Is a qualitative methodology appropriate?	Y	Y	Y	Y	Y	Y	Y	Y	Y	Y	Y	Y	Y	Y	Y	Y
Was the research design appropriate to address the aims of the research?	Y	Y	Y	Y	Y	Y	Y	Y	Y	Y	Y	Y	Y	Y	Y	Y
Was the recruitment strategy appropriate to the aims of the research?	Y	Y	Y	Y	Y	Y	Y	N	Y	N	Y	Y	Y	N	Y	N
Were the data collected in a way that addressed the research issue?	Y	Y	Y	Y	Y	Y	Y	Y	Y	Y	Y	Y	Y	Y	Y	Y
Has the relationship between researcher and participants been adequately considered?	N	N	N	N	N	N	N	N	N	N	N	N	N	N	N	N
Have ethical issues been taken into consideration?	N	N	N	N	N	N	N	N	N	N	N	N	N	N	N	N
Was the data analysis sufficiently rigorous?	N	Y	Y	Y	Y	Y	Y	Y	Y	Y	Y	Y	Y	Y	N	N
Is there a clear statement of findings?	Y	Y	Y	Y	Y	Y	Y	Y	Y	Y	Y	Y	Y	Y	Y	Y
Overall quality rating:	M	H	H	H	H	M	H	M	H	H	H	H	M	M	M	M

Note. Each research study was confronted with every question in the checklist and could be only answered with yes (Y) or no (N). Whenever there was no information available around a specific criterion, it was assumed that the researcher did not take it into consideration. Conclusively, every research was given a quality rating. This rating depended on how they scored on the questions:

- (L) Low: 0–4 times answered yes
- (M) Medium: 4–6 times answered yes
- (H) High: 7–9 times answered yes

If the answers in the first three questions were negative, the study should be excluded, and could be identified as fatally flawed.

Appendix 2.3 Critical appraisal of quantitative research

Criteria for appraising quantitative research	Berg & Chyung, 2008	Coetzer, 2006a	Coetzer, 2007	Doornbos, Simons, & Denessen, 2008	Hicks, Bagg, Doyle, & Young, 2007	Kwakman, 2001	Kwakman, 2003	Kyndt et al., 2009	Livingstone & Raykov, 2008	Livingstone & Stowe, 2007	Lohman, 2006	Lohman, 2009	Lohman, 2005	Ouweneel, Taris, Van Zolingen, & Schreurs, 2009	Richter, Kunter, Klusmann, Lüdtke, & Baumert, 2011	Skule, 2004	Van der Heijden, Boon, Van der Klink, & Meijs, 2009	Van Woerkom, Nijhof, & Nieuwenhuis, 2002
Was there a clear statement of the aims of the research?	Y	Y	Y	Y	Y	Y	Y	Y	Y	Y	Y	Y	Y	Y	Y	Y	Y	Y
Was the research design appropriate to address the aims of the research?	Y	Y	Y	Y	Y	Y	Y	Y	Y	Y	Y	Y	Y	Y	Y	Y	Y	Y
Was the recruitment strategy well described?	Y	Y	Y	Y	Y	Y	Y	Y	Y	Y	Y	Y	Y	Y	Y	Y	Y	Y
Was the sample representative of the source population (i.e., no selection bias) and was the response rate acceptable?	N	Y	Y	Y	Y	N	N	Y	Y	Y	Y	Y	Y	Y	Y	Y	N	Y
Was the selection of explanatory variables based on a sound theoretical basis?	Y	Y	Y	Y	Y	Y	Y	Y	Y	Y	Y	Y	Y	Y	Y	Y	Y	Y
Is the questionnaire valid and reliable?	Y	Y	Y	Y	Y	Y	Y	Y	Y	Y	Y	Y	Y	Y	Y	Y	Y	Y
Have confounding factors been considered?	Y	Y	Y	Y	Y	Y	Y	Y	Y	Y	Y	Y	Y	Y	Y	Y	Y	Y
Is there a clear statement of the findings?	Y	Y	Y	Y	Y	Y	Y	Y	Y	Y	Y	Y	Y	Y	Y	Y	Y	Y
Are the findings generalisable to the source population?	Y	Y	Y	Y	Y	Y	Y	Y	Y	Y	Y	Y	Y	Y	Y	Y	Y	Y
Overall quality rating	H	H	H	H	H	H	H	H	H	H	H	H	H	H	H	H	H	H

Note. Each research study was confronted with every question in the checklist and could be only answered with yes (Y) or no (N). Whenever there was no information available around a specific criterion, it was assumed that the researcher did not take it into consideration. Conclusively, every research study was given a quality rating. This rating depended on how they scored on the questions:

- (L) Low: 0–4 times answered yes
- (M) Medium: 4–6 times answered yes
- (H) High: 7–9 times answered yes

If the answers in the first three questions were negative, the study should be excluded, and could be identified as fatally flawed.

Appendix 2.4 Overview of the categories, subthemes and codes of barriers and facilitators of informal learning

Personal characteristics

General characteristics
- Age
- Tenure
- Experience concentration
- Gender
- Marital status
- Union member
- Levels of English proficiency
- Educational background

Personality
- Outgoing
- Nurturing
- Being open-minded
- Integrity
- Having a teamwork ethic
- Being curious
- Work engagement
- Coping with change

Attitudes concerning learning
- Love of learning
- Interest in the field
- Interest in the development of the field
- Wanting to remain up-to-date in the field
- Commitment to continuous professional development
- Motivation to learn
- Value of learning

Proactivity
- Being proactive
- Showing learning initiative

Other personal factors:
- Self-efficacy
  o Perceived level of competence
  o Professional capability
- Confidence
- Job satisfaction
- Feasibility of collaborative activities
- Feasibility of innovative activities

Work environment characteristics

Organisational features
- Size of the organisation
- Type of industry
- Organisational structure
- Payment system

Reward system
- Monetary rewards
- Recognition
- Rewarding of proficiency

Interaction opportunities
- Structures for teacher interactions
- Creating appropriate work schedules
- Hallway conversations
- Informal meetings
- Arranging morning minglers
- Break-time discussions
- Participation in networks
- Participation in projects
- Participation in workshops
- Other employees that are reluctant to participate
- Old-guard cynicism
- Being territorial when it comes to sharing knowledge

Learning resources
- Colleagues
  o Work in isolation
  o Proximity to other work areas/classes
  o Physical architectural barriers
- Expert others
  o Access to experts
  o Finding availability of a mentor or coach
  o Extensive professional contacts
  o Inaccessibility of subject matter experts
  o Observation
  o Guidance
  o Talking things through
  o Asking questions
- Managers
  o Accessibility of managers
  o Delegation of responsibilities
- Computer technology
  o Access to computers
  o Availability of computer technology
  o Having own computer
- Information sources
  o Location of library
  o Accessibility of information sources
- Lack of own workspace
- Lack of funds
- HRD resources

(continued)

Appendix 2.4 *(continued)*

- Knowing that resources exist
- Participation in formal learning

Social support
- Collegial support
    o Trusting relationship
- Supervisor's support
    o Superior feedback
    o Learning committed leadership
    o Not learning committed leadership
    o Management that supports learning
    o Beliefs of managers
    o Managers that role-model learning
    o Skills and competences of managers
    o Lack of feedback and goals
    o Designating learning facilitators
    o Facilitating access to direct guidance
    o Promotion of communication
- The organisational culture
    o Internal culture that supports learning
    o Unsupportive organisational culture
    o Positive learning culture

Macro environment
- Cultural practices

Job characteristics

Allocation of work:
- Hierarchical position
- Full-time or part-time work
- Managerial responsibilities
- Service responsibilities

Structuring of work
- Amount of change within the job
- Lack of time within the job
- Job demands
    o Workload
    o Emotional demands
    o Job intensification
- Job control
    o Participation in decision making
    o Autonomy
- Job challenge
- Job variety
- Job challenges
- Opportunities to experiment
- Job demands
- Job control

References

NB: References marked with an ★ were included in the analysis.

★Ashton, D.T. (2004). The impact of organisational structure and practices on learning in the workplace. *International Journal of Training and Development, 8*(1), 43–53.

Aveyard, H. (2010). *Doing a literature review in health and social care: A practical guide.* Maidenhead: McGraw-Hill.

Baert, H., De Witte, K., Govaerts, N. & Sterck, G. (2011). *Werk maken van leren. Strategisch VTO-beleid in organisaties. [Making work of learning. Strategic HRD policy in organisations].* Leuven-Apeldoorn: Garant.

Baser, J.A., & Buntat, Y. (2010). Informal learning among engineering technology teachers. *Procedia Social and Behavioural Sciences, 7,* 336–344.

★Berg, S.A., & Chyung, S.Y. (2008). Factors that influence informal learning in the workplace. *Journal of Workplace Learning, 20*(4), 229–244.

Billett, S. (1995). Workplace learning: Its potential and limitations. *Education & Training, 37*(5), 20–27. #

Billett, S. (2001a). A critique of workplace learning discourses: Participation in and continuity of practice. *9th Annual International Conference on post compulsory Education and Training: Knowledge demands of the new economy vol. 1* (pp. 85–92). Surfers Paradise Park Royal, Queensland, Australia, 3–5 December.

Billett, S. (2001b). Learning through work: Workplace affordances and individual engagement. *Journal of Workplace Learning, 13*(5), 209–214.

*Boud, D., Rooney, D., & Solomon, N. (2009). Talking up learning at work: Cautionary tales in co-opting everyday learning. *International Journal of Lifelong Education, 28*(3), 323–334.

CASP (2013). *Qualitative research checklist: 10 Questions to help you make sense of qualitative research*. Retrieved from http://www.casp-uk.net/find-appraise-act/appraising-the-evidence/

Centre for Reviews & Dissemination (2009). *Systematic Reviews: CRD's guidance for undertaking reviews in health care*. York: University of York.

*Coetzer, A. (2006a). Employee learning in New Zealand small manufacturing firms. *Employee Relations, 28*(4), 311–325.

*Coetzer, A. (2006b). Managers as learning facilitators in small manufacturing firms. *Journal of Small Business and Enterprise Development, 13*(3), 351–362.

*Coetzer, A. (2007). Employee perceptions of their workplaces as learning environments. *Journal of Workplace Learning, 19*(7), 417–434.

Colardyn, d., & Bjornavold, J. (2004). Validation of formal, non-formal and informal learning: Policy and practices in EU member states. *European Journal of Education, 39*(1), 69–89.

De Cuyper, N., Mauno, S., Mäkikangas, A., Kinnunen, U., & De Witte, H. (2012). Cross-lagged associations between perceived employability, job insecurity and exhaustion: Testing gain and loss spirals according to the COR theory. *Journal of Organizational Behavior, 33,* 770–788. doi:10.1002/job.1800

Doornbos, A.J. (2004). Work practice, learning worker characteristics and informal learning. *Online submission paper presented at Academy of HRD International Conference*, pp. 130–139.

*Doornbos, A.J., Simons, R.J., & Denessen, E. (2008). Relations between characteristics of workplace practices and types of informal work-related learning: A survey study among Dutch police. *Human Resource Development Quarterly, 19*(2), 129–151.

*Ellinger, A.D. (2005). Contextual factors influencing informal learning in a workplace setting: The case of 'reinventing itself company'. *Human Resource Development Quarterly, 16*(3), 389–415.

*Ellinger, A.D., & Cseh, M. (2007). Contextual factors influencing the facilitation of others' learning through everyday work experiences. *Journal of Workplace Learning, 19*(7), 435–452.

Enos, M.D., Kehrhahn, M.T., & Bell, A. (2003). Informal learning and the transfer of learning: How managers develop proficiency. *Human Resource Development Quarterly, 14*(4), 369–387.

Eraut, M. (2004). Informal learning in the workplace. *Studies in Continuing Education, 26*(2), 247–273.

*Eraut, M. (2007). *Early career learning at work. Insights into professional development during the first job*. TLRP Research Briefing 25, London.

European Commission (2001). *Lifelong learning practices and indicators. Supporting document to the Communication of the Commission 'Making a European Area of Lifelong Learning a Reality'*. Communication from the Commission, COM (2001) 678 Final, Brussels.

European Commission (2007). *Action plan on adult learning: It is always a good time to learn*. Communication from the Commission, COM (2007) 558 Final, Brussels.

*Ha, T.S. (2008). How IT workers learn in the workplace. *Studies in Continuing Education, 30*(2), 129–143.

*Hicks, E., Bagg, R., Doyle, W., & Young, J.D. (2007). Canadian accountants: Examining workplace learning. *Journal of Workplace Learning, 19*(2), 61–77.

Hobfoll, S.E. (1989). Conservation of resources. A new attempt at conceptualizing stress. *American Psychologist, 44,* 513–524.

*Hoekstra, A., Korthagen, F., Brekelmans, M., Beijaard, D. & Imants, J. (2009). Experienced teachers' informal workplace learning and perceptions of workplace conditions. *Journal of Workplace Learning, 21*(4), 276–298.

*Jurasaite-Harbison, E. (2009). Teachers' workplace learning within informal contexts of school cultures in the United States and Lithuania. *Journal of Workplace Learning, 21*(4), 299–321.

*Kwakman, K. (2001). Work stress and work-based learning in secondary education: Testing the Karasek model. *Human Resource Development International, 4*(4), 487–501.

*Kwakman, K. (2003). Factors affecting teachers' participation in professional learning activities. *Teaching and Teacher Education, 19,* 149–170.

Kyndt, E., & Baert, H. (2013). Antecedents of employees' involvement in work-related learning: A systematic review. *Review of Educational Research, 83,* 273–313.

*Kyndt, E., Dochy, F., & Nijs, H. (2009). Learning conditions for non-formal and informal workplace learning. *Journal of Workplace Learning, 21*(5), 369–389.

Kyndt, E., Gijbels, D., Grosemans, I. & Donche, V. (2016). Teachers' everyday professional development: Mapping informal learning activities, antecedents, and learning outcomes. *Review of Educational Research, 86*(4), 1111–1150. doi:10.3102/0034654315627864

Livingstone, D.W. (2001). *Adults' informal learning: Definitions, findings, gaps and future research.* NALL Working Paper No. 21-2001, Toronto.

*Livingstone, D.W., & Stowe, S. (2007). Work time and learning activities of the continuous employed: A longitudinal analysis, 1998–2004. *Journal of Workplace Learning, 19*(1), 17–31.

*Livingstone, D.W., & Raykov, M. (2008). Workers' power and intentional learning among non-managerial workers: A 2004 benchmark survey. *Industrial Relations, 63*(1), 30–56.

*Lohman, M.C. (2000). Environmental inhibitors to informal learning in the workplace: A case study of public school teachers. *Adult Education Quarterly, 50*(2), 83–101.

*Lohman, M.C. (2005). A survey of factors influencing the engagement of two professional groups in informal workplace learning activities. *Human Resource Development Quarterly, 16*(4), 501–527.

*Lohman, M.C. (2006). Factors influencing teachers' engagement in informal learning. *Journal of Workplace Learning, 18*(3), 141–156.

*Lohman, M.C. (2009). A survey of factors influencing the engagement of information technology professionals in informal learning. *Informal Technology Learning & Performance Journal, 25*(1), 43–53.

Marsick, V.J. (2003). Invited reaction: Informal learning and the transfer of learning: How managers develop proficiency. *Human Resource Development Quarterly, 14*(4), 389–395.

Marsick, V.J. (2006). Informal strategic learning in the workplace. In J.N. Streumer (Ed.), *Work-related learning* (pp. 51–69). Dordrecht: Springer.

Marsick, V., & Volpe, M. (1999). The nature and need for informal learning. *Advances in Developing Human Resources, 1*(1), 1–9.

Marsick, V.J., & Watkins, K. (1990). *Informal and incidental learning in the workplace.* London: Routledge.

*Mitchell, L., & Livingstone, D.W. (2002). *'All on your own time learning': Informal learning practices of bank branch workers* (Working Paper No. 64). Toronto: NALL.

*Nawab, A. (2011). Workplace learning in Pakistani schools: A myth or reality? *Journal of Workplace Learning, 23*(7), 421–434.

NICE (National Institute for Health and Clinical Excellence) (2009). *Methods for the development of NICE public health guidance* (2nd ed.). Retrieved 12 February, 2011, from http://www.nice.org.uk/media/2FB/53/PHMethodsManual110509.pdf

*Noble, C., & Hassell, K. (2008). Informal learning in the workplace: What are the environmental barriers for junior hospital pharmacists? *International Journal of Pharmacy Practice, 16*, 257–263.

*Ouweneel, A.P.E., Taris, T.W., Van Zolingen, S.J., & Schreurs, P.J.G. (2009). How task characteristics and social support relate to managerial learning: Empirical evidence from Dutch home care. *Journal of Psychology, 143*(1), 28–44.

*Reardon, R.F. (2004). Informal learning after organizational change. *Journal of Workplace Learning, 16*(7), 385–395.

*Richter, D., Kunter, M., Klusmann, U., Lüdtke, O., & Baumert, J. (2011). Professional development across the teaching career: Teachers' uptake of formal and informal learning opportunities. *Teaching and Teacher Education, 27*, 116–126.

*Sambrook, S., & Stewart, J. (2000). Factors influencing learning in European learning oriented organisations: Issues for management. *Journal of European Industrial Training, 24*(2–4), 209–219.

Sawchuk, P.H. (2008). Theories and methods for research on informal learning and work: Towards cross fertilization. *Studies in Continuing Education, 32*, 1–16.

*Skule, S. (2004). Learning conditions at work: A framework to understand and assess informal learning in the workplace. *International Journal of Training and Development, 8*(1), 8–20.

Svetlik, I. (2009). Assessing, recognizing and certifying informal and non-formal learning: Evolution and challenges. *European Journal of Vocational Training, 3*, 12–27.

*Tikkanen, T. (2002). Learning at work in technology intensive environments. *Journal of Workplace Learning, 14*(3), 89–97.

Tynjälä, P. (2008). Perspectives into learning at the workplace. *Educational Research Review, 3*, 130–154.

*Van der Heijden, B., Boon, J., Van der Klink, M., & Meijs, E. (2009). Employability enhancement through formal and informal learning: An empirical study among Dutch non-academic university staff members. *International Journal of Training and Development, 13*(1), 19–37.

*Van Woerkom, M., Nijhof, W.J., & Nieuwenhuis, L.F.M. (2002). Critical reflective working behaviour: a survey research. *Journal of European Industrial Training, 26*(8), 375–383.

Watkins, K.E., & Marsick, V.J. (1992). Towards a theory of informal and incidental learning in organizations. *International Journal of Lifelong Education, 11*(4), 287–300.

3
EFFECTS OF COMPLEXITY OF WORK TASKS ON INFORMAL LEARNING AT WORK IN THE IT DOMAIN

Katrin Hirschmann and Regina H. Mulder[1]

Introduction

The tasks performed by software designers, namely designing, implementing and maintaining computer systems that gather, manage and analyse information used by organisations, have become critical to the functionality of organisations (Lohman, 2009; Sonnentag, 1995). To accomplish such tasks, software developers work in teams. Teams work autonomously but under time pressure to fulfil their tasks. Software developers are responsible as a team for a product, but work independently to accomplish their individual work tasks. Many work tasks in the domain of IT can be described as "ill-defined" problems (Simon, 1973, in Sonnentag, 1998). This implies incomplete problem specifications, decision making during work processes and a range of possible solutions instead of one ideal way.

To be successful, software developers need a variety of skills and knowledge and must be able to handle a high amount of information processing. A combination of technical knowledge, creative skills and knowledge about economy and marketing is essential (OECD, 2002). Therefore, lifelong learning is essential in this domain. However, the rapid technical developments in the IT-domain, additional requirements to get to know the application domain of the software and the work intensification reduce the time available for formal learning (Lohman, 2005, 2009; Sonnentag, 1995). These challenges apply to other domains as well, such as engineering, but are not as distinct in the daily work of some others, such as lawyers or doctors.

Work tasks in the domain of software developing involve employees in "short-term loops of problem-driven learning", for example, to correct malfunctions or develop new functionalities (Nerland, 2008, p. 65). Research showed the relevance of informal learning in the IT-domain (Lohman, 2005, 2009) to meet the

[1] University of Regensburg, Germany

requirements of short-term technical developments. Employees in various domains consider informal learning more relevant and helpful for meeting job demands than formal learning (Felstead, Fuller, Unwin, Ashton, Butler, & Lee, 2005). Therefore, it is important to identify relevant predictors for informal learning at work in order to be able to develop organisational support for improving the staff's performance. Learning is labelled "informal learning" when it is not organised and structured in terms of learning goals, time for learning, or support for learning. Informal learning happens in daily life, during leisure time, or at work (Marsick & Watkins, 1990). It is important to find out how learning at work is influenced by characteristics of the work task in this domain. Work tasks are, next to the structure of the organisation and the organisational culture, an important part of employees' (organisational) context. A work task serves as a frame for triggering informal learning at work. Research on determinants of informal learning at work focuses on contextual factors, such as autonomy, task variation and time pressure (e.g. Doornbos, Bolhuis, & Denessen, 2004). Hence, content and structure of work tasks are considered important factors for informal learning at work (Ellinger & Cseh, 2007; Lundgren, 2011). Research indicates that informal learning at work depends on the characteristics of the specific work task (e.g. Doornbos et al., 2004). Nevertheless, research is scarce on characteristics of a specific work task and learning activities that emanate from carrying out that work task. For example, the relation between characteristics of work tasks, such as task complexity, and informal learning at work is not clear yet. Characteristics of work tasks can work as triggers that can lead to a variety of activities, such as searching for new information, revising one's initial beliefs, or experimenting with new ideas and behaviours (Watkins & Marsick, 1992). For instance, errors can be triggers (e.g. Leicher, Mulder, & Bauer, 2013; Leicher & Mulder, 2016), as well as feedback (e.g. Mulder, 2013). Work tasks that are novel or challenging and demanding are considered triggers for informal learning (Ha, 2008; Volmer & Sonnentag, 2011). To our knowledge it is so far unknown what the relation is between the complexity of work tasks and informal learning in this domain. Therefore, this contribution focuses on the effects of the complexity of work tasks on informal learning at work in the domain of IT.

The influence of the complexity of work tasks on employee performance and learning is based on the requirements that a complex work task sets on employees' knowledge, skills and resources (Wood, 1986). Complex work tasks are defined as work tasks that require problem solving skills, information processing skills and skill variety for successful accomplishment. For getting insight into the relation between the complexity of work tasks and learning activities that emanate from that, the theories of Piaget (1977) and action theory (Frese & Zapf, 1994) are used to formulate assumptions. Piaget's (1977) concept of disturbances, which is part of the theory of equilibration of cognitive structures, provides the theoretical basis for what is perceived as triggers for informal learning at work and the effect of these triggers on informal learning at work. The theory of Frese and Zapf (1994) helps to explain why people choose specific learning activities as a course of action. Different learning activities are seen as options that the learner can choose from.

A cross-sectional study in the domain of software developing was conducted to answer the following research question: what is the relation between the complexity of a work task and learning activities that emanate from this work task? In the following, the theoretical framework on learning at work and the relation with the complexity of work tasks is presented, before the study design is described. Results are shown and related to research and theoretical implications. The contribution ends with implications for research and practice.

Informal learning at work

Informal learning

As mentioned before, informal learning is not organised and structured in terms of learning goals, time for learning, or support for learning. Learning activities can be planned or not planned (Merriam, Caffarella, & Baumgartner, 2007). Many definitions of informal learning state that informal learning is unplanned, and that this is the distinction between formal and informal learning (e.g. Manuti, Pastore, Scardigno, Giancaspro, & Morciano, 2015). Next to being unplanned, informal learning has no formal outcomes, and there is no formal curriculum (e.g. Hager & Halliday, 2006). Informal learning can be defined along many other features. For example, intention, cognisance, setting, context (Hager, 1998; Marsick & Watkins, 1990; Mulder, Harteis, & Gruber, 2009), and type of activity (Mulder et al., 2009; Simons & Ruijters, 2004). Other examples are experience (e.g. practice and judgement), and the amount of interaction (e.g. learning through mentoring and team work) (Manuti et al., 2015; Marsick & Watkins, 1990). Furthermore, the aims or purposes and the outcomes are also relevant features of informal learning (e.g. Hager & Halliday, 2006). Outcomes of informal learning at the individual level include professional development, knowledge, skills and competences, but not formal qualifications, certifications, or a degree (Merriam et al., 2007; Skule, 2004). Informal learning refers to activities initiated by people in work settings that result in professional knowledge and skills (Cofer, 2000; Lohman, 2005, 2009).

As mentioned before, informal learning can occur in different contexts (Marsick & Watkins, 1990). In the work context, informal learning is embedded in everyday work activities and daily routines (Le Clus, 2011; Marsick & Volpe, 1999), and happens while accomplishing these work tasks. The aim of behaviour at work is to solve a problem, find a new solution, etc. (e.g. Marsick & Watkins, 1990; Manuti et al., 2015). To improve work and not learning as such is the purpose. The employee's aim is to carry out and accomplish work tasks. Thus, employee learning occurs as a side effect. An outcome of informal learning, at task level, is, for instance, a solution to a specific problem at work.

The characteristics of the context are also considered to be of importance. Informal learning activities occur depending on the features of the organisation, such as the organisational culture. In addition, informal learning activities depend on the kind of experiences and activities that, for instance, result from the characteristics of an employee's work tasks. This makes learning situated (e.g. Lave & Wenger, 1991). In addition, informal learning can be influenced by individual conditions such as self-efficacy and motivation. Self-efficacy is defined as people's beliefs about their capabilities to produce designated levels of performance that exercise influence over events that affect their lives. Self-efficacy enhances learning in different ways. When self-efficacy is high, that can influence the selection of activities in a sense that the more difficult activities, with more learning potential, are chosen. It can influence how problems are confronted and solved, and persons with higher self-efficacy see problems as less big and with less emotional distress (Bandura & Locke, 2003). High self-efficacy leads to motivation to carry out informal learning activities (Lohman, 2005).

Learning is considered a process of, for instance, reflection that is caused by experiences and the corresponding activities that are carried out. Learning is a process in which individuals engage in learning activities (e.g. Billett & Choy, 2013). At the level of the learning activities of an individual at work, the individual's intention is relevant. The level of intention to learn is, according to Eraut (2000), one of the basic dimensions to define informal learning. He distinguished deliberative, reactive and implicit learning. Deliberative learning is intentional – time is set aside for it and the learner is aware of the learning process (Eraut, 2000). Reactive learning is near-spontaneous and unplanned in that the learner acts in response to recent, current, or upcoming situations. The learner is aware of the learning, but the level of intentionality varies. Implicit learning is characterised by the absence of intention to learn and the absence of awareness of learning at the time the learning takes place. Because implicit learning cannot be measured, it is not further taken into account in this chapter.

Below, two different aspects that are frequently touched upon in understanding and defining informal learning are briefly discussed, in order to clarify the position that is taken here in relation to the meaning of informal learning, namely features relating to the type and the setting of learning activities.

Type of learning activities

Next to intention, learning activities can be distinguished according the type of activity. Learning contains mental as well as overt activities (Simons & Ruijters, 2004). In addition, learning activities can be physical or cognitive (e.g. Ellström, 2001). It is important to clearly distinguish two different components: learning processes as being observable or not, and learning processes as a cognitive versus physical activity (Mulder, 2013). Although learning is often considered to be a cognitive process, in research, learning activities are often (also) measured with physical activities, such as searching the Internet (e.g. Kwakman, 2003). This might be caused by the fact that cognitive activities are less overt, and therefore more difficult to measure. Awareness of the distinction between physical and cognitive learning activities makes it possible that researchers have both in scope and do not mix them up. An example of a cognitive learning activity is reflecting on former solutions. Furthermore, mere engagement in learning activities is not equal to learning (Dewey, 1933). According to Mulder (2013), "physical learning activities can cause cognitive learning processes, but do not necessarily do so" (p. 52). Physical learning activities are observable. Cognitive learning activities are not necessarily, but can be made observable, for example, by thinking aloud (Mulder, 2013). In this chapter we take into account both physical and cognitive aspects.

Setting of learning activities

The relevance of the context was already touched upon. Informal learning activities can be carried out in a setting where one is alone or where other colleagues are present. Next to the location, another feature is that learning activities can be conducted alone, as well as together with colleagues in a collaborative manner (e.g. Hager & Halliday, 2006). In various definitions of informal learning, a distinction is made between individual and social learning activities. As mentioned, learning activities can be carried out individually (e.g. "analysing the situation", "searching the Internet") or in social interaction with other people (e.g. "reflecting together with colleagues on a prior solution", "discussing ideas with colleagues") (Mulder, 2013). Asking questions or discussing problems with colleagues are other examples of learning activities in a social setting (e.g. Doornbos, Simons, & Denessen, 2008). Software developers choose different ways to develop expertise. They differ regarding the amount of learning and the chosen learning behaviour (Assimakopoulos & Yan, 2006; Ha, 2008). However, in general, employees in the IT-domain tend to learn on their own (Lohman, 2009). Learning activities conducted individually lead to individual learning results. Learning activities occurring in social settings can result in both social and individual learning results. Social learning activities can take place as learning from others or learning together with others in a social setting. However, when someone is in a social setting, individual learning activities can occur. Learning activities leading to an individual learning result are the level of inquiry in the current chapter. As said, this can occur when alone, or in a context with colleagues.

To conclude, in this chapter, informal learning at work is defined as engagement in learning activities embedded in accomplishing work tasks in a specific work context. That engagement can be deliberate or reactive in intention and occur individually or socially outside organised learning settings and lead to changes in individual competences.

Triggering and engaging in learning activities at work

To understand the relationship between triggering and engaging in learning activities at work we use aspects of three different theoretical approaches. Piaget's (1977) concept of disturbances, which is part of the theory of equilibration of cognitive structures, provides the theoretical basis for what is perceived as a trigger for informal learning at work and for the effect of these triggers on informal learning at work. According to Piaget, development is driven by the process of equilibration. Equilibration encompasses assimilation and accommodation. Assimilation means that people transform incoming information so that it fits within their existing thinking (i.e. schemata). Accommodation means that people adapt their thinking to incoming information. Based on the concepts of assimilation and accommodation, which remain at the level of description, Piaget created a general model to explain learning at the individual level. The starting point of the learning process is a disturbance that makes people aware of a shortcoming in their thinking and they are dissatisfied, that is, in a state of disequilibrium and experiencing a disturbance they want to solve. Disturbances emerge through mismatches between the anticipated and the received result of actions (Piaget, 1977). A mismatch becomes a disturbance for the individual when it indicates the lack of an object, the deficiency of conditions necessary to perform an action, or the lack of knowledge that is crucial for accomplishing a (work) task. Work tasks are defined pieces of work that need to be accomplished in order to reach an objective. This objective is assigned to employees and carried out as part of one's duties. Regarding informal learning at work, situations that lead to disturbances are interactions with other people and the work task. Disturbances are perceived by the individual as unexpected results of actions, knowledge gaps, or errors (Piaget, 1977). The individual awareness of disturbances as a result of the interpretation of an experience stimulates activities to solve the disturbance. Therefore, disturbances can lead to modifications of the individual knowledge structure.

Furthermore, the learning process is conceptualised as a problem solving cycle or an action regulation model according to the models of Marsick and Watkins (1990) and Frese and Zapf (1994). Marsick and Watkins' model of informal and incidental learning depicts a process of meaning making (i.e. learning). They argue that learning begins with a trigger. This internal or external stimulus signals dissatisfaction with current ways of thinking or being. The model suggests that people diagnose or frame a new experience that they encounter. They assess what is problematic or challenging about it, examine alternative solutions, decide on one learning strategy, produce this solution and assess the outcomes.

In addition, actions are goal-oriented behaviour that is organised in specific ways by goals, information integration, plans and feedback, and can be regulated consciously or via routines. Action theory is a cognitive theory that is linked to behaviour and is concerned with the process that intervenes between environmental input and behaviour – the regulatory function of cognitions (Frese & Zapf, 1994). The starting point of work actions is the work task and the employee's goal is to accomplish the work task. This process can be disturbed by errors and knowledge gaps. To complete the work task, the employee develops a new goal, for example to correct the error. These actions to correct the error are seen as engagement in learning activities. Learning activities that vary in type and setting are considered possible courses of action. The choice of the learning activity is based on previous experiences and the context, including the work task and its characteristics.

The employee engages in the chosen learning activity, monitors the consequences and evaluates the success of the learning activity.

Work task characteristics are context factors and can therefore influence the choice of learning activity to accomplish the work task. Research showed that complex tasks require a high amount of context-based information and knowledge, which is described as experience-based knowledge. Software engineers try to gain access to this experience-based knowledge by talking to colleagues or through other knowledge-sharing channels.

Action theory not only combines environmental input (work tasks and its characteristics) and behaviour with regard to cognitive processes, but can also be used to depict the link between working and learning, because learning activities can be regarded as activities to accomplish work tasks. The theory of Frese and Zapf (1994) and the model of Marsick and Watkins (1990) further help to explain why people choose specific learning activities as their course of action and produce the chosen learning activities. Piaget's (1977) concept of disturbances provides the theoretical basis for what is perceived as triggers for informal learning at work and helps to describe these triggers.

According to that, the influence of work task characteristics on learning at work can be two sided. Firstly, work tasks and, therefore, their characteristics can lead to the detection of errors or knowledge gaps. Thus, work tasks provide the basis for triggering informal learning at work and therefore influence the extent of informal learning at work. Secondly, complexity of work tasks can influence the choice of learning activity regarding type and setting to accomplish the work task.

Complexity of work tasks

The complexity of work tasks can be interpreted and defined as (a) the structure of a task, and as (b) requirements on employees' skills. Based on the requirements, complex work tasks are interpreted as difficult (Morgeson & Humphrey, 2006) or challenging (Campbell, 1988). This individual experience is regarded as an individual's reaction to the complexity of the work task (Campbell, 1988) and not as a characteristic of the work task itself. Aspects to assess work task complexity objectively refer to the structure of a work task (Vakkari, 1999) which depends on the number of elements and their interrelation (Byström, 2002) which can be assessed objectively. Elements are the number of sub-tasks, the number of aims and the number of possible solutions (Brown & Miller, 2000; Campbell, 1988; Wood, 1986). The complexity of work tasks can be determined by the interconnectedness of these elements, in which a higher number of elements and interrelations between elements indicate higher work task complexity. Related to these characteristics is the non-transparency of adequate problem solving strategies.

Task complexity is regarded as a crucial influencing factor for the performance of employees. The influence on performance and informal learning at work is based on the requirements of complex work tasks on employee's knowledge, skills and resources (Wood, 1986). Based on theories of action regulation, task complexity is interpreted as the extent of the demand on cognition that is necessary to accomplish a task. Cognition is depicted by the aspects of planning, decision making and problem solving (Hacker, 2003). To accomplish a complex work task, an individual must regulate numerous aims and sub-aims. This is related to a high level of information processing. Complex tasks include a high number of sub-tasks. According to Brown and Miller (2000), a sub-task is seen as a single activity that requires specific knowledge and skills. The more numerous the sub-tasks, the more knowledge and skills are required. Therefore, complex work tasks are defined as work tasks which require high problem solving skills, high information processing skills and high skill variety for successful accomplishment.

In the domain of IT, the complexity of work tasks depends on the operation range of the software and, therefore, can vary across work tasks. Here, complexity can be seen as an aspect of the problem level, as an aspect of requirements the software must fulfil, as an aspect of design and as an aspect of the written code of the software. If one aspect indicates higher complexity, the other aspects indicate that as well. The problem level of software represents the complexity of the technical task. The number of interrelations is determined by the connectivity of multiple elements, e.g. the interrelated requirements of the software. Task complexity can be described objectively at this level and can be illustrated by the interconnectedness of the elements. The requirement level includes the complexity of the technical solution as well as business and technical requirements, technical objects, technical interfaces and applications. With an increasing number of specified interrelations, the complexity of the technical solution increases and, thus, the demands on employees' knowledge and their problem solving and information processing skills while working on this task, increase. These demands can be described objectively, too. The level of the design and the written code refer to the solution of the work task and, hence, the developed software.

In the following, the way in which a complex work task influences the extent and setting of learning activities is described. To do so, it is necessary to compare the influence of complex work tasks on the engagement in learning activities with the influence of less complex work tasks. Problem solving, information processing and skill variety as dimensions of the complexity of work tasks are used to illustrate this influence.

Effects of complexity of work tasks on informal learning at work

Work task characteristics can provide opportunities to reveal errors or knowledge gaps (Piaget, 1977). Work task characteristics provide the basis for triggering informal learning at work and therefore influence the extent of informal learning at work. Thus, the way in which problem solving, information processing and skill variety induce disturbances is focused on.

Problem solving reflects the degree to which a work task requires more active cognitive processing. This comprises generating unique or innovative ideas or solutions, diagnosing and solving non-routine problems, and preventing or undoing errors (Wall, Corbett, Clegg, Jackson, & Martin, 1990, in Morgeson & Humphrey, 2006). These cognitive processes lead to the detection of knowledge gaps and an accumulation of errors. Therefore, we expect more engagement in learning activities while accomplishing a complex work task as compared to a less complex work task.

The amount of information processing needed to accomplish a work task reflects the degree to which a job requires attending to and processing data or other information (Morgeson & Humphrey, 2006). If information processing is high (e.g. during evaluation and creating software), important information can easily be disregarded and errors are more likely to occur. Again, the experienced errors in turn lead to more engagement in learning activities, while accomplishing a complex work task compared to a less complex work task.

Skill variety reflects the extent to which a work task requires the use of a variety of skills to complete the work task. The more sub-tasks that must be accomplished, the more skills are required and, consequently, the more knowledge gaps are revealed and errors are made if the skills are not sufficient. The higher the variety of necessary knowledge, the higher is the amount of information (Byström, 2002). Therefore, we expect that high skill variety in a complex work task leads to more engagement in learning activities compared to a less complex work task. Consequently, the first hypothesis is:

> Hypothesis 1: Employees accomplishing a complex work task engage more in individual and social learning activities than employees accomplishing a less complex work task.

Work task characteristics can influence the choice of a learning activity regarding type and setting to accomplish the work task. Objective characteristics are reflected in employees' individual perception (Hacker, 2003), which means that employees choose a learning activity based on the individual perception of objective work task characteristics, the context and previous (learning) experiences. We focus on how employees deal with the need for problem solving, information processing and skill variety while accomplishing complex work tasks.

A complex task requires information on problem solving in order to accomplish the task (Byström & Järvelin, 1995). Byström (2002) showed that the more complex a task is and the higher the variety of necessary knowledge, the higher is the number of information sources and the importance of interaction partners to gain knowledge.

Based on their qualitative analysis in a study with software engineers, Freund, Toms and Waterhouse (2005) concluded that complex tasks require a high amount of context-based information and knowledge, which is described as experience-based knowledge. Software engineers try to gain access to this experience-based knowledge by talking to colleagues or using other knowledge-sharing channels, such as online forums. Opportunities to gain access to experts become important while accomplishing complex work tasks with a high need of different knowledge. In addition, to handle the necessary information processing during planning, decision making and problem solving, employees tend to work together. Therefore, we expect more engagement in social learning activities than in individual learning activities while employees accomplish a complex work task.

With high skill variety, the importance of interaction partners increases, because interaction partners provide the fastest access to the needed knowledge and skills necessary to accomplish the work task. Employees are expected to engage more in social learning activities than in individual learning activities to gain access to knowledge and skills while accomplishing a complex work task. Therefore, the second hypothesis is formulated as follows:

> Hypothesis 2: Employees accomplishing a complex work task engage more in social learning activities than in individual learning activities.

Research design

Domain

In the IT-domain, there are mainly small and medium-sized enterprises. The average information and communication technology service provider employs about ten people (Statistisches Bundesamt, 2013). According to Ruiz Ben (2007), the gender distribution is in favour of male employees (14 per cent female compared to 86 per cent male). Women are underrepresented, especially in small enterprises. Employees are characterised as "knowledge workers". Generally, IT-employees acquired high educational qualifications, work autonomously on projects and enjoy a high status in the labour market. Employees with lower qualification levels mostly work in the area of technical support (Hall, 2007). Software developers can be employed by enterprises, can work in IT-departments or can work as freelancers.

Design and sample

In a cross-sectional study, software developers were asked to fill out an online questionnaire. The domain of software developing was selected because it fulfils the requirements a domain has to meet for investigating work task complexity and informal learning at work. These requirements are (a) informal learning at work must be part of the daily work life and (b) employees must experience work tasks with varying degrees of complexity.

(a) Software developers in general rely on informal learning (Lohman, 2005, 2009) because of job intensification, which leads to the need for more knowledge and skills and simultaneously to a reduction of time for learning, fast knowledge development in the domain and the necessity to get to know the application domain of the software. Work contexts in the domain of software developing that lead to learning are characterised by challenging and demanding tasks employees find in their normal work routines, such as troubleshooting at work, and the installation of hardware and software components and projects (Ha, 2008).

(b) In the domain of software developing, the degree of work task complexity depends on the software and can be investigated objectively. The problem level of software applies to the objective characteristic of the work task and, thus, the structure of the work task. The structure of the work task can be illustrated by the number of links and knots, such as the interconnectedness of elements. The level of requirements refers to the complexity of accomplishing a work task. It includes subject-specific and technical requirements, interfaces and applications. With an increasing number of links and knots at the problem level, the complexity of the solution for this work task rises. Along with this, requirements regarding problem solving and information processing increase. Summing up, the extent of work task complexity depends on the requirements of the programmed software and therefore can vary between complex and less complex.

The sample was recruited from small- and medium-sized for-profit companies that provide information technology services, including programming, planning and designing of information systems, running data processing equipment for third parties and other IT-services, such as software installation or data recovery. The data were collected in autumn 2012 and spring 2013 with an online questionnaire distributed to employees of such enterprises (range of software developers: 3–100). Fifty-seven enterprises were contacted; in the end 38 participated in the study in that they distributed the cover letter to their employed software developers. Therefore, the enterprises functioned as access to software developers only. Enterprise affiliation was not gathered, in order that the participants maintain anonymity. Participation was voluntary.

Thus, 1,017 software developers received the cover letter via e-mail and were invited to fill out the online questionnaire. In the end, data of 182 software developers could be used for analysis (response rate = 18 per cent). Forty-nine per cent of the participants completed the questionnaire with the complex work task and 51 per cent completed the questionnaire with the less complex work task. The average age was $M = 35.32$ ($SD = 9.03$) and the participants had worked in the domain for $M = 10.13$ years ($SD = 8.11$) (i.e. professional age). Due to the gender distribution in this domain, mainly men participated (12.6 per cent women, 87.4 per cent men). Regarding age and work experience, both groups showed no differences and therefore can be compared to each other.

Instrument

The questionnaire consisted of different parts: a vignette and questions for measuring the control variables. To acknowledge the importance of the context, researching informal learning at work has to be bound to authentic situations, since the individual, isolated from the context, is not the appropriate level to analyse the interaction between the trigger for informal learning at work and individual learning. A context-bound measurement is necessary to guarantee content validity. The Vignette Technique is used to measure learning at work. This technique is context bound and at the same time allows a controlled variation of work task complexity.

The vignette contains a simulation of realistic, authentic situations or events (Wilks, 2004), requires questions or instructions (as stimulus) and some kind of answering mode (Mulder, 2015). It thus ensures a link between the participants' reaction and the fictive situation. The stimulus presented to the participants can be texts of different lengths, an image, or a video. Vignettes should be based on authentic, realistic situations that need problem solving (Finch, 1987). A vignette should be based on literature, be written in collaboration with professionals of the work context and be validated by these professionals (e.g. Mulder, 2015). Below, the operationalisation of the complexity of work tasks with the vignettes and the development of the vignettes is described.

Complexity of work tasks

Vignettes as presentations of a work task with a variation of work task complexity were developed to be able to investigate the learning activities that emanate from the complexity of work tasks. The vignettes were designed based on the operationalisation of the construct of work task complexity and the findings of an explorative interview study in the domain of software developing ($N = 7$, all men, $M_{age} = 27.28$ years, $SD_{age} = 2.69$; $M_{work\ experience} = 2.57$ years; $SD_{work\ experience} = 2.22$). The interview study should ensure insight into the domain of software developing. Therefore, the participants worked in different fields (counselling, development and research) and at different hierarchical levels. The level of analysis was the level of the disturbance that triggers informal learning at work. Therefore, the sample consisted of the reported disturbances and related learning activities ($n = 27$). The sample size was sufficient to identify typical disturbances in the domain of software developing as the basis for designing vignettes. In addition, the resulting vignettes were analysed in terms of their authenticity – the complexity and extent of the described work task as well as the participants' possible reactions, as indicated by three software developers (one expert and two semi-experts) with whom the vignettes were piloted and who provided feedback for improving the vignettes.

The topic of the work tasks concerns the development and integration of software. An error served as a disturbance that emphasised the need for informal learning. To ensure a clear operationalisation of the complexity of the work tasks, only two domain-specific vignettes were designed, one complex and one less complex work task (Figures 3.1 and 3.2). Between these two vignettes, the differences concerning tasks complexity were maximised.

The vignettes differ regarding the interconnectedness of the software requirements (7 knots and 6 links versus 12 knots and 16 links) (Ketterl, 2013) and therefore indicate different levels of complexity. Additionally, requirements regarding the employees' problem solving skills, information processing skills and skill variety were based on the varying software requirements described in the vignettes. The requirements for accomplishing the less complex work task were low. Web shops can be built with modular construction systems. This presupposes fewer skills because the requirements are limited to installing programs and applying passive

> In the following, an authentic, but hypothetical example of your daily work is presented. Please, read it thoroughly. Try to imagine the situation.
>
> The producer of toys 'Woodtoy' would like to display and sell his wooden toys through a web shop. The product range comprises wooden figures of different kinds as well as building blocks which are provided in different sets. You take employment to program the web shop. The following features should be implemented:
>
> - Presentation of the goods, with appealing layout
> - Consumer basket
> - Payment, without the use of a third-party-supplier (*note: necessary for accepting credit cards, etc.*)
> - No storage of addresses necessary
>
> While feeding in the data, you face a problem.
> What would you do?

FIGURE 3.1 Less complex work task vignette

> In the following, an authentic, but hypothetical example of your daily work is presented. Please, read it thoroughly. Try to imagine the situation.
>
> The producer of tools 'Toolmaster' would like to extend their enterprise. The product range comprises different tools of the renowned producer as well as possible equipment. You take employment to program the web shop. The following features should be implemented:
>
> - Presentation of the goods, with appealing layout
> - Consumer basket
> - Suggestions of additional products
> - Payment, with the use of a third-party-supplier (*note: necessary for accepting credit cards, etc.*)
> - Database for addresses, also for international customers, with plausibility check
> - Recognition of customers and list of recommendations based on previous purchases
> - Integration with stock system, including inventory audit and direct enter on stock
> - Possibility to contact
>
> During accomplishing the work task, you detect a process that could not be integrated into the software concept.
> What would you do?

FIGURE 3.2 Complex work task vignette

interfaces. Therefore, the necessary information processing is also low. Due to the low requirements and the low interconnectedness of the elements, the requirements for problem solving are also low.

The requirements for accomplishing the complex work task are higher. Additionally, the employee needs knowledge and skills in hardware and IT-infrastructure. Moreover, skills in database applications and its links are necessary. Information processing is higher because of the higher interconnectedness of all elements (feedbacks and database connections). Active interfaces are necessary;

therefore, problem solving is needed, because the integration of different components can lead to errors (Ketterl, 2013).

Each participant was randomly assigned one out of the two vignettes and was asked to picture such a situation as described.

Learning activities

In combination with the vignette, learning activities adapted to the domain of software developing were presented, and each participant was asked what he/she would do to solve the problem described in the vignette (e.g. reflecting on known literature). The participants were asked to rate all learning activities as potential options of action (see Table 3.1 for all learning activities). To cover the wide range of possible learning activities in this domain that may emanate from the complexity of a task, different learning activities from the different parts of the framework of learning activities (i.e. social and individual, physical and cognitive) were presented. Based on our insight from literature, the interviews and piloting the vignettes, and by systematically using the framework, we selected those learning activities that seemed most relevant in the domain of software developing. That led to in total 24 learning activities which were presented (12 individual learning activities and 12 social learning activities). The answering mode was a 6-point Likert-scale ranged from 1 (totally disagree) to 6 (totally agree).

Control variables

The scale of Jerusalem and Schwarzer (1981) was applied to collect information about self-efficacy (10 items, Cronbach's $\alpha = .80$). In addition, data on the age and work experience of the participants was collected with open questions.

Analysis

Informal learning at work in both conditions was analysed by calculating frequencies and totals. Due to the non-normally distributed nature of the data on the engagement in learning activities, differences concerning the engagement in learning activities that were carried out in the complex condition and the less complex condition (Hypothesis 1) were tested with the Mann-Whitney-U-Test. Differences concerning the engagement in individual and social learning activities in the complex condition (Hypothesis 2) were tested with the Wilcoxon Signed Rank Test. In this regard, the sum of all rated individual learning activities and the sum of all rated social learning activities for each participant were compared.

Learning activities at work in IT

The results showed that all presented learning activities were reported by the respondents (see Table 3.1). That means that engagement in all kinds of learning activities emanated from the work tasks that were covered by the vignettes. There were, however, differences concerning the engagement in different learning activities: the scores run from 2.43 to 5.57 on a range from 1 to 6. Overall, the scores indicated that the respondents would engage in many learning activities. The software developers mentioned the learning activity "analysing the situation" the most, and the learning activity "reading a professional journal" the least.

Employees accomplishing a complex work task engage more in learning activities than employees accomplishing a less complex work task (Hypothesis 1)

Participants in the complex condition engaged more in 'individual-cognitive learning activities' compared to participants in the non-complex condition, except for the learning activity "specifying the problem". In contrast to our expectation, the less complex task resulted in more problem specification. These differences concerning the engagement in "individual-cognitive learning" activities between the two work tasks (i.e. complex vs. less complex), however, were not statistically significant. Moreover, participants in the complex condition stated more intended engagement in "individual-physical learning activities" compared to participants in the non-complex condition. However, for the engagement in "individual-physical learning activities", no statistically significant differences between the complex and non-complex work tasks were found either.

In general, participants whose responses were based on the complex work task reported more intended engagement in "'social-cognitive learning activities" than participants whose responses were based on the less complex work task. Among all presented "social-cognitive learning activities", statistically significant differences between the two work tasks (i.e. complex vs. less complex) were found for the learning activities "reflecting together with colleagues on a prior solution", "reflecting together with colleagues on a prior discussion about a similar topic" and "reflecting together with colleagues on a prior expert discussion". Moreover, participants stated more intended engagement in "social-physical learning activities" in relation to accomplishing the complex work task than in relation to accomplishing the non-complex work task. However, for the intended engagement in the different "social-physical learning activities", no statistically significant differences between the two conditions (i.e. complex vs. less complex work tasks) were found, except for the learning activity "drawing notes during an expert discussion with a colleague". In general, participants stated that they would engage significantly more in a small number of social learning activities if their responses were based on the complex work task vignette compared to participants whose responses were based on the less complex work task vignette.

Thus, the first hypothesis, stating that employees accomplishing a complex work task engage more in learning activities than employees accomplishing a less complex work task, is partially supported. Only few statistically significant differences concerning the engagement in learning activities as a result of the complexity of the work task were found. Specifically, statistically significant differences were found for three learning activities that are examples of "social-cognitive learning activities".

In Table 3.1, the mean and standard deviation are listed for each learning activity and the results of the Mann-Whitney-U-Test between the two conditions. The two groups did not differ regarding the background variables age and work experience.

TABLE 3.1 Extent of agreement with the question "what would you do" to solve the described trigger for informal learning at work (mean, standard deviation and Mann-Whitney-U-Test)

Learning activities	Complex work task N = 89 M	SD	Less complex work task N = 93 M	SD	Mann-Whitney-U-Test P
Individual-cognitive					
Reflecting on known literature.	2.96	1.49	2.92	1.46	.92
Specifying the problem.	5.12	1.33	5.57	.82	.05*
Reflecting on prior experiences.	4.90	1.14	4.76	1.18	.38
Reflecting on learned things.	4.22	1.41	4.01	1.37	.26
Thinking about possible solutions.	5.27	1.02	5.12	1.00	.14
Analysing the situation.	5.40	.95	5.44	.90	.87
Individual-physical					
Drawing notes.	4.18	1.60	4.38	1.37	.39
Repeating the task.	3.29	1.59	3.44	1.59	.52
Searching the Internet.	5.16	1.23	4.96	1.36	.27
Reviewing existing materials.	3.88	1.38	3.91	1.45	.85
Reading a book.	2.96	1.48	2.73	1.44	.31
Reading a professional journal.	2.67	1.42	2.43	1.44	.19
Social-cognitive					
Reflecting together with colleagues on a prior solution.	4.76	1.29	4.38	1.37	.03★
Reflecting together with colleagues on a prior discussion about a similar topic.	4.16	1.61	3.66	1.52	.01★
Reflecting together with colleagues on feedback.	4.09	1.45	4.03	1.43	.64
Reflecting together with colleagues on prior suggestions.	4.04	1.47	3.66	1.52	.07
Reflecting together with colleagues on prior expert discussions.	3.88	1.58	3.31	1.70	.02★
Reflecting together with colleagues on support another colleague received.	3.70	1.47	3.52	1.50	.44

(continued)

TABLE 3.1 Extent of agreement with the question "what would you do" to solve the described trigger for informal learning at work (mean, standard deviation and Mann-Whitney-U-Test) *(continued)*

	Complex work task N = 89		Less complex work task N = 93		Mann-Whitney-U-Test
Learning activities	M	SD	M	SD	P
Social-physical					
Talking about this problem with a colleague.	5.01	1.28	4.97	1.03	.27
Discussing ideas with colleagues.	5.11	1.09	5.09	.98	.50
Working together with colleagues to solve the problem.	4.67	1.33	4.60	1.25	.51
Exchanging information with colleagues.	5.06	1.08	5.03	1.05	.79
Discussing with colleagues.	4.61	1.34	4.32	1.46	.20
Drawing notes during an expert discussion with a colleague.	3.96	1.58	3.49	1.63	.05★

Range 1–6
1 – I totally disagree
6 – I totally agree
★ $p \leq .05$

Employees accomplishing a complex work task engage more in social learning activities than in individual learning activities (Hypothesis 2)

The second hypothesis stated that employees would engage more in social learning activities than in individual learning activities while accomplishing a complex work task. To test this hypothesis a Wilcoxon Signed Rank Test was conducted. Thus, the sum scores of all 12 individual and all 12 social learning activities (each can range from 12 to 72) were calculated. Results showed a significantly higher engagement in social learning activities than in individual learning activities for participants in the complex condition (Z = –3.203; p < .01). This result supports the second hypothesis.

Concerning control variables, no statistically significant correlation between self-efficacy and engagement in learning activities was found for the less complex work task. On the contrary, self-efficacy correlated significantly with four learning activities in the complex work task condition. These learning activities were "analysing the situation" (r = .21, p < .05), "reading a book" (r = .21, p < .05), "reflecting on learned things" (r = .26, p < .05) and "thinking about possible solutions" (r = .27, p < .05). This means that self-efficacy can have a positive effect on the engagement in at least part of the learning activities, however without showing a clear pattern. Because of these sparse correlations, no further analyses were carried out. In addition, no statistically significant correlations for the background variables (age and work experience) and the engagement in learning activities were found.

Conclusion

The tasks of software developers seem to involve employees in the engagement in learning activities. The learning activities "analysing the situation" and "specifying the problem" are the activities the employees would engage in the most. It is noticeable, that employees in the domain of software developing would engage less in learning activities concerning written material (e.g. "reading a professional journal", "reading a book"), but showed a high intention to search the Internet. In general, employees would engage more in different components of social learning activities than in components of individual learning activities. It is not surprising that participants stated their high engagement in learning activities such as "analysing the situation" and "specifying the problem". Both activities are seen as the first step of problem solving, regardless of the complexity of a work task. This result is opposite to what Lohman (2009) stated in her study on factors influencing the engagement of information technology professionals in informal learning activities. In her study, employees would engage most strongly in the learning activity "searching the Internet", followed by "talking with others". Furthermore, participants in her study added the learning activity "reading professional literature" as an additional learning activity in which they would engage in.

Statistically significant differences concerning the engagement in learning activities as a result of the complexity of work tasks were found for different activities belonging to the categories "individual-cognitive learning activities" and "social-cognitive learning activities". Interesting is the fact that employees who are presented a less complex work task intend to engage more in the learning activity "specifying the problem". Also, in general, few statistically significant differences concerning the engagement in learning activities were found. Thus, there was only partial support for the first hypothesis. On the contrary, we found support for the second hypothesis which stated that employees would engage more in social learning activities than in individual learning activities while accomplishing a complex work task.

Software developers need a combination of technical knowledge, creative skills and knowledge of business and marketing. This knowledge is not entirely codified in various media (e.g. manuals), but exists as implicit knowledge (Assimakopoulos & Yan, 2006). Along with that, the results indicated the importance of social learning activities in the domain of software developing. The higher the complexity of the work tasks and the more knowledge and problem solving skills are required, the more sources are used and the greater is the use of people inside the organisation as a source (Byström, 2002). This is reflected in the results. In both conditions of complexity, the employees stated a high intention to engage in social learning activities. In addition, in the complex condition, the intended engagement in social learning activities was significantly higher compared to the less complex condition and compared to the engagement in individual learning activities in the complex condition.

Limitations and implications for further research

Due to the selective sample, generalisation of the results is limited to domains in which employees encounter complex work tasks and rely on informal learning at work. Research in other domains of engineering is conceivable and it would be worthwhile to investigate work task complexity and its effect on informal learning in other domains as well.

In addition, to better understand learning at work in IT, the Vignette Technique was used to (a) measure learning in a context-bound manner and (b) with built-in variation in the complexity of work tasks. Regarding the content of the stimulus, the space for interpretation can thus be reduced and the comparability of reactions can be increased. The design of the stimulus, however, must be aligned to the aim of the research. Therefore, using the Vignette Technique allows a systematic, controlled variation of variables during the research. There are some examples of usage of this technique in investigating and fostering informal learning (and professional development) (e.g. Bernabeo, Reddy, Ginsburg, & Holmboe, 2014; Leicher & Mulder, online first), but these are scarce. Instead of researching complexity as a general work task characteristic as is usually done, this project investigated the effect of the complexity of a specific work task on learning activities that emanate from them. In addition, in this study, a selection of all kinds of possible learning activities that can occur in jobs in this domain was used. This was done with the objective to cover the wide variety of possibilities, but not to systematically represent the full range of activities. Therefore, the activities used in this study do not form a scale that can be used in various domains. For every study, the learning activities should be selected fitting to the specific domain.

Employees redefine their work tasks individually (Hacker, 2003) and therefore, the individual perception of a situation (e.g. the complexity of the work task) is crucial for the chosen course of action. Thus, in future research, the perceived complexity of work tasks should be taken into account, in addition to the objectively measured complexity of work tasks in order to be able to control if the objective complexity is interpreted as intended. Therefore, it would be interesting to consider the relation with prior knowledge and work experience as well.

Self-efficacy is an important predictor of job performance (Bandura and Locke, 2003) and enhances the motivation to conduct informal learning activities (Lohman, 2005). In the presented study, self-efficacy correlated significantly with a few individual (and mostly cognitive) learning activities in the complex work task condition. In contrast, while accomplishing a less complex work task, no statistically significant correlations between self-efficacy and engagement in learning activities were found. It could be assumed that self-efficacy becomes especially important in challenging situations.

Practical implications for fostering informal learning at work

Based on the results, practical implications are derived for fostering informal learning at work in the domain of software developing. The learning activity "specifying the problem" emanates more from less complex tasks. This indicates that managers need to support that aspect less when there are less complex problems, and more in situations where there are more complex work tasks, namely by creating awareness of the characteristics of complex work tasks and by providing opportunities to handle these work tasks. That may be applied to other domains in which complex work tasks play a pivotal role as well. In general, literature, journals and books are rarely used in these situations. That can be encouraged by providing opportunities and the time to use these resources. Generally, to foster informal learning at work while accomplishing a work task, the organisation and structure of the workplace should allow the employee to engage in social-physical learning activities (e.g. discussing ideas with colleagues) and individual-cognitive learning activities (e.g. analysing the situation). Employees need time to analyse problems and reflect on previous experiences and to interact not only with colleagues but also with other experts in the field in order to learn informally. In addition, if employees have to accomplish a complex work task, even more important for fostering informal learning at work is access to the experiences of a team (i.e. memory), for example, to be involved in problem solving strategies concerning the work of one's colleagues and having the time to reflect on the interactions while accomplishing complex work tasks. Consequently, the supervisor should be aware of the importance of reflection for the learning process and arrange enough time for reflection. Moreover, the supervisor should be aware of how to benefit best from teamwork. Time to talk is crucial, but also the support of information and knowledge exchange is helpful for successful learning. To define specialised contact persons (experts) might support the knowledge exchange and therefore foster informal learning at work. At the organisational level, the implementation of these recommendations would lead to an established learning culture and therefore to better learning conditions for employees – conditions employees should take advantage of in order to learn informally.

The physical learning activities that were investigated seem to be carried out more frequently than the cognitive activities. Physical learning activities, however, do not necessarily lead to cognitive learning processes that, in turn, lead to further professional development (i.e. long term development, instead of one problem solution). That means that in practice there needs to be awareness of the difference and importance of explicitly using physical learning activities more often for (long-term) cognitive learning processes. Managers and employees (supervisors and subordinates) can play a role in this by discussing these aspects on a regular basis, for instance, in appraisal interviews or by implementing (peer-) mentoring and coaching phases.

References

Assimakopoulos, D. & Yan, L. (2006). Sources of knowledge acquisition for Chinese software engineers. *R&D Management*, *36*(1), 97–106.
Bandura, A., & Locke, E. A. (2003). Negative self-efficacy and goal effects revisited. *Journal of Applied Psychology*, *88*(1), 87–99. doi:10.1037/0021-9010.88.1.87

Bernabeo, E. C., Reddy, S. G., Ginsburg, S., & Holmboe, E. S. (2014). Professionalism and maintenance of certification: Using vignettes describing interpersonal dilemmas to stimulate reflection and learning. *Journal of Continuing Education in the Health Professions, 34*(2), 112–122. doi:10.1002/chp.21228

Billett, S., & Choy, S. (2013) Learning through work: emerging perspectives and new challenges. *Journal of Workplace Learning, 25*(4), 264–276 doi:10.1108/13665621311316447

Brown, T. M., & Miller, C. E. (2000). Communication networks in task-performing groups. Effect of task complexity, time pressure, and interpersonal dominance. *Small Group Research, 31*(2), 131–157. doi:10.1177/104649640003100201

Byström, K., & Järvelin, K. (1995). Task complexity affects information seeking and use. *Information Processing and Management, 31*(2), 191–213. doi:10.1016/0306-4573(94)00041-Z

Byström, K. (2002). Information and information source in tasks of varying complexity. *Journal of the American Society for Information Science and Technology, 53*(7), 581–591. doi:10.1002/asi.10064

Campbell, D. J. (1988). Task complexity: A review and analysis. *Academy of Management Review, 13*(1), 40–52. doi:10.5465/AMR.1988.4306775

Cofer, D. (2000). *Informal workplace learning* (Practice application brief. No. 10). US Department of Education: Clearinghouse on Adult, Career, and Vocational Education.

Dewey, J. (1933). *How we think. A restatement of the relation of reflective thinking to the educative process.* Boston, MA: D. C. Heath.

Doornbos, A., Bolhuis, S., & Denessen, E. (2004). Exploring the relation between work domains and work-related learning: The case of the Dutch police force. *International Journal of Training and Development, 8*(3), 174–190. doi:10.1111/j.1360-3736.2004.00207.x

Doornbos, A., Simons, R.-J., & Denessen, E. (2008). Relations between characteristics of workplace practices and types of informal work-related learning: A survey study among Dutch Police. *Human Resource Development Quarterly, 19*(2), 129–151. doi:10.1002/hrdq.1231

Ellinger, A., & Cseh, M. (2007). Contextual factors influencing the facilitation of others' learning through everyday work experiences. *Journal of Workplace Learning, 19*(7), 435–452. doi:10.1108/13665620710819384

Ellström, P.-E. (2001). Integrating learning and work: Problems and prospects. *Human Resource Development Quarterly, 12*(4), 421–435.

Eraut, M. (2000). Non-formal learning and tacit knowledge in professional work. *British Journal of Educational Psychology, 70*(1), 113–136. doi:10.1348/000709900158001

Felstead, A., Fuller, A., Unwin, L., Ashton, D., Butler, P., & Lee, T (2005). Surveying the scene: Learning metaphors, survey design and the workplace context. *Journal of Education and Work, 18*(4), 359–383. doi:10.1080/13639080500327857

Finch, J. (1987). The vignette technique in survey research. *Sociology, 21*(1), 105–111.

Freund, L., Toms, E. G., & Waterhouse, J. (2005). Modeling the information behaviour of software engineers using a work-task framework. *Proceedings of the American Society for Information Science and Technology, 42*(1), n/a. doi:10.1002/meet.14504201181

Frese, M., & Zapf, D. (1994). Action as the core of work psychology: A German approach. In H. C. Triandis, M. D. Dunnette, & L. M. Hough (Eds.), *Handbook of industrial and organizational psychology* (pp. 271–340). Palo Alto, CA: Consulting Psychologists Press.

Ha, T. S. (2008). How IT workers learn in the workplace. *Studies in Continuing Education, 30*(2), 129–143. doi:10.1080/01580370802097728

Hacker, W. (2003). Action regulation theory: A practical tool for the design of modern work processes? *European Journal of Work and Organizational Psychology, 12*(2), 105–130. doi:10.1080/13594320344000075

Hager, P., & Halliday, J. S. (2006). *Recovering informal learning: Wisdom, judgement and community*. Dordrecht: Springer.

Hager, P. (1998), Understanding workplace learning: general perspectives. In D. Boud (Ed.), *Current issues and new agendas in workplace learning* (pp. 30–42). Springfield, VA: NCVER.

Hall, A. (2007). *Tätigkeiten und berufliche Anforderungen in wissensintensiven Berufen: Empirische Befunde auf Basis der BIBB/BAuA-Erwerbstätigkeitenbefragung 2006* [Activities and job requirements in knowledge-intensive jobs: Empirical evidences based on the BIBB/BAuA employee survey 2006]. Bonn: BIBB.

Jerusalem, M., & Schwarzer, R. (1981). Selbstwirksamkeit (WIRK) [Self-efficacy (WIRK)]. In R. Schwarzer (Ed.), *Skalen zur Befindlichkeit und Persönlichkeit* [Scales on state and personality] (Research Report No. 5, pp. 15–28). Berlin: Freie Universität, Institut für Psychologie.

Ketterl, K. (2013). *Informelles Lernen im Arbeitsprozess: Eine Untersuchung kontextueller Einflussfaktoren auf Lernaktivitäten von Softwareentwicklern* [Informal learning at work: An investigation of contextual factors that influence the learning activities of software developers]. Hamburg: Kovac Verlag.

Kwakman, K. (2003). Factors affecting teachers' participation in professional learning activities. *Teaching and Teacher Education, 19*(2), 149–170. doi:10.1016/S0742-051X(02)00101-4

Lave, J., & Wenger, E. (1991). *Situated learning: Legitimate peripheral participation*. Cambridge: Cambridge University Press.

Le Clus, M. (2011). Informal learning in the workplace: A review of the literature. *Australian Journal of Adult Learning, 51*(2), 355–373.

Leicher, V., & Mulder, R. H. (2016). Individual and contextual factors influencing engagement in learning activities after errors at work: A replication study in a German Retail Bank. *Journal of Workplace Learning, 28*(2), 66–80. doi:10.1108/JWL-03-2015-0022

Leicher, V., & Mulder, R. H. (online first). Development of vignettes for learning and professional development. *Gerontology and Geriatrics Education*. doi:10.1080/02701960.2016.1247065

Leicher, V., Mulder, R. H., & Bauer, J. (2013). Learning form errors at work: A replication study in elder care nursing. *Vocations and Learning, 6*(2), 7–20. doi:10.1007/s12186-012-9090-0.

Lohman, M. C. (2005). A survey of factors influencing the engagement of two professional groups in informal workplace learning activities. *Human Resource Development Quarterly, 16*(4), 501–527. doi:10.1002/hrdq.1153

Lohman, M. C. (2009). A survey of factors influencing the engagement of information technology professionals in informal learning activities. *Information Technology, Learning and Performance Journal, 25*(1), 43–53. doi:10.1108/13665620610654577

Lundgren, S. (2011). Learning opportunities for nurses working within home care. *Journal of Workplace Learning, 23*(1), 6–19. doi:10.1108/13665621111097227

Manuti, A., Pastore, S., Scardigno, A. F., Giancaspro, M. L., & Morciano, D. (2015), Formal and informal learning in the workplace: A research review. *International Journal of Training and Development, 19*(1), 1–17. doi:10.1111/ijtd.12044

Marsick, V. J., & Volpe, M. (1999). The nature and need for informal learning. *Advances in Developing Human Resources, 1*(3), 1–9.

Marsick, V. J., & Watkins, K. E. (1990). *Informal and incidental learning in the workplace*. London: Routledge.

Merriam, S., Caffarella, R. S., & Baumgartner, L. M. (2007). *Learning in adulthood: A comprehensive guide*. San Francisco, CA: Jossey-Bass.

Morgeson, F. P., & Humphrey, S. E. (2006). The Work Design Questionnaire (WDQ): Developing and validating a comprehensive measure for assessing job design and the nature of work. *Journal of Applied Psychology*, *91*(6), 1321–1339. doi:10.1037/0021-9010.91.6.1321

Mulder, R. H. (2013). Exploring feedback incidents, their characteristics and the informal learning activities that emanate from them. *European Journal of Training and Development*, *37*(1), 49–71. doi:10.1108/03090591311293284

Mulder, R.H. (2015). Using critical incidents and vignette technique in HRD research to investigate learning activities and behaviour at work. In P. Tosey & M. Saunders (Eds.), *Handbook of research methods on human resource development* (pp. 258–272). Cheltenham: Edward Elgar Publishing.

Mulder, R. H., Harteis, C., & Gruber, H. (2009). Lernen von Lehrenden im Arbeitsprozess [Learning of educators in their work]. In O. Zlatkin-Troitschanskaia, K. Beck, D. Sembill, R. Nickolaus, & R. Mulder (Eds.), *Lehrprofessionalität. Bedingungen, Genese, Wirkungen und ihre Messung* [Teaching professionalism. Conditions, genesis, effects, and its measurement] (pp. 567–576). Weinheim: Beltz.

Nerland, M. (2008). Knowledge cultures and the shaping of work-based learning: The case of computer engineering. *Vocations and Learning*, *1*(1), 49–69. doi:10.1007/s12186-007-9002-x

OECD (2002). *OECD information technology outlook: ICTs and the information economy*. Paris: OECD.

Piaget, J. (1977). *The development of thought: Equilibration of cognitive structures*. Oxford: Basil Blackwell.

Ruiz Ben, E. (2007). Defining expertise in software development while doing gender. *Gender, Work and Organization*, *14*(4), 312–332. doi:10.1111/j.1468-0432.2007.00346.x

Simons, P. R.-J., & Ruijters, M. C. P. (2004). Learning professionals: Towards an integrated model. In H. P. A. Boshuizen, R. Bromme, & H. Gruber (Eds.), *Professional learning: Gaps and transitions on the way from novice to expert* (pp. 207–229). Dordrecht: Kluwer.

Skule, S. (2004). Learning conditions at work: A framework to understand and assess informal learning in the workplace, *International Journal of Training and Development*, *8*(1), 8–20. doi:10.1111/j.1360-3736.2004.00192.x

Sonnentag, S. (1995). Excellent software professionals: Experience, work activities, and perception by peers. *Behaviour & Information Technology*, *14*(5), 289–299. doi:10.1080/01449299508914648

Sonnentag, S. (1998). Expertise in professional software design: A process study. *Journal of Applied Psychology*, *83*(5), 703–15. doi:10.1037/0021-9010.83.5.703

Statistisches Bundesamt (2013). *IKT-Branche in Deutschland: Bericht zur wirtschaftlichen Entwicklung* [ICT branch in Germany: Report on the economic development]. Wiesbaden: Statistisches Bundesamt.

Vakkari, P. (1999). Task complexity, problem structure and information actions: Integrating studies on information seeking and retrieval. *Information Processing and Management*, *35*(6), 819–837. doi:10.1016/S0306-4573(99)00028-X

Volmer, J., & Sonnentag, S. (2011). The role of star performance in software design teams. *Journal of Managerial Psychology*, *26*(3), 219–234. doi:10.1108/02683941111112659

Watkins, K. E., & Marsick, V. J. (1992). Towards a theory of informal and incidental learning in organizations. *International Journal of Lifelong Education*, *11*(4), 287–300. doi:10.1080/0260137920110403

Wilks, T. (2004). The use of vignettes in qualitative research into social work values. *Qualitative Social Work*, *3*(1), 78–87. doi:10.1177/1473325004041133

Wood, R. E. (1986). Task complexity: Definition of the construct. *Organizational Behaviour and Human Decision Processes*, *37*(1), 60–82. doi:10.1016/0749-5978(86)90044-0

4
DELIBERATE PRACTICE AS A LEVER FOR PROFESSIONAL JUDGEMENT

Lessons from informal workplace learning

Therese Grohnert, Roger Meuwissen, and Wim H. Gijselaers[1]

Introduction and theoretical framework

Organisations across professional environments rely on their employees' expertise to make high-quality judgements and decisions. From radiologists viewing mammograms to detect tumours, to auditors who monitor clients' financial statements for cues of fraud, professionals rely on their experience to make judgements in the workplace (Kahneman and Klein, 2009). However, experience is not the same as expertise. Across a wide range of environments, research has shown that not all professionals perform at similar levels when they possess the same amount of experience (Elmore, Wells and Howards, 1998; Payne and Ramsay, 2005). For example, Elmore et al. (1994) find that when presenting the same mammograms to experienced radiologists, recommendations for follow-up vary significantly between radiologists (in up to 33 per cent of the cases). Similar behaviour was found within professionals. When evaluating the same scans a second time, judgements differed in up to 9 per cent of the cases. The internal consistency of radiologists' judgements seems therefore limited. In the audit environment, a recent review of 989 audits of the six largest audit firms has shown that in the period of one year, 1,260 flaws were found, despite the fact that each audit is conducted and checked by multiple auditors with different levels of experience (International Forum of International Audit Regulators (IFIAR), 2016). This raises the question of what distinguishes professionals' performance within the same levels of experience.

In their review on two decades of expertise research, Salas and Rosen (2010) find that deliberate practice is a crucial determinant of performance. Deliberate practice was first defined by Ericsson, Krampe and Tesch-Römer as a "highly structured

---

1 Maastricht University, The Netherlands

activity, the explicit goal of which is to improve performance" (1993, p. 368), that is guided by a teacher, continuously challenging, including immediate feedback and requiring high cognitive effort. Recently, two reviews have been conducted on the relationship between the number of hours spent on deliberate practice (as defined by Ericsson, Krampe and Tesch-Römer (1993)), and professional performance (Hambrick et al., 2014; Macnamara, Hambrick and Oswald, 2014). In the environments of games, sports and music, deliberate practice was found to predict between 18 and 34 per cent of variance in performance. In education and the professions (e.g. aviation, medicine) however, deliberate practice was found to explain between less than 1 and 4 per cent only across a review of seven effect sizes. Macnamara, Hambrick and Oswald (2014) present a potential explanation for this discrepancy: the underlying assumption behind the concept of deliberate practice is that it has been defined for environments with high validity. Kahneman and Klein (2009, p. 520) define environmental validity as "the causal and statistical structure of the relevant environment". However, most professions are characterised by limited validity: the same information may not be indicative of the same judgement at all times. Professionals therefore need to learn to distinguish valid from invalid information to make high-quality judgements (Kahneman and Klein, 2009).

This chapter follows up on Macnamara, Hambrick and Oswald's (2014) suggestion to apply deliberate practice to environments characterised by limited validity to get a better understanding of how experience and deliberate practice relate to performance. To achieve this goal, we first discuss how professionals form judgements in limited validity environments. Next we discuss deliberate practice in these environments by taking into account characteristics of workplace learning specified by the informal learning literature.

Making high-quality judgements in limited validity environments

Making high-quality judgements, especially in limited validity environments, requires taking into account both the process as well as the outcome of professional judgements (Emby and Gibbins, 1988; Knechel and Messier Jr, 1990). Croskerry (2009) proposes a model of diagnostic reasoning that conceptualises both components. Following Croskerry's model, when faced with a situation that requires a judgement, the first step is to collect relevant information. The second step is the interpretation of the retrieved information based on prior experiences, followed by the making of a judgement. Judgement quality then takes into account both the process of collecting information as well as the outcome, the actual judgement made. This is reflected in professional practice, for example, by the requirement for auditors to document the information they collected for each judgement made, specified in their analytical procedures, and the checklists provided to medical professionals in many different functions. We therefore formulate the following underlying hypothesis with respect to judgement quality:

> H1: Information search is positively related to judgement accuracy.

Croskerry (2009) highlights that professionals require extensive knowledge to effectively translate information from a situation into an accurate judgement. This knowledge is often operationalised as years of experience with a specific task; both Kahneman and Klein (2009) as well as Shanteau (1992) however, explicitly state that under certain conditions, experience is not sufficient for high judgement quality: when validity is limited, experience supports the making of high-quality judgements in some, but not all situations, depending on the degree to which information is valid. Kahneman and Klein (2009) suggest that in addition to amount of experience, professionals need to have sufficient opportunity to learn about the validity of their respective environment in order to make high-quality judgements. This requires learning to distinguish relevant from irrelevant information, to recognise relevant knowledge, and to interpret the information in the current context (Elmore et al., 1994; Wright and Wright, 1997; Kahneman and Klein, 2009). The degree to which professionals are enabled to make high-quality judgements therefore depends on (1) the validity of the environment and its characteristics (Shanteau, 1992), (2) the degree to which professionals engage in learning (Kahneman and Klein, 2009), and (3) characteristics of the individual professional as a driver of learning and performance (Shanteau, 1988). In this chapter, we focus on the second determinant specified in extant literature, as an environment's validity is stable, as are most conceptualisations of individual differences, while learning can be actively supported and facilitated by organisations. To define and operationalise this learning, we build on two theoretical frameworks: deliberate practice as defined by Ericsson, Krampe and Tesch-Römer (1993) and Salas and Rosen (2010), as well as on informal workplace learning as discussed by Marsick and Volpe (1999) and Eraut (2004).

Conceptualising deliberate practice for environments with limited validity

To translate the concept of deliberate practice to environments with limited validity, two assumptions underlying the original concept need to be considered. Firstly, deliberate practice as a concept was developed for environments with high validity, such as chess and music. In these settings, the objective of learning is known in advance, and curricula exist through which a teacher or coach can guide the learner (Eraut, 2004). In environments with limited validity by contrast, neither the knowledge necessary for future high performance nor the optimal way of developing this knowledge is known in advance (Tannenbaum, 2001). Secondly, deliberate practice has previously been described as separate from work processes and performance (van de Wiel and Van den Bossche, 2013). Extant literature on professional learning and development, however, demonstrates that most professional learning takes place as part of daily work activities, not separately (Marsick and Volpe, 1999; Eraut, 2004): it takes place informally. Therefore, to realise the benefits of deliberate practice in professional environments with limited validity, it needs to take into account findings on informal workplace learning. Based on these assumptions, we propose a re-conceptualisation of deliberate practice in line with current perspectives on informal workplace learning.

Marsick and Volpe (1999, p. 5) characterise informal workplace learning by the following elements: "integrated with daily routines, . . . triggered by an internal or external jolt, . . . not highly conscious, . . . haphazard and influenced by chance, . . . an inductive process of reflection and action, . . . linked to learning of others". In contrast to deliberate practice, with its focus on which kind of activities lead to optimal learning, informal workplace learning is concerned with drivers of ongoing professional learning across different activities. This distinction is rooted in an important difference between environments with high and limited validity. In valid environments, it is possible to design specific activities that can be exercised repeatedly to improve a specific skill, because the objective of this learning is known in advance. For example, in order to play a certain piano piece, it is necessary to develop flexible and strong dexterity. By contrast, in environments with limited validity, the objective of learning and the knowledge necessary for high judgement quality is unknown. For example, to become a high-performing auditor, one needs to take into account constant changes in regulation, work organisation and differences between clients. Work in limited validity environments is not proceduralised, standardised, or repetitive enough to comply with the characteristics of deliberate practice as formulated by Ericsson, Krampe and Tesch-Römer (1993). In this study, we illustrate the difference between learning in high and limited validity environments, by bridging the differences between deliberate practice and informal workplace learning. We will discuss the four characteristics of deliberate practice as mechanisms in relation to informal learning in turn.

The starting point of the learning process in deliberate practice is the repeated exercise of tasks crucial to performance in an environment (Ericsson, Krampe and Tesch-Römer, 1993). While these experiences would be consciously designed by a teacher in valid environments, we propose that in the workplace, critical experience provides professionals with important triggers for learning (Salas and Rosen, 2010). Critical experience is described by Cope and Watts (2000, p. 113) in the context of entrepreneurship learning as a "complex phenomenon that does not occur independently of the entrepreneur, but in many cases is a change in perception and awareness that stimulates the entrepreneur into action". Examples of critical experience can be e.g. missing a cancer diagnosis based on a mammography, or discovering fraud while auditing a client's financial statements. Through critical experience, professionals learn about unexpected outcomes of their judgements, and in turn can learn to distinguish valid from invalid cues, contributing to judgement quality. Research on critical incidents, a more formalised research stream (Flanagan, 1954), has demonstrated the value of critical incidents for learning and future performance improvement (Cope, 2003; Clarke, 2008). We therefore hypothesise that professionals who have acquired critical experience will be able to make higher-quality judgements, leading to the following hypothesis:

> H2: Task experience including critical experience moderates the relationship between information search and judgement accuracy.

The second element of deliberate practice that the guidance learners receive from a dedicated teacher is unlikely in most professions to occur in the same way observed in music or chess (Salas and Rosen, 2010). On the one hand, as mentioned above, the knowledge necessary for future success is unknown both to the learner as well as to his or her colleagues. On the other hand, learning is not a core purpose in most professional environments – judgement quality is (Edmondson, 2008). Therefore, instead of a designated teacher who designs and supports learning from experience, at the workplace, this guidance may come from multiple sources, such as coaches, colleagues and clients/patients (Salas and Rosen, 2010). An organisation's learning climate will then determine the role learning plays in daily work (Marsick and Watkins, 2003; Edmondson, 2008). In an organisation with a supportive learning climate, learning is valued as part of daily work for continuous performance improvement (Marsick and Watkins, 2003). We therefore expect that professionals who acquire task experience in a supportive learning climate are more likely to develop the necessary knowledge to make high-quality judgements, leading to our third hypothesis:

> H3: Task experience made in a positive learning climate moderates the relationship between information search and judgement accuracy.

The third element of deliberate practice is continuous feedback, provided both by the task as well as the teacher or coach (Ericsson, Krampe and Tesch-Römer, 1993). The concept of feedback is highly relevant both in high and limited validity environments, as highlighted by Kahneman and Klein (2009) and Shanteau (1992). In addition to the feedback received from teacher and task in deliberate practice, feedback in the workplace is likely to come from a variety of sources, both within and outside the organisation. We therefore expect that a professional will make higher-quality judgements when he or she acquired task experience including feedback, leading to our fourth hypothesis:

> H4: Task experience including feedback moderates the relationship between information search and judgement accuracy.

The final element of deliberate practice is the high mental demand placed on the learner by a learning activity (Ericsson, Krampe and Tesch-Römer, 1993). This high demand stems from two sources: the effort with which the task is executed to learn, as well as the awareness of the learning process itself. Relating this statement to Marsick and Volpe's (1999) conceptualisation of informal learning as happening unconsciously as well as consciously, we follow Eraut's (2004) suggestion to allow for learning from activities with varying mental demands. We therefore represent high cognitive effort through the concept of meta-cognition (Sternberg, 1998; Feltovich, Prietula and Ericsson, 2006): knowing about one's own knowledge, judgement processes and one's actual performance (Flavell, 1979). Several studies have demonstrated the importance of engaging in meta-cognitive processes, such as reflection, for learning and performance (Anseel, Lievens and Schollaert, 2009; Gabelica et al., 2014), leading to our fifth and final hypothesis:

> H5: Task experience including meta-cognition moderates the relationship between information search and judgement accuracy.

Methods

Sample and participants

The professional environment of auditing was chosen as the context for this study because it requires professionals to make diagnostic judgements in a highly regulated environment with limited validity (Shanteau, 1992), and because experience is highly valued, as represented by the strong reliance on hierarchy in the design of auditor's professional organisations (Bédard, 1991). Additionally, the auditing profession has clearly defined procedures and indicators that allow us to measure both the process of information search, as well as the resulting judgement's accuracy (Brown, Peecher and Solomon, 1999). Finally, formal education, certification and training for aspiring and practising auditors are standardised profession-wide on the national level, allowing us to focus on the contributions of informal learning on judgement quality. In collaboration with a Dutch branch of a Big 4 audit firm, we were granted access to 54 Dutch auditors across all function levels on three locations, forming one business unit. Our sample represents the hierarchical structure of the organisation, with 11 of the 13 partners (with an average of 17.64 years of task experience), 21 of the 68 managers (with an average of 13.76 years of task experience) and 21 of 123 juniors (with 1.95 years of average task experience) participating in this study. Our sample covers 17 female and 37 male professionals, with most female auditors on the junior and manager level.

Procedure

This study was designed in line with classic cognitive expertise research, by measuring performance through a task representative of the characteristics of the professional environment (Claessen and Boshuizen, 1985; Hobus, Schmidt and Boshuizen, 1987; Ericsson and Smith, 1991). This approach has the advantage of allowing control over the stimuli presented to participants within a specific environment. This study makes use of two measurement tools: a case to capture judgement quality, and a questionnaire capturing task experience and informal workplace learning based on deliberate practice. Both measures were administered online directly following each other, in individual settings at the auditors' office location, with a researcher present to debrief each participant and to help with technical challenges.

The case

The case for this study was created by the research team in collaboration with the participating audit firm, based on data of an actual client. A task was chosen that all auditors participating in this study are familiar with – auditing a client's accounts receivable – and that is characterised by a standardised approach to its analysis, while at the same time never providing absolute certainty to auditors, leading to limited validity in line with Shanteau (1992). In the case, participants learn that their client is still waiting on payment from two buyers, and that these outstanding positions have already been accounted for as revenue. Participants are requested to judge the likelihood of both buyers to settle their positions, and to advise the client whether the missing sums should rather be recorded as outstanding debt. In auditing, this task is known as auditing a client's accounts receivable, and previous studies on auditor performance often report this task to be associated with poor auditor judgements (Beasley, Carcello and Hermanson, 2001; Payne and Ramsay, 2005). Participants worked on the case in an online environment using MouselabWEB (Willemsen and Johnson, 2008), and were presented with twenty information items from different sources on which they could freely decide to base their judgement. MouselabWEB captured which of the items participants accessed, allowing us to operationalise the evidence collection process. This case included both relevant (60 per cent) and irrelevant information (40 per cent), but no false information, in order to increase case authenticity (Boshuizen, 1989). Participants were not given a time limit to investigate information, but were informed that time spent on the information items would be charged to their hypothetical time budget for the client in line with general audit practice. Overall, participants are able to make a relative, but not an absolute judgement. To capture the final judgement, participants were asked to evaluate how likely the two buyers in the case were to settle their outstanding positions.

Measurement of judgement quality

The judgement process: information search

The first element of judgement quality is operationalised in this study as the standard deviation of time spent accessing the different information items. This measure was chosen to represent the differential time participants are expected to spend investigating the relevant and irrelevant information presented in the case. A low standard deviation would indicate that participants spent equal time accessing all items, representing limited processing of the information content. A high standard deviation would indicate a clear focus on few (relevant) items, indicating purposeful processing of the information. Descriptives for this variable are reported in Table 4.1. To control for this assumption, we ran an ANOVA to compare time spent on relevant versus irrelevant information between auditors who made an accurate versus inaccurate judgement. We indeed find that those participants who made accurate judgements spent significantly (F=11.851, p<.001, ω^2 =0.170) more time on relevant information (M=2.332 minutes, SD=2.306) compared to participants with inaccurate judgements (M=0.768 minutes, SD=0.890). We did not find a significant difference in time spent on irrelevant information between the two groups (F=0.287, ω^2=−0.014).

The judgement outcome: judgement accuracy

In the case, participants were asked to judge the likelihood of two buyers settling their outstanding positions, in percentage. Information in the case was designed to indicate a high likelihood of payment for one, and a low likelihood of payment for the other buyer. Subtracting the percentage rating of the weaker buyer from the stronger buyer results in a percentage measure of the perceived difference between the two buyers. A positive difference indicates an increasingly accurate judgement of the two buyers, and a negative difference indicates an increasingly inaccurate judgement. Descriptives for this variable are reported in Table 4.1.

Measurement of deliberate practice

The four different mechanisms of deliberate practice in limited validity environments, as well as the amount of task experience, were measured through previously validated scales mostly. To measure critical experience, we were interested in participants' experiences requiring them to adjust their approach towards a certain client. Participants were therefore asked whether they had experienced at least one material error or fraud with any of their three main clients within the past three years. The resulting variable ranges from 0 (no incident with any client across the last three years), and 3 (at least one incident per client across the last three years). To measure learning climate, Marsick and Watkins' (2003) 6-item Likert-type "Inquiry & Dialogue" scale from the "Dimensions of the Learning Organization Questionnaire" was used to measure participants' perception of the audit firm's learning climate (Cronbach alpha 0.856) on a scale from 1 to 6. Feedback received in the workplace is measured using Ashford's (1986) amount of feedback received scale, measured on a 5-point Likert scale, with a Cronbach alpha of 0.721. Participants' tendency to engage in meta-cognition is measured using the 7-item Likert-type cognitive self-consciousness scale from Cartwright-Hatton and Wells' (1997) "Meta-Cognition Questionnaire" (Cronbach alpha 0.773). Task experience was measured in this study as the number of years participants had conducted audit tasks. Descriptives for these variables are reported in Table 4.1.

Analysis

After confirming normality for all variables except for amount of task experience, one outlier was identified based on their high number of years of task experience, and the subject was removed from the sample. Next to descriptives and correlations, we used Hayes's (2013) PROCESS macros to conduct moderation analysis with a dichotomous moderator. Moderators were created by median-splitting the participants' scores on (1) years of task experience, and (2) the interaction terms of years of task experience with each of the four measures of deliberate practice. Using a dichotomous moderator allows us to contrast the influence of task experience and deliberate practice on judgement quality, taking into account the available sample. Due to the same reason, omega squared is reported for each model.

Results

Descriptives and correlations

Table 4.1 reports the minimum, maximum and mean scores, as well as the standard deviation, for each of the variables included in this study, both across the entire sample as well as for those participants with below- and above-median years of task experience (seven years). The participants with more than seven years of experience score higher on critical experience, information search and judgement accuracy, but also score lower on the four variables making up deliberate practice. Correlations between the variables (Table 4.2) reveal that information search correlates positively and significantly with task experience (r=0.398, p<0.01) and feedback amount (r=0.365, p<0.01). In turn, judgement accuracy correlates positively with critical experience (r=0.325, p<0.05). The measures of deliberate practice, as well as the two variables making up judgement quality, do not significantly intercorrelate.

Hypothesis 1: information search, judgement accuracy and task experience

To investigate the first hypothesis, we ran a simple regression predicting judgement accuracy by information search (Table 4.2, Model 1). We find a positive (yet insignificant) coefficient, and a small effect size of $\omega^2=0.060$. Running a second

TABLE 4.1 Descriptives

	Overall sample (N=53)				Low experience (N=25)		High experience (N=28)	
	Min.	Max.	M	SD	M	SD	M	SD
Task experience	0.000	36.000	9.890	9.001	2.560	2.142	16.430	7.608
Critical experience	0.000	3.000	0.528	0.799	0.440	0.821	0.607	0.786
Learning climate	2.500	5.670	4.296	0.765	4.533	0.805	4.083	0.672
Feedback amount	1.600	4.000	2.955	0.494	3.024	0.456	2.893	0.526
Meta-cognition	1.290	3.570	2.523	0.494	2.600	0.385	2.454	0.573
Information search	0.000	0.990	0.368	0.217	0.309	0.234	0.421	0.190
Judgement accuracy	−40.000	60.000	2.830	24.525	−4.400	24.509	9.286	23.083

TABLE 4.2 Correlations

	(1)	(2)	(3)	(4)	(5)	(6)	(7)
(1) Task experience	1						
(2) Critical experience	0.118	1					
(3) Learning climate	−0.141	−0.045	1				
(4) Feedback amount	−0.082	−0.065	0.206	1			
(5) Meta-cognition	−0.155	0.059	−0.108	0.178	1		
(6) Information search	0.398**	0.272	0.190	0.365**	−0.026	1	
(7) Judgement accuracy	0.172	0.325*	−0.030	−0.078	−0.043	0.201	1

Note: Significance of correlations indicated as *p<.05, **p<.01

model (Table 4.2, Model 2) with below- and above-median years of task experience as the moderator, we find a significant interaction between task experience and information search: auditors with more than seven years of task experience make increasingly accurate judgements when they pay attention to the relevant over the irrelevant information (B=66.390, p<0.05). For participants with below-median task experience, the attention paid across information items was not related to judgement accuracy (B=−13.915, p>0.05). The moderation model is significant (F=3.916, p<0.05), and a medium effect size of $\omega^2=0.081$. The change in ω^2 due to the interaction of information search and task experience is 0.060. We therefore accept hypothesis 1 only for those participants with above-median task experience. The direct relationship of model 1 and the conditional effects of model 2 are illustrated in Figure 4.1, Panels A and B respectively.

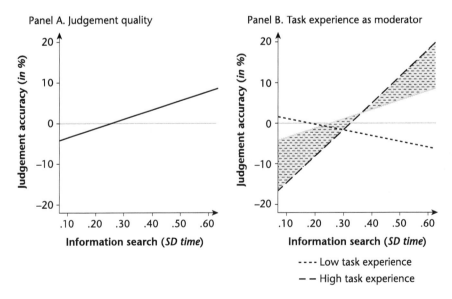

FIGURE 4.1 The relationship between information search and judgement accuracy

Hypotheses 2–5: the leverage effect of deliberate practice on task experience

Table 4.2 also reports the results for hypotheses 2 to 5. For each hypothesis we ran a regression model in which the relationship between information search and judgement accuracy is moderated by experience and one of the four variables making up deliberate practice. For each hypothesis we look at the overall interaction, as well as the conditional effects of the dichotomous moderators. To test hypothesis 2, we looked at the effect of having task experience that contains critical experience (Table 4.2, Model 3). We find a significant and positive interaction term (B=82.628, p<0.05), with those participants scoring above-median on task experience with critical experience displaying more accurate judgements with increasingly focused information search (B=67.544, p<0.02), while the coefficient is negative, if not significant, for the below-median group (B=−23.615, p>0.05). The model is significant (F=4.682, p<0.01), with a large effect size of ω^2=0.178. The ω^2 change due to the interaction is ω^2=0.106, with a difference of 0.046 compared to only task experience as the moderator, a small effect. We therefore accept hypothesis 2. Hypothesis 3 is tested in the same manner, investigating task experience and learning climate's influence on judgement quality (Table 4.2, Model 4). In this model, both information search and the interaction between task experience and learning climate are close to threshold of p=0.05, with p<0.10. The interaction term with information is again significant (r=80.628, p<0.05). As with the earlier models, a significant relationship between information search and judgement accuracy exists for those participants scoring above the median of task experience with learning climate (B=59.0745, p<0.05), while the same relationship is negative and insignificant for below-median scoring participants (B=−13.083, p>0.10). The overall model is significant (F=3.095, p<0.05) with a medium effect size of ω^2=0.110. The change in ω^2 due to the interaction is ω^2=0.090, a medium effect, and the difference in this change between models 2 and 4 is 0.030, a small effect. We therefore accept hypothesis 3. Results for hypothesis 4, addressing amount of feedback received (Table 4.2, Model 5), reveal similar results to hypothesis 2. We find a significant interaction term (B=88.636, p<0.01) and again a positive and significant relationship between information search and judgement accuracy for those auditors scoring above-median on task experience with amount of feedback received (B=74.677, p<0.01), and an insignificant and negative relationship is found for the below-median scoring group (B=−13.959, p>0.10). The overall model is significant (F=3.464, p<0.05), and a medium effect size of ω^2=0.127. The change in ω^2 due to the interaction is ω^2=0.110. Compared to model 2, this is an improvement of 0.050, a small effect. We therefore accept hypothesis 4. Finally, the model investigating hypothesis 5, and meta-cognition (Table 4.2, Model 6) again reveals similar results, with a significant interaction term (B=81.618, p<0.05), a positive coefficient for above-median scoring participants (B=66.985, p<0.05) and a negative coefficient for below-median scoring participants (B=−14.633, p>0.10). Again the model is significant (F=3.473, p<0.05, R^2=0.182; ω^2=0.127). The difference in ω^2 change between

74 Grohnert, Meuwissen, and Gijselaers

model 2 and model 6 is 0.038, thus we accept hypothesis 5. The conditional effects of models 3 to 6 are illustrated in Figure 4.2.

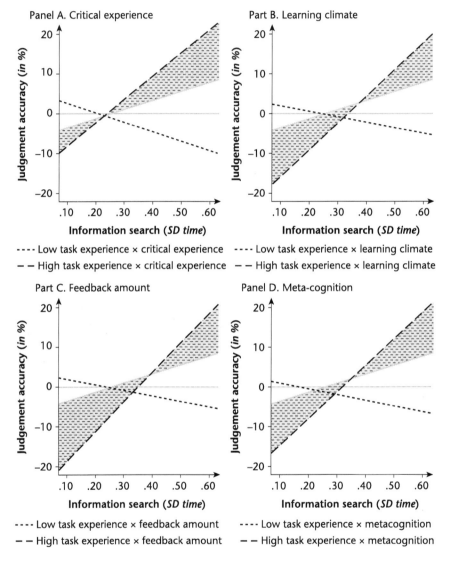

FIGURE 4.2 The relationship between information search and judgement accuracy by the interaction between task experience and deliberate practice

Discussion

Discussion of findings

Kahneman and Klein (2009) as well as Shanteau (1992) observe that task experience is a key determinant of professional judgement quality. At the same time, the authors emphasise that when faced with making judgements in limited validity environments, task experience may not be sufficient to ensure high judgement quality. In this chapter, we investigated whether deliberate practice can leverage the effect of task experience on professionals' judgement quality. Addressing theoretical concerns with the concept of deliberate practice as introduced by Ericsson, Krampe and Tesch-Römer (1993), as specified by Hambrick et al. (2014) and Macnamara, Hambrick and Oswald (2014), as well as the recommendations by Sonnentag and Kleine (2000), we broadened the concept to take into account characteristics of informal learning at the workplace (Marsick and Volpe, 1999). Viewing deliberate practice in terms of underlying learning mechanisms rather than specific activities allows translating the concept to tasks with limited validity, and to investigate its contribution to professional judgement quality. We find that critical experience, learning climate, feedback received and meta-cognition interact with task experience, leveraging the degree to which participants' information search is associated with judgement accuracy. This means that even with few years of experience spent engaging in (informal) workplace learning, participants could outperform more experienced colleagues who did not benefit from the same learning mechanisms. The effect size improvement by these interactions ranges from 0.090 to 0.110, and variance explained as indicated by ω^2 for the overall models range from 0.081 to 0.178, higher than the average finding by Macnamara, Hambrick and Oswald (2014) for professional environments (<1 per cent). We therefore conclude that learning as part of daily work is a promising avenue for understanding how to improve professional judgement quality.

Limitations and future research

This study is subject to several limitations that should be considered when interpreting the findings. First, the set-up of this study is very contingent on the characteristics of the research setting, Data were collected within three locations of one firm's business unit. This has the advantage that noise in variables such as the learning climate is reduced, in line with earlier studies on informal learning (Eraut, 2004), but limits the ability to generalise the findings. Moreover, in auditing, formal education and training are standardised on the national level, allowing us to exclude it in this study, while in less regulated contexts, measures capturing formal learning should be added for a more complete picture. In addition, tenure and task experience correlate very highly in the audit environments (in our sample, the correlation is r=0.968, p<0.001), because it is unusual for auditors to switch employers in the Netherlands. In environments where professionals change employers, tasks, or fields more often, measures need to be included that capture the different kinds of experiences in their respective learning contexts. Under these conditions, critical experience can also be measured in different ways, e.g. through experience with a specific challenge (e.g. fraud) or in a specific task. In addition, performance is measured using a case carefully created to mirror a realistic audit judgement situation. In line with classic cognitive research on expertise (Ericsson and Smith, 1991), this approach allows us to carefully capture the process of searching for information and controlling inputs for the judgement to be taken. Though beyond the scope of the current study, future research can expand on the operationalisation of information search processes, e.g. by taking into account the order in which information is sought and the resulting belief revision (e.g. Tubbs, Messier and Knechel, 1990), as well as by taking into account actual work performance on similar tasks, where available. Next to the environment-specific features of the design, characteristics of the sample as well as the choice of variables need to be considered. While the sample includes most higher-level auditors from the participating offices, the overall number still results in a small sample. Therefore, generalisation is limited and findings need to be substantiated by future research. In this future research, an important next step is to investigate the role of individual characteristics previously associated with engagement in learning, such as self-regulation (e.g. Zimmerman, 2006) and cognitive abilities (e.g. Shanteau, 1992). We expect that individuals with these properties would take more advantage of the learning mechanisms discussed in this study, further leveraging the effect of task experience on judgement quality.

Implications for practice

Based on the existing research on deliberate practice as well as informal workplace learning, the choice of the variables in this study lend themselves to the formulation of specific implications for practice. At the organisational level, leaders can create a supportive learning climate through role modelling (Edmondson, 2012). Communicating your own critical experiences, asking for honest input from different levels of the hierarchy, and publicly rewarding the learning of colleagues, they communicate values supportive of learning. A positive climate is expected to encourage individuals to utilise critical experience and feedback as effective triggers for learning (Marsick and Watkins, 2003; Edmondson, 2012). Moreover, according to Anseel, Lievens and Schollaert (2009), organisations can actively facilitate the use of feedback through reflection, a meta-cognitive activity. Members of the organisation need to know how to effectively provide and receive feedback, and how and when to reflect. Moreover, learners require time to exchange feedback and to reflect, which can be both reactive as well as deliberative (Eraut, 2004), flexibly meeting the learning needs of professionals in the moment. The actual undertaking of informal learning activities under these conditions will then depend on characteristics of the individual, as well as on the degree to which the organisation's climate supports learning. Designing an environment in which professionals can improve their judgement quality then requires that organisations consciously create conditions for learning to occur, so that professionals not only accumulate years of experience, but actually learn from their experience.

References

Anseel, F., Lievens, F. and Schollaert, E. (2009) 'Reflection as a Strategy to Enhance Task Performance after Feedback', *Organizational Behavior and Human Decision processes*. Elsevier Inc., 110(1), pp. 23–35. doi: 10.1016/j.obhdp.2009.05.003

Ashford, S. J. (1986) 'Feedback-Seeking in Individual Adaptation: A resource perspective', *Academy of Management Journal*, 29(3), pp. 465–487.

Beasley, M., Carcello, J. and Hermanson, D. (2001) 'Top 10 Audit Deficiencies', *Journal of Accountancy*, (April), pp. 63–67.

Bédard, J. (1991) 'Expertise and Its Relation to Audit Decision Quality', *Contemporary Accounting Research*, 8(1), pp. 198–222. doi: 10.1111/j.1911-3846.1991.tb00842.x

Boshuizen, H. (1989) 'The Development of Medical Expertise: A Cognitive-psychological Approach', PhD thesis. Maastricht University.

Brown, C. E., Peecher, M. E. and Solomon, I. (1999) 'Auditors ' Hypothesis Testing in Diagnostic Inference Tasks', *Journal of Accounting Research*, 37(1), pp. 1–26.

Cartwright-Hatton, S. and Wells, A. (1997) 'Beliefs about Worry and Intrusions: The Meta-Cognitions Questionnaire and its correlates', *Journal of Anxiety Disorders*, 11(3), pp. 279–296.

Claessen, H. and Boshuizen, H. (1985) 'Recall of Medical Information by Students and Doctors', *Medical Education*, 84, pp. 1022–1028.

Clarke, I. (2008) 'Learning from Critical Incidents', *Advances in Psychiatric Treatment*, 14(6), pp. 460–468. doi: 10.1192/apt.bp.107.005074

Cope, J. (2003) 'Entrepreneurial Learning and Critical Reflection. Discontinuous events as triggers for "higher-level" learning', *Management Learning*, 34(4), pp. 429–450. doi: 10.1177/1350507603039067

Cope, J. and Watts, G. (2000) 'Learning by Doing. An exploration of experience, critical incidents and reflection in entrepreneurial learning', *International Journal of Entrepreneurial Behavior & Research*, 6(3), pp. 1335–2554.

Croskerry, P. (2009) 'A universal model of diagnostic reasoning.', *Academic Medicine: Journal of the Association of American Medical Colleges*, 84(8), pp. 1022–1028. doi: 10.1097/ACM.0b013e3181ace703

Edmondson, A. (2012) *Teaming. How organizations learn, innovate, and compete in the knowledge economy*. San Francisco, CA: Jossey-Bass.

Edmondson, A. C. (2008) 'The Competitive Imperative of Learning.', *Harvard Business Review*, July–August, pp. 1–10. Available at: www.ncbi.nlm.nih.gov/pubmed/18681298.

Elmore, J., Wells, C. and Howards, D. (1998) 'Does Diagnostic Accuracy in Mammography Depend on Radiologists' Experience?', *Journal of Women's Health*, 7(4), pp. 443–449.

Elmore, J., Wells, C., Lee, C., Howard, D. and Feinstein, A. (1994) 'Variability in Radiologists' Interpretations of Mammograms', *New England Journal of Medicine*, 331(22), pp. 1493–1499.

Emby, C. and Gibbins, M. (1988) 'Good Judgement in Public Accounting: Quality and justification.', *Contemporary Accounting Research*, 4(2), pp. 287–313. doi: 10.1111/j.1911-3846.1987.tb00668.x

Eraut, M. (2004) 'Informal Learning in the Workplace', *Studies in Continuing Education*, 26(2), pp. 37–41. doi: 10.1080/158037042000225245

Ericsson, K. A., Krampe, R. T. and Tesch-Römer, C. (1993) 'The Role of Deliberate Practice in the Acquisition of Expert Performance', *Psychological Review*, 100(3), pp. 363–406.

Ericsson, K. and Smith, J. (1991) 'Prospects and Limits of the Empirical Study of Expertise: An introduction', in Ericsson, K. and Smith, J. (eds) *Toward a General Theory of Expertise: Prospects and limits*. Cambridge, MA: Cambridge University Press, pp. 1–38.

Feltovich, P., Prietula, M. and Ericsson, A. (2006) 'Studies of Expertise from Psychological Perspectives', in Ericsson, A., Charness, N., Feltovich, P. and Hoffman, R. (eds) *The Cambridge Handbook of Expertise and Expert Performance*. New York: Cambridge University Press, pp. 41–68.

Flanagan, J. C. (1954) 'The Critical Incident Technique', *Psychological Bulletin*, 51(4), pp. 327–58. Available at: www.ncbi.nlm.nih.gov/pubmed/13177800.

Flavell, J. (1979) 'Metacognition and Cognitive Monitoring: A new area of cognitive-developmental inquiry', *American Psychologist*, 34(10), pp. 906–911.

Gabelica, C., Bossche, P. Van Den, Segers, M. and Gijselaers, W. (2014) 'Dynamics of Team Reflexivity after Feedback', *Frontline Learning Research*, 5, pp. 64–91.

Hambrick, D. Z., Oswald, F. L., Altmann, E. M., Meinz, E. J., Gobet, F. and Campitelli, G. (2014) 'Deliberate Practice: Is that all it takes to become an expert?', *Intelligence*. Elsevier Inc., 45, pp. 34–45. doi: 10.1016/j.intell.2013.04.001

Hayes, A. F. (2013) *Introduction to Mediation, Moderation and Conditional Process Analysis*. New York: Guilford Press.

Hobus, P., Schmidt, H. and Boshuizen, H. (1987) 'Contextual Factors in the Activation of First Diagnostic Hypotheses: Expert-novice differences', *Medical Education*, 21(6), pp. 471–476.

IFIAR (2016) *Report on 2014 Survey of Inspection Findings*. New York.

Kahneman, D. and Klein, G. (2009) 'Conditions for Intuitive Expertise: A failure to disagree.', *American Psychologist*, 64(6), pp. 515–526. doi: 10.1037/a0016755

Knechel, W. R. and Messier Jr, W. F. (1990) 'Sequential Auditor Decision Making: Information search and evidence evaluation', *Contemporary Accounting Research*, 6(2), pp. 386–406. Available at: http://search.ebscohost.com/login.aspx?direct=true&db=buh&AN=10939067&site=ehost-live.

Macnamara, B. N., Hambrick, D. Z. and Oswald, F. L. (2014) 'Deliberate Practice and Performance in Music, Games, Sports, Education, and Professions: A meta-analysis.', *Psychological Science*, 25(8), pp. 1608–1618. doi: 10.1177/0956797614535810

Marsick, V. J. and Volpe, M. (1999) 'The Nature and Need for Informal Learning', in Marsick, V. J. and Volpe, M. (eds) *Informal Learning on the Job*. San Francisco, CA: Berrett Kohler, pp. 1–9.

Marsick, V. J. and Watkins, K. E. (2003) 'Demonstrating the Value of an Organization's Learning Culture: The dimensions of the Learning Organization Questionnaire', *Advances in Developing Human Resources*, 5(2), pp. 132–151. doi: 10.1177/1523422303251341

Payne, M. and Ramsay, R. (2005) 'Fraud Risk Assessments and Auditors' Professional Skepticism', *Managerial Auditing Journal*, 20(3), pp. 321–330.

Salas, E. and Rosen, M. A. (2010) 'Experts at Work: Principles for developing expertise in organizations', in Kozlowski, S. W. J. and Salas, E. (eds) *Learning, Training, and Development in Organizations*. New York: Routledge, pp. 99–134.

Shanteau, J. (1988) 'Psychological Characteristics and Strategies of Expert Decision Makers', *Acta Psychologica*, 68, pp. 203–215.

Shanteau, J. (1992) '"Competence in Experts": The role of task characteristics', *Organizational Behavior and Human Decision Processes*, 53, pp. 252–266.

Sonnentag, S. and Kleine, B. (2000) 'Deliberate Practice at Work: A study with insurance agents', *Journal of Occupational and Organizational Psychology*, 73, pp. 87–102.

Sternberg, R. J. (1998) 'Abilities are Forms of Developing Expertise', *Educational Researcher*, 27(3), pp. 11–20.

Tannenbaum, S. (2001) 'Enhancing Continuous Learning: Diagnostic findings from multiple companies', *Human Resource Management*, 36(4), pp. 437–452.

Tubbs, R., Messier, W. and Knechel, W. (1990) 'Recency Effects in the Auditor's Belief-revision Process', *The Accounting Review*, 65(2), pp. 452–460.

van de Wiel, M. W. J. and Van den Bossche, P. (2013) 'Deliberate Practice in Medicine: The motivation to engage in work-related learning and its contribution to expertise', *Vocations and Learning*, 6(1), pp. 135–158. doi: 10.1007/s12186-012-9085-x

Willemsen, M. and Johnson, E. (2008) 'MouselabWEB'. Available at: www.mouselabweb.org.
Wright, A. and Wright, S. (1997) 'The Effect of Industry Experience on Hypothesis Generation and Audit Planning Decisions', *SSRN Electronic Journal*. doi: 10.2139/ssrn.42913
Zimmerman, B. (2006) 'Development and Adaptation of Expertise: The role of self-regulatory processes and beliefs', in Ericsson, A., Charness, N., Feltovich, P. and Hoffman, R. (eds) *The Cambridge Handbook of Expertise and Expert Performance*. New York: Cambridge University Press, pp. 705–722.

5

INFORMAL LEARNING AT WORK AS A FACILITATOR OF EMPLOYEES' INNOVATIVE WORK BEHAVIOUR

Maike Gerken,[1] Gerhard Messmann,[2] Dominik E. Froehlich,[3] Simon A. J. Beausaert,[4] Regina H. Mulder,[5] and Mien Segers[6]

Introduction

Increased competition requires organisations to keep on developing new ideas, products, and procedures – in short: to innovate (Damanpour & Schneider 2006; Govaerts et al. 2011; Scott & Bruce 1994). Innovation is described as "all intentional results of action (products or processes) that bring about perceived change within the organisation" (Krause 2004, p. 79). "Innovations are products or processes that are new for a particular organisational or work context and that help to maintain or improve the current state of this context" (Messmann & Mulder 2015, p. 125). These innovations are developed by employees in the organisation (Kanter 1988; West & Wallace 1991). More specifically, a set of tasks leads to the development of innovations. These tasks include the exploration of opportunities to generate ideas, and promoting and realising these ideas in the organisation (Janssen 2000, 2003; Kanter 1988; Messmann & Mulder 2012; Scott & Bruce 1994). Employees' fulfilment of the tasks is referred to as innovative work behaviour (Messmann & Mulder 2012). It includes all work activities that lead to the development of innovations. Although organisations might stimulate employees to engage in innovative work behaviour, evidence on its determinants is lacking. The purpose of this contribution is to better understand the factors that make employees engage in innovative work behaviour in the workplace.

---

1 University of Witten/Herdecke, Germany
2 University of Regensburg, Germany
3 University of Vienna, Austria
4 Maastricht University, the Netherlands
5 University of Regensburg, Germany
6 Maastricht University, the Netherlands

Literature suggests that in order to stimulate employees to engage in innovative work behaviour, they need to learn at work (Amabile 1998; Carmeli & Spreitzer 2009). Employees who develop new competences and capabilities through work are more likely to see the possibilities for new ways of doing and trying things. Professional development is not only a result of participating in formal training programs. A review by Tynjälä (2008) indicates that people learn at work not only through formal education but by doing the job itself, through informal learning. Informal learning at work includes different informal learning behaviours such as interaction with colleagues, reflection, reading professional literature, and collaboration (Froehlich et al. 2014; Haider & Kreps 2004; Lohman 2006) that take place during daily work (Marsick et al. 1999; Tannenbaum et al. 2010). Informal learning is defined as learning that occurs as a by-product of other activities and at the employee's own initiative (Eraut 2004; Marsick et al. 1999; Watkins & Marsick 1992). A distinction is made between individual informal learning and informal learning in social interaction (e.g. Kyndt & Baert 2013; Mulder 2013). In this respect, Noe et al. (2013) refers to learning from oneself and learning from non-interpersonal sources as individual informal learning, and learning from others as informal learning in social interaction. Learning from oneself refers to reflection and experimenting with new ways of thinking and acting. Learning from non-interpersonal sources implies learning from information in written material, or via the Internet. Learning from others involves interaction with peers, supervisors, and relevant others in the learner's network by information, help, or feedback seeking behaviours. Although many authors refer to these different types of informal learning and the related informal learning behaviours, previous research measured informal learning in a rather holistic way, including a range of behaviours, and did not clearly make a distinction between specific informal learning behaviours (e.g. Kwakman 2003; Lohman 2006). For example, a clear distinction between cognitive informal learning, learning from oneself (e.g. reflection), and learning from others (e.g. feedback exchange with colleagues) was not always made. Moreover, to date, research hardly offers insights into which specific informal learning behaviours contribute to employees' engagement in innovative work behaviour. The aim of this chapter is to investigate the extent to which informal learning can foster employees' innovative work behaviour. In the following, we first discuss innovative work behaviour. Second, we examine the role of informal learning for engaging in innovative work behaviour. We then present the results of two studies in which the relationships between different types of informal learning and innovative work behaviour were examined. We conclude with practical implications and suggestions for future research.

Theoretical framework

Innovation

Innovation is a source for competitive advantage. In this respect, companies look for ways to encourage employee-driven innovation. Innovation has been studied in several disciplines and refers to all initiatives concerning the creation and application of useful ideas (Damanpour & Schneider 2006; Kanter 1988; Ramamoorthy et al. 2005; Scott & Bruce 1994; West & Farr 1989) with the intention to benefit the organisation (Damanpour & Schneider 2008; West & Farr 1989). Yet, new ideas are not only developed in one specific unit of the organisation but are often generated at the work floor when dealing with or anticipating problems. In this respect, researchers in the domain of innovation have been addressing the concept of innovative work behaviour of employees (De Jong & Den Hartog 2010; Janssen 2003; Messmann & Mulder 2012).

The concept of innovative work behaviour

Innovative work behaviour is defined as "the sum of all physical and cognitive work activities employees carry out in their work context, either individually or in social interaction, in order to accomplish a set of interdependent innovation tasks required for the development of an innovation" (Messmann & Mulder 2012, p.45). Four tasks of innovative work behaviour can be distinguished (Messmann & Mulder 2012). *Opportunity exploration* refers to seeing opportunities for change and improvement. *Idea generation* refers to the creation of new ideas, generating solutions for problems, but also seeking out new working methods or instruments. *Idea promotion* means to mobilise support and to acquire approval for innovative ideas and to make important organisational members enthusiastic for innovative ideas. *Idea realisation* is defined as transforming innovative ideas into useful applications, introducing innovative ideas into the work environment in a systematic way, and evaluating the utility of innovative ideas (Janssen 2000; Kanter 1988; Messmann & Mulder 2011; West & Farr 1989). These tasks can depend on one another. However, not necessarily every employee carries out all tasks, and these tasks are not necessarily carried out in a specific sequence (Dorenbosch et al. 2005; Messmann & Mulder 2015). For instance, when promoting ideas employees might see new opportunities or generate different ideas.

Informal learning at the workplace

Informal learning is defined as "cognitive and physical learning activities (that lead to cognitive activities) that can be deliberate or reactive, and that lead to competences but not to formal qualifications" (Mulder 2013, p. 52). In line with this, Noe et al. (2013, p. 3) define informal learning as learner-initiated behaviour that involves action and reflection. Both definitions imply that informal learning is learner-initiated and provides opportunities for learner interaction in the workplace. Furthermore, reflection helps individuals to uncover insights from their experiences. In this respect, Noe et al. (2013) propose to differentiate between learning from oneself and learning from others. Learning from oneself refers to reflection on, for instance, the effectiveness and efficiency of one's ideas. Reflection plays a major role during innovation processes as a linking element within and between the specific innovation tasks that have to be accomplished. That is, reflection enables employees to become aware of dynamic relations among innovation tasks (e.g., how new ideas in an advanced innovation process change the current strategy used for realising existing ideas) (Messmann & Mulder 2012). Informal learning from others entails talks and discussions between employees (Meirink et al. 2007). Employees exchange ideas and information as well as seeking feedback and help (Froehlich et al. 2014).

Innovative work behaviour represent interdependent innovation tasks that can take place simultaneously and repeatedly (Dorenbosch et al. 2005; Messmann & Mulder 2012). Consequently, behaviours that link these different innovation tasks and the corresponding work activities employees carry out in the innovation process are crucial. Such linking behaviours can be informal learning such as collaborating with colleagues or asking questions and reflection (Cunningham & Iles 2002). In the following we will elaborate on acting upon feedback, information seeking, help seeking, and reflection.

Learning from others: acting upon feedback, information seeking, and help seeking

Employees learn in a social context by working together with colleagues, participating during group activities, and consulting each other (Conlon 2004; Eraut 2004, 2007). In this sense, learning from others is the proactive seeking for relevant others in the workplace to share information and expertise (Eraut 2007). Informal learning from others has been operationalised in different concrete learning activities in the workplace (Kyndt et al. 2009).

A first informal learning activity is acting upon feedback. Seeking feedback is described as a core informal learning activity (Marsick et al. 1999; Noe et al. 2013). Employees seek feedback in order to identify the adequacy of their behaviour to secure certain goals. It has an evaluative character and might evoke negative emotions that in turn impede dealing with or acting upon the feedback. If the feedback seeker does not act upon the feedback, no learning will happen. Therefore, acting upon feedback is a crucial phase in the feedback seeking process. In this respect, research has shown that it is especially the extent to which an employee is acting upon feedback that contributes to employees' performance at work (Anseel et al. 2007; Gupta 1999; Salas & Rosen 2010; Shute 2008).

A second informal learning activity is help seeking. Based on a review of study on informal learning, Marsick and Watkins (2001) state that informal learning is a result of "everyday encounters while working and living in a given context. A new life experience may offer a challenge, a problem to be resolved . . ." (p. 29). In order to deal with challenges and problems, employees often engage in help seeking behaviour. Help seeking behaviour involves proactively consulting others on task-related issues or asking for assistance at work. More than feedback and information seeking, it is problem-focused (Karabenick & Knapp 1988; Lee 1997; Van der Rijt et al. 2013a; Veenman 2005). Research on help seeking behaviour emphasises that employees gather missing information, assess different alternatives to solve problems, expand resources, or receive social support (Lee 1997; Ryan & Pintrich 1997; Van der Rijt et al. 2013a). It is considered a key component to achieve success (Hofmann et al. 2009; Van der Rijt et al. 2013a) and employees mainly seek help to solve problems that can lead to further development of expertise (Lee 1997).

Third, employees engage in informal learning by proactively seeking information (Grant & Ashford 2008; Morrison 2002). According to Mills, Knezek and Khaddage (2014), information seeking is a major component of facilitating the shift from formal to informal learning. This informal learning activity is more neutral and refers to proactive searching for information or knowledge from others (Borgatti & Cross 2003; Cross & Sproull 2004). The main goal is to gain specific resources (Ashford & Cummings 1983; Eraut 2004; Froehlich et al. 2014; Karabenick 2004; Lee 1997). Information seeking allows employees to understand factors in an organisation that lead to higher performance (Borgatti & Cross 2003; Morrison 2002).

There is evidence that learning from others has an influence on employees' innovative work behaviour (Carmeli & Spreitzer 2009; Scott & Bruce 1994). In an early study, Scott and Bruce (1994) looked at the supervisor–employee relationship for stimulating innovative work behaviour. Employees that perceived the quality of the relationship with the supervisor as trustful and supportive and thus sought help, reported to engage more in innovative work behaviour. In addition, good relationships among employees in the work group also positively affected innovative work behaviour. In a cross-sectional study among 172 employees from different organisations, Carmeli and Spreitzer (2009) found that trust and connectivity between colleagues were important factors relating to innovative work behaviour. High-quality connectivity means that colleagues are open to new ideas and proactively seek each other to discuss opportunities and ideas (Carmeli & Spreitzer 2009). Therefore, we expect that learning from others will stimulate innovative work behaviour. Study 1 focuses on employees' informal learning behaviours from others, i.e. acting upon feedback, help seeking, and information seeking, and how these behaviours relate to innovative work behaviour. The following hypotheses are formulated:

> *Hypothesis 1:* Employees' acting upon feedback will have a significant positive effect on their innovative work behaviour.
> *Hypothesis 2:* Employees' information seeking behaviour will have a significant positive effect on their innovative work behaviour.
> *Hypothesis 3:* Employees' help seeking behaviour will have a significant positive effect on their innovative work behaviour.

Innovation-specific reflection

Reflection has been described as the engagement in thoughtful consideration about one's experience to uncover insights and see connections and consequences (Tannenbaum et al. 2010). Reflection is a critical component as it provides an understanding of the performance of past experiences (Kolb 1984; Segers & Van der Haar 2011; Tannenbaum et al. 2010) and helps individuals to seek further experiences

(Anseel et al. 2009; Marsick et al. 1999). With respect to innovation processes, reflection is defined as the sum of all work activities carried out individually or collectively to examine one's performance and its underlying goals and assumptions and the surrounding context, in order to adjust and improve it for future situations (Kolb 1984; Watkins & Marsick 1992). Innovation-specific reflection may take place *in* action as well as *on* action, that is, before, during, and after the different innovation tasks are accomplished.

Reflection during innovation processes represents an important possibility for employees to learn from ongoing events during the innovation process, such as sociopolitical barriers or unexpected outcomes. Because these events may represent unfamiliar, unexpected, or ambiguous experiences for employees, innovation-specific reflection enables them to make sense of these experiences and use them to expand their knowledge and skills, and become more flexible in finding solutions for problems and challenges during the innovation process. Furthermore, without innovation-specific reflection, innovation tasks (i.e., opportunity exploration, idea generation, idea promotion, idea realisation) would remain isolated and the social and context-bound reality of an innovation process would remain unrecognised (Messmann & Mulder 2015). Consequently, we expect that reflection facilitates employees' engagement in and their accomplishment of all innovation tasks encompassed in innovative work behaviour. Study 2 focuses on this role of innovation-specific reflection for enhancing innovative work behaviour and addresses the corresponding hypothesis:

> *Hypothesis 4:* Employees' innovation-specific reflection will have a significant positive effect on their innovative work behaviour.

To address our research question and the corresponding hypotheses, two studies were conducted in which effects of acting upon feedback, information seeking, help seeking, and innovative-specific reflection were investigated. Some research has already been done in the domain of vocational education (Messmann et al. 2010). This calls for further research in other domains where innovations in terms of processes and/or products are important. For this study, we wanted to cover a wide range of domains. Therefore, employees working in different sectors in the Netherlands and Germany represent the research setting for these studies. Employees deal with all kinds of innovations and therefore represent a natural setting for testing our hypotheses.

Study 1: Learning from others and innovative work behaviour

Method

Sample and data collection

In April 2014, an online questionnaire was distributed in a postgraduate programme, linked to a business school in the south of the Netherlands as well as in the network of the postgraduate school. The employees enrolled in the postgraduate school were working full-time. These employees and people in the broader network of the school (i.e., other employees working in organisations) were invited to participate anonymously via the website and the monthly electronic newsletter.

The school and the broader network of the postgraduate school contain employees working in different sectors: energy, IT, banking, consulting, and health. After a period of four weeks, 493 employees filled in the questionnaire, of which 243 answered the complete questionnaire. A strict data cleaning procedure was conducted to delete respondents who filled out the questionnaire multiple times (i.e., based on IP address and the combination of background characteristics) and persons with suspicious response patterns (e.g., no variance in their responses). The final sample consisted of $N = 215$ employees.

The mean *age* of the sample was 42.7 ($SD = 11.78$). Regarding *gender*, 45 percent of the respondents were female. On average, 48 percent of the respondents worked between 1 and 3 years in their *current function*. With regard to the number of *job functions* employees had worked in so far, 68 percent had between 1 and 6 job functions. The majority (72 percent) had worked for 2 to 6 different *organisations* in the past including their current organisation.

Measures

Innovative work behaviour

Employees' engagement in innovative work behaviour was measured with a self-report scale adapted from Messmann and Mulder (2012) which consisted of the shortened version of 17 items and four dimensions tapping employees' engagement in opportunity exploration (4 items, sample item: 'Keeping oneself informed about the latest developments within the company'), idea generation (4 items, sample item: 'Addressing the things that have to change directly'), idea promotion (6 items, sample item: 'Promoting new ideas to colleagues in order to gain their active support'), and idea realisation (3 items, sample item: 'Introducing colleagues to the application of a developed solution'). The items were rated on a 6-point Likert scale ranging from *does not apply at all* (1) to *fully applies* (6). Respondents were instructed to state how adequately each item described their actual behaviour in the workplace.

Learning from others: Seeking for information and help, and acting upon feedback

We measured these informal learning behaviours with a previously validated composite scale of employees' seeking for information and help, and acting upon feedback (Froehlich et al. 2014). The scale consists of 10 items measured on a 5-point Likert scale. A confirmatory factor analysis was performed among 895 employees in different sectors in the original validation study. The results showed four informal learning behaviours: information seeking (2 items, sample item:

'I meet employees from other organisations by participating in conferences, workshops, and lectures'), acting upon feedback from the supervisor (3 items, sample item: 'The feedback I receive from my supervisor motivates me to reflect'), acting upon feedback from colleagues (3 items, sample item: 'Feedback from colleagues makes me act'), and help seeking (2 items, sample item: 'Getting help would be one of the first things I would do if I were having trouble at work'). We confirmed this factor structure also in our sample: Comparative Fit Index (CFI) = .98, Root Mean Square Error of Approximation (RMSEA) = .05, and Standardised Root Mean Square Residual (SRMR) = .03 (Hu & Bentler 1999). However, due to the low reliability of the help seeking scale (α = .55), we removed the help seeking items from further analyses. The remaining three scales show acceptable reliabilities (α = .79 - .89).

Data analyses

A first exploration of the relationship between learning from others and innovative work behaviour was conducted through correlational analysis and multiple hierarchical regression analyses with opportunity exploration, idea generation, idea promotion, and idea realisation as dependent variables. For the hierarchical regression analyses, background characteristics were entered in step 1, and learning from others in step 2. To complement the analysis and to investigate the three hypotheses, path analysis was applied with robust generalised least squares procedures based on the significant direct effects that emerged from the hierarchical regression analyses (Knight 2000). When applicable, modification indices were inspected to apply changes (Wald and Lagrange Multiplier tests). The path analysis was conducted in EQS version 6.2 (Bentler and Wu 2002; Bentler 2005).

Results

The descriptive statistics in Table 5.1 provide an overview of all variables. The data indicate that the scales for all variables have acceptable internal consistencies. The mean score of acting upon feedback from colleagues was the highest among the scales (M = 4.23, SD = .67) and information seeking had the lowest score (M = 3.33, SD = 1.13). Concerning innovative work behaviour, the mean of opportunity exploration was slightly higher compared to the scores of the three other dimensions (M = 4.78, SD = .83). The correlational analysis showed that all three informal learning behaviours were significantly positively related to all four dimensions of innovative work behaviour.

Next, multiple hierarchical regression analyses were conducted to investigate relationships that served as an input for the following path analysis. The results are depicted in Table 5.2. Both information seeking and acting upon feedback from colleagues had a significant effect on opportunity exploration, idea generation, and idea promotion. The effect of acting upon feedback from the supervisor was not significant. Therefore, acting upon feedback from the supervisor was not integrated

TABLE 5.1 Descriptive statistics and correlations for learning from others and innovative work behaviour

		M	SD	1.	2.	3.	4.	5.	6.	7.
1.	Information seeking	3.33	1.13	(.79)						
2.	Acting upon feedback supervisor	4.08	.82	.20**	(.89)					
3.	Acting upon feedback colleagues	4.23	.67	.30**	.61**	(.87)				
4.	Opportunity exploration	4.78	.83	.32**	.31**	.36**	(.77)			
5.	Idea generation	4.72	.82	.24**	.21**	.35**	.45**	(.80)		
6.	Idea promotion	4.73	.86	.23**	.28**	.33**	.47**	.70**	(.88)	
7.	Idea realisation	4.34	1.10	.13*	.18**	.25**	.44**	.51**	.64**	(.85)

Note. *p < .05, **p < .01. N = 215. Values for Cronbach's α are presented in parentheses in the diagonal of the correlation matrix.

in the follow-up path analysis. The number of jobs was positively related to opportunity exploration and idea realisation. In addition, the number of organisations was negatively related to idea generation and idea realisation.

Path analysis was conducted in order to investigate the three hypotheses. Based on the results of the hierarchical regression analyses, we could identify the relationships between two independent variables (information seeking, acting upon feedback from colleague), two background variables (number of job functions, number of organisations), and the four tasks of innovative work behaviour. Non-significant parameters were removed and modifications were implemented in two areas as suggested by the Wald test: the relations between the number of jobs and opportunity exploration and the relation between the number of organisations and idea generation were dropped. The correlations between the independent variables ranged from −0.02 to 0.62. The relationships are presented in Figure 5.1. Information seeking, and acting upon feedback from colleagues positively affected opportunity exploration. Acting upon feedback from colleagues and information seeking also affected idea generation and idea promotion. The results suggest that learning from others is especially important for the act of exploring and generating ideas. There was no effect on idea realisation. The results show that both behaviours are related to innovative work behaviour. Thus, the results confirm hypotheses 1 and 2. No evidence could be obtained for hypothesis 3 since the help seeking scale was removed from further analysis due to low reliability.

Looking at the background characteristics, we found that the number of jobs an employee had during work life was significantly positively related to idea realisation indicating that the more functions an employee held, the more they indicate to

TABLE 5.2 Multiple hierarchical regression analysis

Independent variables		Dependent variables			
		Opportunity exploration	Idea generation	Idea promotion	Idea realisation
Step 1					
	Gender	0.08	−0.01	−0.01	−0.11
	Age	0.08	0.16	0.02	−0.01
	Number of jobs	0.19*	0.16	0.15	0.26**
	Number of organisations worked for	−0.14	−0.24**	−0.17	−0.29**
	Years in current function	0.06	−0.07	−0.12	0.05
Step 2					
	Information seeking	0.24**	0.16*	0.14*	0.07
	Acting upon feedback supervisor	0.15	0.00	0.13	0.05
	Acting upon feedback colleagues	0.18*	0.28**	0.19*	0.16
Step 1 ΔR^2		0.019	0.02	0.01	0.05
Step 2 ΔR^2		0.18	0.13	0.12	0.09
R^2		0.21	0.16	0.15	0.13

Note. $*p < 0.05$, $**p < 0.01$. $N = 215$. Standardised regression coefficients (Beta) are reported.

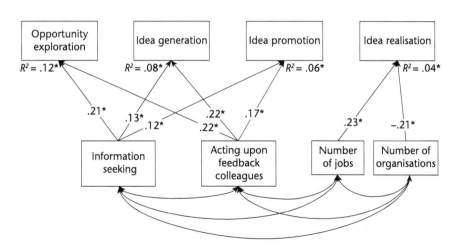

FIGURE 5.1 Standardised estimates for effects of learning from others and background characteristics on innovative work behaviour

transform ideas into useful applications. Interestingly, the number of organisations an employee worked for was significantly negatively related to idea realisation. This means that employees that worked for more organisations find it difficult to realise ideas and put them into practice in the organisation.

Study 2: Reflection and innovative work behaviour

Method

Sample and data collection

The sample of study 2 consisted of employees of a German automotive supply company working in two factories, one in Germany and one in the USA. Employees were invited by email to participate in the study and to answer an online questionnaire containing questions about innovative work behaviour, reflection, and background characteristics. By this means, a total target sample of 1,095 or 51.7 per cent of all employees in both factories was determined. Altogether, $N = 225$ employees (163 in the German factory and 62 in the US factory; response rate = 20.6 per cent) completed the questionnaire.

With respect to background characteristics of participants, no differences between the German and US subsamples were found. Concerning *gender*, 11.7 per cent were female. Regarding *age*, 35.2 per cent were between 30 and 39 years old; 43.7 per cent were between 40 and 49 years old; 8.5 per cent were below 30; and 12.7 per cent were over 50. In terms of *education*, 86.8 per cent had a higher education degree. With regard to *tenure*, 62.9 per cent worked for the company between 3 and 12 years, 34.3 per cent for over 12 years, and 2.8 per cent for less than 3 years. Regarding *organisational function*, 67.3 per cent worked in R&D while 32.7 per cent worked in other units, such as support or production. Finally 27.3 per cent of the employees had a *management* position.

Measures

Innovative work behaviour

Innovative work behaviour was measured with the IWB scale developed by Messmann and Mulder (2012) and consisted of 21 items and four subscales: opportunity exploration (5 items), idea generation (6 items), idea promotion (5 items), and idea realisation (5 items). Data were gathered with self-reports. The answering mode for all items was a 6-point Likert scale that ranged from *does not apply at all* (1) to *fully applies* (6). Respondents indicated how adequately each item described their actual behaviour during the recalled innovation episode they had participated in. The recall of this episode of innovation development was supported by asking questions regarding the status, the duration, the number of persons involved, and the number of goals achieved in this innovation process.

Innovation-specific reflection

Employees' reflection taking place during processes of innovation development was measured with a self-constructed scale consisting of six items. Using existing measures of work-related reflection as a starting point (e.g., Van Woerkom 2003), we deliberately constructed a new scale that targets reflection in the context of an innovation process. The basic idea in this respect was that the dynamics of developing an innovation, such as the increased amount of knowledge creation, also make corresponding reflection more dynamic. All items started with the introductory sentence 'To what extent do the following work activities apply to you?' A sample item is: 'Assessing the progress while putting ideas into practice'. Exploratory factor analysis (principal axis, promax rotation) yielded one distinct factor for innovation-specific reflection. In conjunction with the measurement of innovative work behaviour displayed during one's involvement in an innovation process, the scale assesses the degree to which respondents also reflected on the current state as well as on changes concerning their knowledge, skills, and performance during this process. Respondents also answered items on a 6-point Likert scale from *does not apply at all* (1) *to fully applies* (6).

Data analyses

The data were analysed using correlations to determine the relationship between reflection and the four tasks of innovative work behaviour. Next, path analysis was conducted to address hypothesis 4 on the influence of reflection on innovative work behaviour. The path analysis was conducted using the software M*plus* 6 with robust ML estimation (Muthén and Muthén 2010).

Results

Preliminary scale analyses showed satisfactory internal consistencies for all scales (Table 5.3). Descriptive statistics indicated that the employees were engaged in all dimensions encompassed in innovative work behaviour and reflection. However, they were engaged more strongly in idea generation, promotion, and realisation than in opportunity exploration as well as in reflection. Furthermore, correlations showed that reflection was significantly related to all dimensions of innovative work behaviour.

Finally, two of the above mentioned background characteristics of participants and of the recalled innovation episodes explained mean differences in the engagement in innovative work behaviour. That is, employees in a management position were more engaged in idea promotion. Also, with a longer duration of the experienced innovation process, significantly more engagement in all dimensions of innovative work behaviour was found. And with a more positive evaluation of the goals accomplished in the innovation process, employees were more engaged in opportunity exploration.

TABLE 5.3 Descriptive statistics and correlations for reflection and innovative work behaviour

	M	SD	1.	2.	3.	4.	5.
1. Innovation-specific reflection	4.10	1.06	(.83)				
2. Opportunity exploration	4.13	1.06	.63**	(.79)			
3. Idea generation	4.90	.89	.59**	.55**	(.86)		
4. Idea promotion	4.74	1.01	.61**	.58**	.68**	(.85)	
5. Idea realisation	4.77	.91	.57**	.60**	.65**	.69**	(.82)

Note. *p < .05, **p < .01. N = 225. Values for Cronbach's α are presented in parentheses in the diagonal of the correlation matrix.

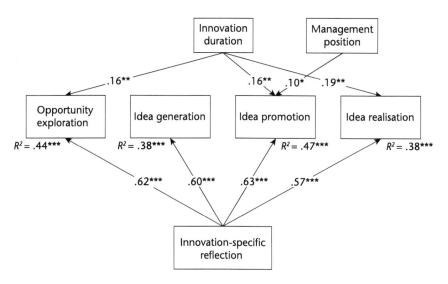

FIGURE 5.2 Standardised estimates for effects of innovation-specific reflection on innovative work behaviour

To address our research question and the stated hypothesis 4, we measured the effects of reflection on innovative work behaviour (Figure 5.2). We controlled for the above mentioned correlational effects of 'management position', 'innovation duration', and 'goal achievement'.

Results show that, after controlling for effects of background characteristics, reflection has significantly positive effects on all dimensions of innovative work behaviour. The direct effects also indicate that there is no difference between the four dimensions in relation to the role of reflection. This means that innovation-specific reflection plays the same role for opportunity exploration, idea generation, idea promotion, and idea realisation. The results confirm hypothesis 4.

Discussion

The aim of this contribution was to investigate how acting upon feedback supervisor, acting upon feedback colleagues, information seeking, help seeking, and reflection can support employees' engagement in innovative work behaviour. We hypothesised a direct relation between these behaviours and all dimensions of innovative work behaviour. However, the role of help seeking could not be tested due to the low internal consistency of the measurement scale. Two studies were conducted: the first study looked into the relationship between acting upon feedback and information seeking and innovative work behaviour. The second study examined the relationship between reflection and innovative work behaviour.

The results of the first study show that two learning-from-others components, that is, acting upon feedback from colleagues and information seeking, are significantly related to opportunity exploration, one dimension of innovative work behaviour. The results underline the importance of proactively seeking information and using the feedback of colleagues to recognise and explore opportunities for change and improvement. Acting upon feedback from colleagues and information seeking also relates to idea generation showing that the quality of feedback is important to substantiate an idea. Next, acting upon feedback from supervisors was not related to innovative work behaviour. Employees turn to their colleagues and use their feedback, as well as seeking information to promote their ideas. Colleagues are perceived as credible sources of feedback and are approached more easily than, for example, supervisors (Van der Rijt et al. 2013b). The lack of this relationship might also be explained by the fact that innovation is seen as a bottom-up process where the knowledge is with employees, who can be motivated to share their ideas for numerous improvements of current processes or products. In this respect, previous research recognised the learning climate as having an influence on informal learning (Marsick et al. 1999). Therefore, future research could investigate whether the learning climate plays a role for informal learning and, in turn, innovative work behaviour. Prior research on innovative work behaviour has focused on the importance of connectivity among colleagues in a more general way (Carmeli & Spreitzer 2009). Literature also suggests that contact and interaction with external others brings new perspectives to one's mind-set (Kanter 1988) and, in turn, increases innovative work behaviour (De Jong & Den Hartog 2010). Furthermore, the study reveals that learning from others does not affect idea realisation, the fourth dimension of innovative work behaviour. Rather, the number of job functions is positively related to idea realisation. It seems that employees who worked in different job functions are more likely to know the structures in an organisation necessary to transform innovative ideas into useful applications and to evaluate the usefulness of that idea. A certain level of experience in different job functions might help to transform ideas into useful applications. Interestingly, the number of organisations an employee worked for relates negatively to idea realisation. In other words, employees who have worked in many different organisations are less likely to realise ideas and put them into practice in the organisation. This might be because employees who change organisations are unfamiliar with the procedures, do not have an elaborated network in the organisation, and lack the necessary knowledge to realise ideas within existing structures. This opposes prior research stating that experiences from working in different organisations increases innovative outcomes (Taylor & Greve 2006).

The results of study 2 reveal that employees' engagement in innovation-specific reflection enhances their engagement in innovative work behaviour. Reflection is beneficial for opportunity exploration, idea generation, idea promotion, and idea realisation. The results of the second study contribute evidence to prior research that innovation-specific reflection relates to employees' innovative work behaviour (Messmann & Mulder 2015). Those employees that reflect more during the innovation process have the skills to adopt innovative work behaviour and are able to carry out the tasks that lead to innovation. It is worth noting the influence of some control variables on dimensions of innovative work behaviour. Innovation duration relates positively to opportunity exploration. This means that the longer an innovation process endures, the more employees engage in exploring opportunities for innovation. At the same time, the management position is positively related to idea promotion indicating that the higher the position of an employee is, the easier it is to promote ideas in the organisation. This might be because employees in higher management positions know key persons in the organisations for mobilising support and acquiring approval and making them enthusiastic for their innovative ideas.

Limitations and future research

The findings in the studies are subject to a number of limitations that should be addressed in future research. First, innovative work behaviour is a context-bound construct, meaning that innovation tasks are integrated in the work context in which they are carried out (cf. Messmann & Mulder 2012). The results of the studies can only be generalised to work contexts that are similar to the works context of this study (i.e., automobile, energy, IT, banking, consulting, and health) characterised by rapidly changing work environments and the need to continuously improve their products or services to secure long-term success and survival. While this study did not research contextual antecedents, future research could study in more detail how these antecedents, such as learning climate, trust, or task variety influence informal learning and in turn innovative work behaviour in various contexts.

Second, self-report measures were used to assess informal learning and innovative work behaviour. This provides the advantage that employees indicate most properly to what extent they were engaged in this behaviour. However, using different data sources would be beneficial to prevent common method bias (Conway & Lance 2010). In this respect, if in a given work context supervisors are closely monitoring the daily work of their subordinates, they should be considered as an additional data source. Social network analysis (SNA) is another method to provide useful insights. SNA permits the study of informal learning behaviour on an interpersonal level (Cross et al. 2002; Van den Bossche et al. 2014), and could be used by the organisation to map isolated networks with the goal of stimulating cooperation among employees for innovation. In addition, the number of innovations per employee or the return of investment for implemented innovations can be attained from participating organisations. Third, the help seeking scale was removed from the analysis due to low reliability. Although previous studies have found acceptable reliability coefficients (e.g., Froehlich et al. 2014; Karabenick 2003), future research may further improve the scale in terms of measurement. Future research would also benefit from further developing and disentangling the concept of informal learning during daily work activities and innovation processes. Finally, future studies could combine acting upon feedback of the supervisor, acting upon feedback of a colleague, information seeking, help seeking, and reflection in one single study to further explore their relationship with innovative work behaviour and adding to the results of these studies.

Practical implications

Organisations can use the research results to pay attention to reflection and learning from others both during daily work and in conjunction with ongoing innovation processes to enhance employees' engagement in innovative work behaviour. For instance, it is important to realise that innovation-specific reflection, acting upon feedback of colleagues, and information seeking contribute to opportunity exploration. A work environment that stimulates employees to easily connect, to discuss opportunities for innovation and explore ideas, makes employees valuable by seeking opportunities to work with others and tapping into the expertise those colleagues possess to help carry out innovation tasks. Supervisors could stimulate this development by acting as broker in the beginning of the innovation process. Colleagues should also be aware of their feedback to employees during the innovation process. Likewise, organisations should illustrate how employees can use reflection as a powerful tool to smoothen the accomplishment of work tasks during innovation processes. For instance, supervisors may encourage employees to examine their performance and underlying assumptions during and after work tasks. This could be done by supporting their ideas through feedback but also by providing on-demand support for their questions. The results of these studies highlight the vital role of reflection and learning from others to enhance innovative work behaviour.

References

Amabile, T. M. (1998). How to kill creativity at work. *Harvard Business Review*, 76, 77–87.

Anseel, F., Lievens, F., & Levy, P. E. (2007). A self-motive's perspective on feedback-seeking behavior: Linking organisational behaviour and social psychology research. *International Journal of Management Reviews*, 9(3), 211–236. doi:10.1111/j.1468-2370.2007.00210.x

Anseel, F., Lievens, F., & Schollaert, E. (2009). Reflection as a strategy to enhance task performance after feedback. *Organisational Behaviour and Human Decision Processes*, 110(1), 23–35. doi:10.1016/j.obhdp.2009.05.003

Ashford, S. J., & Cummings, L. L. (1983). Feedback as an individual resource: Personal strategies of creating information. *Organisational Behaviour and Human Performance*, *32*(3), 370–398. doi:10.1016/0030-5073(83)90156-3

Bentler, P. M., & Wu, E. J. C. (2002). *EQS for Windows: Users' guide*. Encino, CA: Multivariate Software, Inc.

Bentler, P. M. (2005). *EQS 6 Structural Equations Program Manual*. Encino, CA: Multivariate Software, Inc.

Borgatti, S. P., & Cross, R. (2003). A relational view of information seeking and learning in social networks. *Management Science*, *49*(4), 432–445. doi:10.1287/mnsc.49.4.432.14428

Carmeli, A., & Spreitzer, G. M. (2009). Trust, connectivity, and thriving: Implications for innovative behaviours at work. *The Journal of Creative Behaviour*, *43*(3), 169–191. doi:10.1002/j.2162-6057.2009.tb01313.x

Conlon, T. J. (2004). A review of informal learning literature, theory and implications for practice in developing global professional competence. *Journal of European Industrial Training*, *28*(2/3/4), 283–295. doi:10.1108/03090590410527663

Conway, J. M., & Lance, C. E. (2010). What reviewers should expect from authors regarding common method bias in organisational research. *Journal of Business and Psychology*, *25*(3), 325–334. doi:10.1007/s10869-010-9181-6

Cross, R., Borgatti, S. P., & Parker, A. (2002). Making invisible work visible: Using social network analysis to support strategic collaboration. *California Management Review*, *44*(2), 25–47.

Cross, R., & Sproull, L. (2004). More than an answer: Information relationships for actionable knowledge. *Organisation Science*, *15*(4), 446–462. doi:10.1287/orsc.1040.0075

Cunningham, P., & Iles, P. (2002). Managing learning climates in a financial services organisation. *Journal of Management Development*, *21*(6), 477–492. doi:10.1108/02621710210430632

Damanpour, F., & Schneider, M. (2006). Phases of the adoption of innovation in organisations: Effects of environment, organisation and top managers. *British Journal of Management*, *17*(3), 215–236. doi:10.1111/j.1467-8551.2006.00498.x

Damanpour, F., & Schneider, M. (2008). Characteristics of innovation and innovation adoption in public organisations: Assessing the role of managers. *Journal of Public Administration Research and Theory*, *19*(3), 495–522. doi:10.1093/jopart/mun021

De Jong, J. P. J., & Den Hartog, D. N. (2007). How leaders influence employees' innovative behaviour. *European Journal of Innovation Management*, *10*(1), 41–64. doi:10.1108/14601060710720546

De Jong, J. P. J., & den Hartog, D. N. (2010). Measuring innovative work behaviour. *Creativity and Innovation Management*, *19*(1), 23–36. doi:10.1111/j.1467-8691.2010.00547.x

Dorenbosch, L., Engen, M. L. Van, & Verhagen, M. (2005). On-the-job innovation: The impact of job design and human resource management through production ownership. *Creativity and Innovation Management*, *14*(2), 129–141. doi:10.1111/j.1476-8691.2005.00333.x

Eraut, M. (2004). Informal learning in the workplace. *Studies in Continuing Education*, *26*(2), 247–273. doi:10.1080/158037042000225245

Eraut, M. (2007). Learning from other people in the workplace. *Oxford Review of Education*, *33*(4), 403–422. doi:10.1080/03054980701425706

Froehlich, D. E., Beausaert, S. A. J., Segers, M. S. R., & Gerken, M. (2014). Learning to stay employable. *Career Development International*, *19*(5), 508–525. doi:10.1108/CDI-11-2013-0139

Govaerts, N., Kyndt, E., Dochy, F., & Baert, H. (2011). Influence of learning and working climate on the retention of talented employees. *Journal of Workplace Learning*, *23*(1), 35–55. doi:10.1108/13665621111097245

Grant, A. M., & Ashford, S. J. (2008). The dynamics of proactivity at work. *Research in Organisational Behavior, 28*, 3–34. doi:10.1016/j.riob.2008.04.002

Gupta, A., Govindarajan, V., & Malhotra, A. (1999). Feedback-seeking behaviour within multinational corporations. *Strategic Management Journal, 20*(3), 205–222. doi:10.1002/(SICI)1097-0266(199903)20:3<205::AID-SMJ17>30.0.CO;2-H

Haider, M., & Kreps, G. L. (2004). Forty years of diffusion of innovations: Utility and value in public health. *Journal of Health Communication, 9*(1), 3–11. doi:10.1080/10810730490271430

Hofmann, D. A., Lei, Z., & Grant, A. M. (2009). Seeking help in the shadow of doubt: the sense making processes underlying how nurses decide whom to ask for advice. *Journal of Applied Psychology, 94*(5), 1261–1274. doi:10.1037/a0016557

Janssen, O. (2000). Job demands, perceptions of effort-reward fairness and innovative work behaviour. *Journal of Occupational and Organisational Psychology, 73*(3), 287–302. doi:10.1348/096317900167038

Janssen, O. (2003). Innovative behaviour and job involvement at the price of conflict and less satisfactory relations with co-workers. *Journal of Occupational and Organisational Psychology, 76*(3), 347–364. doi:10.1348/096317903769647210

Kanter, R. (1988). When a thousand flowers bloom: Structural, collective, and social conditions for innovation in organisations. *Research in Organisational Behaviour, 10*, 169–211.

Karabenick, S. A. (2003). Seeking help in large college classes: A person-centered approach. *Contemporary Educational Psychology, 28*(1), 37–58. doi:10.1016/S0361-476X(02)00012-7

Karabenick, S. A. (2004). Perceived achievement goal structure and college student help seeking. *Journal of Educational Psychology, 96*(3), 569–581. doi:10.1037/0022-0663.96.3.569

Karabenick, S. A., & Knapp, J. R. (1988). Help seeking and the need for academic assistance. *Journal of Educational Psychology, 80*(3), 406–408. doi:10.1037//0022-0663.80.3.406

Knight, K. (2000). *Mathematical statistics*. New York, NY: Chapman & Hall.

Kolb, D. (1984). *Experiential Learning: Experience as the source of learning and development*. Englewood Cliffs, NJ: Prentice-Hall.

Krause, D. E. (2004). Influence-based leadership as a determinant of the inclination to innovate and of innovation-related behaviors. *The Leadership Quarterly, 15*(1), 79–102. doi:10.1016/j.leaqua.2003.12.006

Kwakman, K. (2003). Factors affecting teachers' participation in professional learning activities. *Teaching and Teacher Education, 19*(2), 149–170. doi:10.1016/S0742-051X(02)00101-4

Kyndt, E., & Baert, H. (2013). Antecedents of employees' involvement in work-related learning: A systematic review. *Review of Educational Research, 82*(3), 273–313. doi:10.3102/0034654313478021

Kyndt, E., Dochy, F., & Nijs, H. (2009). Learning conditions for non-formal and informal workplace learning. *Journal of Workplace Learning, 21*(5), 369–383. doi:10.1108/13665620910966785

Lee, F. (1997). When the going gets tough, do the tough ask for help? Help seeking and power motivation in organisations. *Organisational Behaviour and Human Decision Processes, 72*(3), 336–63. doi:10.1006/obhd.1997.2746

Lohman, M. C. (2006). Factors influencing teachers' engagement in informal learning. *Journal of Workplace Learning, 18*(3), 141–156. doi:10.1108/13665620610654577

Marsick, V. J., & Watkins, K. E. (2001). Informal and incidental learning. *New Directions for Adult Continuing Education, 89*, 25–34. doi:10.1002/ace.5

Marsick, V. J., Volpe, M., & Watkins, K. E. (1999). Theory and practice of informal learning in the knowledge era. *Advances in Developing Human Resources, 1*(3), 80–95. doi:10.1177/152342239900100309

Meirink, J. A., Meijer, P. C., & Verloop, N. (2007). A closer look at teachers' individual learning in collaborative settings. *Teachers and Teaching*, *13*(2), 145–164. doi:10.1080/13540600601152496

Messmann, G., & Mulder, R. H. (2011). Innovative work behaviour in vocational colleges: Understanding how and why innovations are developed. *Vocations and Learning*, *4*(1), 63–84. doi:10.1007/s12186-010-9049-y

Messmann, G., & Mulder, R. H. (2012). Development of a measurement instrument for innovative work behaviour as a dynamic and context-bound construct. *Human Resource Development International*, *15*(1), 43–59. doi:10.1080/13678868.2011.646894

Messmann, G., & Mulder, R. H. (2015). Reflection as a facilitator of teachers' innovative work behaviour. *International Journal of Training and Development*, *19*(2), 125–137. doi:10.1111/ijtd.12052

Messmann, G., Mulder, R. H., & Gruber, H. (2010). Relations between vocational teachers' characteristics of professionalism and their innovative work behaviour. *Empirical Research in Vocational Education and Training*, *2*(1), 21–40.

Mills, L., Knezek, G., & Khaddage, F. (2014). Information seeking, information sharing, and going mobile: Three bridges to informal learning. *Computers in Human Behavior*, *32*, 324–334. doi:10.1016/j.chb.2013.08.008

Morrison, E. W. (2002). Information seeking within organisations. *Human Communication Research*, *28*(2), 229–242. doi:10.1093/hcr/28.2.229

Mulder, R. H. (2013). Exploring feedback incidents, their characteristics and the informal learning activities that enanate from them. *European Journal of Training and Development*, *37*(1), 49–71. doi:10.1108/03090591311293284

Muthén, L. K., & Muthén, B. O. (2010). *Mplus User's Guide* (6th ed.). Los Angeles, CA: Muthén & Muthén.

Noe, R. A., Tews, M. J., & Marand, A. D. (2013). Individual differences and informal learning in the workplace. *Journal of Vocational Behavior*, *83*(3), 327–335. doi:10.1016/j.jvb.2013.06.009

Ramamoorthy, N., Flood, P. C., Slattery, T., & Sardessai, R. (2005). Determinants of innovative work behaviour: Development and test of an integrated model. *Creativity and Innovation Management*, *14*(2), 142–150. doi:10.1111/j.1467-8691.2005.00334.x

Ryan, A. M., & Pintrich, P. R. (1997). Should I ask for help? The role of motivation and attitudes in adolescents' help seeking in math class. *Journal of Educational Psychology*, *89*(2), 329–341.

Salas, E., & Rosen, M. A. (2010). Experts at work: Principles for developing expertise in organisations. In S. W. J. Kozlowski & E. Salas (Eds.), *Learning, Training, and Development in Organisations* (pp. 99–134). New York: Routledge.

Scott, S., & Bruce, R. (1994). Determinants of innovative behavior: A path model of individual innovation in the workplace. *Academy of Management Journal*, *37*(3), 580–607. doi: 10.2307/256701

Segers, M. S. R., & Van der Haar, S. (2011). The experiential learning theory: D. Kolb and D. Boud. In F. Dochy, D. Gijbels, M. S. R. Segers, & P. Van den Bossche (Eds.), *Theories of Learning for the Workplace: Building blocks for training and professional development programs* (pp. 52–65). New York: Routledge.

Shute, V. J. (2008). Focus on formative feedback. *Review of Educational Research*, *78*(1), 153–189. doi:10.3102/0034654307313795

Tannenbaum, S. I., Beard, R. L., McNall, L. A., & Salas, E. (2010). Informal learning and development in organisations. In S. W. J. Kozlowski & E. Salas (Eds.), *Learning, Training, and Development in Organisations* (pp. 303–331). New York: Routledge.

Taylor, A., & Greve, H. H. R. (2006). Superman or the fantastic four? Knowledge combination and experience in innovative teams. *Academy of Management Journal*, *49*(4), 723–740. doi:10.5465/AMJ.2006.22083029

Tynjälä, P. (2008). Perspectives into learning at the workplace. *Educational Research Review*, *3*(2), 130–154. doi:10.1016/j.edurev.2007.12.001

Van den Bossche, P., van Waes, S., & Van der Rijt, J. (2014). Feedback, development, and social networks. In K. Kraiger, J. Passmore, N. Rebelo dos Santos, & S. Malvezzi (Eds.), *The Wiley Blackwell Handbook of the Psychology of Training, Development, and Performance Improvement* (pp. 503–520). Oxford: Wiley-Blackwell.

Van der Rijt, J., Van den Bossche, P., Van de Wiel, M. W. J., Maeyer, S., Gijselaers, W. H., & Segers, M. S. R. (2013a). Asking for help: A relational perspective on help seeking in the workplace. *Vocations and Learning*, *6*(2), 259–279. doi:10.1007/s12186-012-9095-8

Van der Rijt, J., Van den Bossche, P., & Segers, M. S. R. (2013b). Understanding informal feedback seeking in the workplace: The impact of the position in the organisational hierarchy. *European Journal of Training and Development*, *37*(1), 72–85. doi:10.1108/03090591311293293

Van Woerkom, M. (2003). *Critical Reflection at Work: Bridging individual and organisational learning*. PhD thesis, University of Twente, Enschede, the Netherlands.

Veenman, S. (2005). Effects of a cooperative learning program on the elaborations of students during help seeking and help giving. *American Educational Research Journal*, *42*(1), 115–151.

Watkins, K. E., & Marsick, V. J. (1992). Towards a theory of informal and incidental learning in organisations. *International Journal of Lifelong Education*, *11*(4), 287–300. doi:10.1080/0260137920110403

West, M. A., & Farr, J. L. (1989). Innovation at work: Psychological perspectives. *Social Behaviour*, *4*(1), 15–30.

West, M. A., & Wallace, M. (1991). Innovation in health care teams. *European Journal of Social Psychology*, *21*(4), 303–315. doi:10.1002/ejsp.2420210404

6

VITAL BUT NEGLECTED

The informal learning of new teachers in Scotland

Rachel Shanks[1]

Introduction

Student-centred learning has been the focus of school teaching for many years in many countries but teachers' own professional learning has not, in turn, changed to be learner-centred. Teacher professional learning often entails one-off activities that can be understood as one-size-fits-all. This study, however, focused on the situated learning of new teachers, in particular, their informal learning as they moved from being a novice on the periphery of communities of practice in their schools. This informal learning builds on the new teachers' past experiences and learning histories, may be triggered by their classroom experiences and interactions with their colleagues, and can result in increases in their confidence and changes in their practice. Important factors in their learning include the workplace learning environment, the support of their head teacher, their mentor and other colleagues. The teachers' own individual learning dispositions may also be a significant factor in their learning.

This mixed methods study arose as part of the research project around an undergraduate teacher education programme called "Scottish Teachers for a New Era" (STNE). The programme was designed to change the way trainee and new teachers are educated and supported, creating a six-year continuum spanning initial teacher education and early career learning.

The study involved questionnaires and semi-structured interviews with two cohorts of new teachers. The teachers explained how they learnt from classroom experience and from and with their colleagues. Antecedents to learning include the school workplace learning environment and the teachers' individual learning dispositions. These antecedents can also be triggers alongside other catalysts for learning

---

1 University of Aberdeen, United Kingdom

such as having a pupil with additional support needs and teaching a new topic. There are individual and organisational consequences of the teachers' informal learning, such as a teacher's increased confidence and increased opportunities for learning between colleagues.

Learning is understood here as changes in social practices as a new teacher becomes more experienced, and moves from being a novice to being a more active participant in their communities of practice. This can be seen as a way of learning as becoming (Hodkinson et al. 2008). There have been arguments relating to the importance of everyday or informal learning as opposed to formal learning in professional development programmes for teachers (Webster-Wright 2009). While learning in formal contexts is important, by concentrating on this alone, much of the learning that takes place in workplaces is undervalued (Eraut et al. 2000). Learning at the beginning of a career will include both informal conversations with colleagues, formal organised events and individual personal reflection. This study began with a focus on formal continuing professional development (CPD), until pilot interviews and questionnaire run-throughs with new teachers highlighted the importance of their informal learning.

While more attention is being paid to the informal learning of teachers, for example participation in work groups, discussing and sharing learning (HMIE 2009), this may be more related to budgetary pressures than an acceptance of the central role of informal learning in the workplace. In the public sector in the UK, there is evidence of a shift away from using expensive external providers due to financial pressures (Jewson et al. 2014). Current policies on teacher learning in Scotland still favour more formal types of CPD over informal or incidental learning (Kennedy 2011). Formal learning is seen as taking place off-the-job and informal learning occurring on-the-job whereas both happen on- and off-the-job with formal learning such as mentoring by a designated mentor and observation happening at work (Eraut 2007) and informal learning happening at formal off-site events. Much informal learning does take place at work involving a "combination of learning from other people and learning from personal experience, often both together" (Eraut 2004, p. 248). By recognising and supporting informal learning, organisations could improve workplace practices throughout the development of new and different strategies (Boud et al. 2009). With austerity measures following the 2008 financial crash, there are also budgetary reasons for encouraging informal learning at work rather than formal training by external providers. While year-on-year reductions in formal learning participation in the education sector in the UK have been traced to before the 2008 economic crisis (Jewson et al. 2014, p. 7), this pattern is likely to continue.

People who complete initial teacher education in Scotland and fulfil other eligibility criteria are guaranteed a one-year contract as a new teacher in a school in Scotland. Their class contact or teaching time is meant to be 80% of that of a fully registered teacher. Non-teaching time is when colleagues can spend time together and learn and develop together (Hodkinson and Hodkinson 2005), and can be both an antecedent and a trigger for learning. The new teachers are assigned an official mentor who is based in their school or the education authority and who they are meant to meet weekly to discuss progress in relation to satisfying the Standard for Full Registration (GTCS 2012). The mentor and the head teacher must observe the new teacher during the year and decide if they have met the required standard.

The Teacher Induction Scheme was introduced in Scotland in 2002 with new teacher learning understood as formal CPD to be recorded first in an interim and then a final profile document. However, new teacher learning can also be understood as informal learning on the periphery of a community of practice with workplace colleagues. "Legitimate peripheral participation" is the term used by Lave and Wenger (1991) to explain the process of becoming a member of a community of practice providing "a way to speak about the relations between newcomers and old-timers, and about activities, identities, artefacts, and communities of knowledge and practice. It concerns the process by which newcomers become part of a community of practice" (p. 29).

Communities of practice and situated learning

The concepts of communities of practice and legitimate peripheral participation provide an explanation of how novices learn. The action of participating in a social practice, such as working as a teacher in a school, is a way of belonging to a community. The fact of becoming a member allows participation, and thus learning, to take place. The learning can be viewed as changing participation through changing practice (Lave and Wenger 1991). As practice develops and changes in and through social relationships, the new teacher learns how to be a teacher in that community of practice and moves away from the periphery towards the centre. This may be in strongly or weakly framed communities of practice (Boud and Middleton 2003).

Criticisms of situated learning theory include the lack of reference to power relations or to individual agency or formal learning, the absence of explanation of how new knowledge is created or what is learnt rather than what is happening and that workplaces differ (Hodkinson and Hodkinson 2005; Edwards 2005; Cairns 2011; Fuller and Unwin 2011). People are often involved in many different and changing groups of people at work (Boud and Middleton 2003) or other learning opportunities outside of work, so "place" must incorporate a wider sense of workplace (Evans et al. 2006). It has been argued that adaptive learning or preservation takes place in communities of practice rather than new or expansive learning (Gustavsson 2009).

Furthermore, learning to teach is not a technical undertaking but also "a political endeavour entailing the negotiation of complex organisations with multiple actors who may resist the idea of newcomers" (Curry et al. 2008, p. 661). Research into workplace learning will not always highlight positive examples of learning as workplace practices may support or obstruct learning (Webster-Wright 2009). This is important as "Workplaces are contested terrain, and access to activities and guidance are not uniformly distributed across those in the workplace. Therefore, although learning at work is inevitable and ongoing, it is selective and contested" (Billett 2001, p. 20).

Learning to teach can be thought of as an isolating and individual pursuit, with reflection playing an important role in making sense of what is happening in the classroom. The ability to reflect on one's own actions seems to be vital for informal learning (Marsick 1987). This may include "reflection-in-action" and "reflection-on-action" (Schön 1983 and 1987). Teaching yourself appears to be an underestimated but important way to learn (Felstead et al. 2005). Individual learning is closely related to how much an individual participates, how trusted and confident they feel and the kinds of support they receive (Eraut et al. 2000, Skår 2010). Workers may develop the art of "learning-by-walking-around" and dropping in on someone and asking what they were doing or discussing current problems (Granath et al. 1995, cited in Collin 2008, p. 381).

As part of the Scottish Teachers for a New Era programme at the University of Aberdeen, this project set out to explore the learning of teachers in their first year of teaching. Initially, it was planned to research the formal continuing professional development of those who had graduated from the redeveloped initial teacher education programme. However, after reviewing the literature and piloting initial questionnaires and interviews with new teachers, it became apparent that learning from their own and others' practice should be an important focus of the research. Informal learning from the teachers' experience in the classroom, from discussions with colleagues and observations of others' practice, and the support of colleagues and head teachers were identified as potential factors in how the new teachers learnt about their professional practice. Therefore, the following research question and subquestions were devised:

How do new teachers learn in the workplace?

a) What are the antecedents to their learning?
b) What are the triggers for their learning?
c) What are the consequences of their learning?

Methodology

A mixed methods approach was adopted for three reasons: firstly, to offset the limitations in using only one method; secondly, to use the quantitative data to inform the development of questions in the interview schedules; and finally, to provide a more comprehensive understanding of new teacher learning (Plano Clark and Ivankova 2016). The quantitative data highlighted key areas to explore in depth through the qualitative data collection phase. This can be explained as: [quan + qual -> QUAL].

The study follows a sequential explanatory design with questionnaires producing quantitative and qualitative data which were used to develop the qualitative research instrument, namely a semi-structured interview schedule. The advantages of a sequential explanatory design are that it is straightforward and allows opportunities for the exploration of the quantitative results in more detail, while the

TABLE 6.1 Visual model for mixed methods sequential explanatory design (adapted from Ivankova et al. 2006)

Phase	Procedure	Product
Quantitative data collection	Self-selecting web-based and paper questionnaire	Numeric and text data (interview transcripts, documents)
	Data screening Frequencies Chi square test SPSS quantitative software v.18	Descriptive statistics, missing data Text data from open-ended questions
Connecting quantitative and qualitative phases	Coding text data from open-ended questions Developing interview questions	Emerging themes Interview protocol
Qualitative data collection	Individual in-depth telephone or face-to-face interviews CPD documentation	Text data (interview transcripts, documents)
Qualitative data analysis	Coding and thematic analysis Within-interview participant and across-interview participant theme development Cross-thematic analysis Developing questionnaire and interview questions QSR NVivo qualitative software v.8	Visual model of interview participant analysis Similar and different themes and categories Cross-thematic matrix
Quantitative data collection	Self-selecting web-based questionnaire	Numeric and text data
Quantitative data analysis	Data screening Frequencies Chi-square test SPSS quantitative software v.18	Descriptive statistics, missing data Text data from open-ended questions
Connecting quantitative and qualitative phases	Coding text data from open-ended questions Developing interview questions	Emerging themes Interview protocol
Qualitative data collection	Individual in-depth telephone or face-to-face interviews CPD documentation	Text data (interview transcripts, documents)
Qualitative data analysis	Coding and thematic analysis Within-interview participant and across-interview participant theme development Cross-thematic analysis QSR NVivo qualitative software v.8	Visual model of interview participant analysis Similar and different themes and categories Cross-thematic matrix
Integration of quantitative and qualitative results	Interpretation and explanation of the quantitative and qualitative results	Discussion Implications, future research

disadvantages can be the length of time and amount of resources needed to collect and analyse both types of data (Ivankova et al. 2006).

Table 6.1 shows the different stages of the mixed methods study and where and how the data was integrated.

Design of the research instruments

To understand the study, it is necessary to explain the design of the questionnaires and interviews and how each of the research instruments was analysed. A number of previous questionnaire studies of beginning teachers were taken into account when devising the instrument for this study in terms of how questions had been phrased and how to uncover information (Jones 2002, Williams 2003, Burn et al. 2003, Johnson and Birkeland 2003, Hodkinson and Hodkinson 2003, Hodkinson and Hodkinson 2005, Pearson and Robson 2005, Clarke et al. 2007 and Hagger et al. 2008). In particular, the studies by Meirink et al. 2009 and Mcgregor 2003 were useful and a question from each of these studies was adapted and included in the questionnaires. Teachers were asked about what they did when they were considering changing their practice, to establish whether they learnt on their own or with and from colleagues (adapted from Meirink et al. 2009). Teachers were asked about how often they undertook various activities with colleagues in their school. This was to provide an insight into the level of collegiality in the school and how much informal learning it was possible for the new teacher to be engaged in and was adapted from one in the Mcgregor study (2003). Questions were asked about the new teachers' involvement in learning at work, about the support they received from their mentor, head teacher and other workplace colleagues. For example, in the questionnaires, respondents were asked "How have you been learning to be a teacher in your induction year?" and "Who have you learnt from the most in your induction year?"

Interview design

Each of the two sets of interviews started with background questions to put the interview participants at ease (Kvale and Brinkmann 2009). They were asked the same questions in both interviews: about their involvement in professional development and learning at work and about workplace politics, their appointed supporter/mentor, head teacher and other colleagues, including non-teaching staff. Participants were asked if they received peer support from other induction-year teachers including their university peers. Questions were asked about their school if this had not already been covered. The final section of the interview looked back at their initial teacher education and looked ahead to their future learning as a fully registered teacher.

Interview sample

As representative a sample as possible was sought but was dependent on who volunteered. Male teachers were approached and asked to be interviewed as initially all the volunteers were women. Thus, as well as volunteer sampling, where participants are sought on a voluntary basis from a pool of potential participants (Cohen et al. 2007), quota and purposive sampling, where participants with particular traits or characteristics are sought (ibid.), were implemented.

Questionnaire design

The questionnaires were devised using Snap software and then analysed using the Statistical Package for Social Sciences (SPSS) (Kinnear and Gray 2009). In order to provide some information on the proportions of respondents answering questions in a particular way, a simple frequency-based analysis was implemented. Associated open response questions provided some qualitative insights into these quantitative response profiles. In addition, a Chi squared analysis (Kinnear and Gray 2009) was implemented to investigate any relationships between data items – for example, to establish if respondents' opinions on the induction year and associated support were related to the position held by their mentor, or if there was a relationship between the position of the mentor and how often the induction year teacher and mentor met. For the items investigated, there were no statistically significant relationships uncovered.

The first questionnaire responses to open-ended questions were grouped together; these answers were used as the basis for some of the closed questions in the second questionnaire. The primary purpose of the questionnaires was to provide useful information in preparation for the interviews. Analysis was developmental and complementary in that the methods were used sequentially, thus the descriptive statistics provided a picture of the sample and provided areas for further exploration with the interviewees, but the quantitative and qualitative data gathered from the questionnaires were also integrated with the interview data at a later stage in the analysis of the research findings.

Interview analysis

The interview transcripts and the qualitative data from the questionnaires were imported into NVivo (a computer assisted qualitative data analysis software programme) and coded line by line both inductively and deductively until no new codes emerged. The researcher chose to work "manually" by reading the texts and choosing categories that seemed to be mentioned rather than starting with the most frequently used words. By categorising and sorting the data in this way, it was possible to produce a list of key themes (Taylor-Powell and Renner 2003). Although there is no guarantee that first impressions will be avoided altogether, easy access to the data meant that documentation could be revisited easily and as every action in NVivo can be dated, it is possible to see whether, for example, one particular code was used only at a particular stage of the coding process. While qualitative data analysis software like NVivo can facilitate the coding process, the software cannot actually perform the data analysis (Holton, 2010). The researcher still has to interpret the data and make sense of it. To ensure the validity, trustworthiness and thoroughness of the research, the coding process was repeated and coding and recoding was performed in an iterative way (Holton 2010). Coding and codes were reviewed throughout the process and the codes and the coding structure were refined and adjusted in order to reflect the data as accurately as possible. It is hoped that the researcher was able to remain objective and open to different possible answers to the research questions and that there were no expectations strong enough to cause researcher bias. Nine codes were created after reading and re-reading the interview transcripts and the responses to open-ended questions in the questionnaires. These codes and short descriptions are provided in the Appendix to this chapter.

Mixed methods analysis

In the study, analysis was developmental and complementary in that the quantitative and qualitative data were used in sequence, and the descriptive statistics provided a picture of the questionnaire respondents' views and supplied areas for further exploration with the interviewees. Then the qualitative data gathered from the open-ended questions in the questionnaires was integrated with the interview data at a later stage of the analysis. The individual learning dispositions were created from a combination of answers to the interview questions after it became apparent that there were very different views emerging in relation to the teachers' attitudes towards learning. This part of the analysis was done on paper, with each interviewee's answers to particular questions laid out in a table for ease of comparison.

Response rates and demographics of research participants

Questionnaires were sent out to former students from the previous year who had agreed to be contacted by the University of Aberdeen for research purposes and a subset who had volunteered to be interview participants. In the first year of the study 267 new teachers were sent the questionnaires. The first questionnaire was completed by 39 new teachers (response rate = 14.6%) and the second completed by 102 new teachers (response rate = 38.2%). Eight teachers were interviewed twice. In the second year of the study, 170 new teachers were sent the questionnaires. The first questionnaire was completed by 54 new teachers (response rate = 31.7%) and the second completed by 48 new teachers (response rate = 28.2%). In the second year, ten teachers were interviewed.

The lower response rates can be partly explained by the long working hours of new teachers. They have sole responsibility for their class for the whole year for the first time and must satisfy the requirements of the Standard for Full Registration with assessments made by their mentor and their head teacher. They are in a vulnerable situation with a temporary post, with many hoping to work in the same school or education authority the following year (Shanks 2014). As Sax et al. (2003) have noted in relation to university students, there are lower and lower response rates with online and paper-based questionnaires. Interviewees needed to

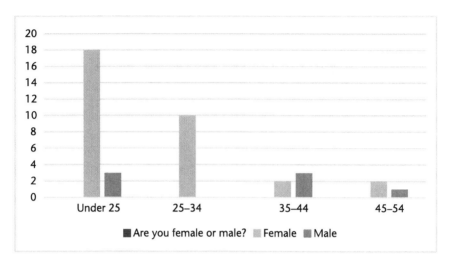

FIGURE 6.1 Age of respondents by gender (questionnaire one, year one)

be reassured about their anonymity so that there could be no repercussions from their participation in the study. Thus data has been anonymised and no identifying details of the teachers or schools have been disclosed in accordance with ethical guidelines (SERA 2005).

For the first questionnaire in the first year of the study, the personal demographic data collected from the respondents, for example, their age, gender and sector, had similarities in the proportions of attributes in each category as the total population of induction year teachers in Scotland (GTCS 2009, pp. 24–27). The Chi-square test was performed to check how confident it was possible to be concerning the similarity of the respondent attributes. It is possible to be 95% confident that the dataset is similar in terms of age, gender and sector.

Although the second questionnaire in the first year of the study had more respondents they did not reflect the demographics of the total population.

The findings and discussion section below is organised according to the themes of the antecedents, triggers and consequences of informal learning.

Findings and discussion

The findings cover how the new teachers thought they were learning to be a teacher, who they said they were learning from, which activities they learnt from, their previous learning experiences and how they had changed as a result of their learning.

Both the interview participants and the questionnaire respondents were asked whether they learnt from their colleagues. For example, in the second questionnaire of the first year of the study, in order to determine if the new teachers recognised or were aware of learning from colleagues, they were asked to rate the statement "I learn from my colleagues." The response was 100% agreement broken down into

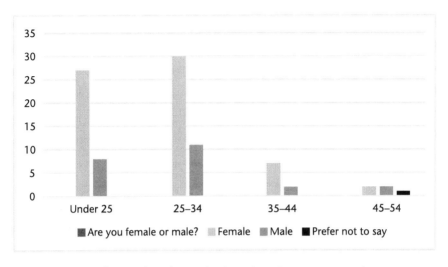

FIGURE 6.2 Age of respondents by gender (questionnaire two, year one)

63.4% strongly agreed and 36.6% agreed. Similarly, in response to the statement "I use feedback from others to further my learning", there was 100% agreement with 62.2% strongly agreeing and 37.8% agreeing.

In answering the question "How have you been learning to be a teacher in your induction year?", colleagues were referred to directly or indirectly (for example, observation of others) many times (see Table 6.2 below). Pupils were referred to in two responses to do with assessment and one response of getting to know the children.

TABLE 6.2 How have you been learning to be a teacher in your induction year? (questionnaire two, year one)

How have you been learning to be a teacher in your induction year?	*Open ended responses with statements grouped (n=40)*
Observation of others	28
Being in class or being a teacher	26
Reflection/self-assessment/self-evaluation/learning from mistakes	17
Discussions with colleagues	15
Formal CPD and meetings	15
Mentor	11
Asking questions or advice	10
Reading	9
Trying new ideas/ taking risks	9
Others observing me	6
Preparation/planning/organisation	6

A key issue in relation to the learning of induction year teachers appeared to be their informal learning. However, the new teachers did not identify it as informal learning, for example, they referred to discussions with their mentor or another key colleague, support and advice from colleagues, discussions with colleagues in general, and observing others teaching.

The new teachers did not talk of formal continuing professional development as being their most important learning and even when the new teachers were at formal CPD events it was actually the social activities that were the most important:

> So it's a chance to socialise with other probationers in the area, which is just, it's, it's really nice, because then you kind of, that's when you really open up. That's, that's probably the best part of the day to be honest.

While the interviewees' CPD documentation contains many references to formal learning, both in school and outside school, it was examined to investigate to what extent informal learning was documented in their official profiles and action plans. Continuing professional development has to be recorded against the Standard for Fully Registration under the headings "Local Authority CPD", "School CPD" and "Personal CPD", for example "Managing Pupil Behaviour". Although the majority of entries are to do with formal events, CPD sessions or meetings, under Personal CPD teachers did include entries such as "professional discussion", "share ideas", "collaborative conversation" and "collaborative discussion" (teachers in year one of the study). Much of this informal learning was taking place with the new teachers' colleagues.

The antecedents to the teachers' learning included their initial teacher education at university and formal professional learning events such as courses on Moving Image Education and teacher conferences. An important antecedent to informal learning was the workplace learning environment which included the support of the head teacher, the induction mentor and other colleagues. The teachers' own individual learning dispositions were a significant factor behind their learning. Antecedents were also triggers for learning with a supportive learning environment being a precursor to learning as well as the catalyst for learning. The learning environment will be considered as an antecedent and individual learning disposition as a trigger but they are interrelated.

Antecedents

As an antecedent to learning, new teachers found support from colleagues more important than support from their official mentor. For specific areas of their jobs – planning and preparation, pupil assessment and subject knowledge – they preferred to go to colleagues for advice and support. This may be because the mentor is in a promoted role rather than being a classroom teacher and because the mentor has an assessment role alongside their support role. The teachers were learning from their mentor, but they were learning more from their colleagues and their pupils.

Discussions with colleagues

Discussions with colleagues were found to be important for new teachers and indicated how informal workplace learning appeared to play a more significant part in their professional learning than formal CPD events. In questionnaire one of the second year of the study, 100% of respondents agreed that they learnt by talking to colleagues (71.7%, strongly agreed and 28.3% agreed). In the second questionnaire that year, every respondent agreed with the statement "I learn by talking to colleagues", with 60.4% strongly agreeing and 39.6% agreeing. This shows that the new teachers continue to understand that they are learning in their conversations with colleagues, although the proportion strongly agreeing has gone down over the year. This may be because the induction year teachers have become more confident in the five months between questionnaires.

In the first questionnaire of the second year, respondents were asked to choose the three types of experience that they had found the most useful so far in their induction year. This question was used to elicit information on which type of professional learning experience appears most useful to new teachers after three months in post.

Useful and important learning activities

In questionnaire two of the second year, respondents were asked to indicate how important certain activities had been to their learning in the induction year rather than asking for the three most useful activities. This was to uncover the induction year teachers' views on all the different types of activity that are available. The

TABLE 6.3 Three most useful experiences (questionnaire one, year two)

Which *three* types of experience have you found the most useful so far? Please click on three.	(n=53)
Doing the job (classroom experience)	94.3%
Discussions with colleagues	52.8%
Having a mentor	35.8%
Trying out new ideas/taking risks	32.1%
Reflection/self-evaluation	26.4%
Local Authority Core Support Days	22.6%
Observing other teachers	20.8%
Others observing me teach	15.1%
Being shown how to do things	5.7%
Courses and/or conferences	3.8%
School in-service days	1.9%
Research on the Internet	1.9%
Reading	1.9%

TABLE 6.4 Percentages of respondents rating specific activities as very important (questionnaire two, year two)

Activity	Very important
Doing the job/classroom experience	95.8
Trying out new ideas/taking risks	72.3
Discussions with colleagues	70.8
Observing others	58.3
Reflection/self-evaluation	56.3
Having a mentor	52.1
Others observing me	37.5
Being shown by others how to do things	35.4
Local Authority Core Support/Probationer Days	25
Courses and conferences	22.9
School in-service days	10.4

activities have been placed in descending order of percentages of the very important response.

Table 6.4 shows that the overwhelming majority of respondents view *doing the job/classroom experience* as very important for their learning. In comparison, more formal activities such as school in-service days, courses and conferences have the lowest percentages of very important. Informal activities appear more important to the respondents than formal activities.

Relationships with adults and children

Relationships with adults and children were an important antecedent to learning.

In the first questionnaire the new teachers regarded informal learning – doing the job and discussions with colleagues – as the most useful professional learning. Interviewed teachers' three most important learning activities were working with other teachers, talking over problems and being observed and receiving feedback and, as an interviewee put it, "getting on with it."

Professional development activities

At both interviews in both years of the study, participants were asked about the professional development they had been involved in. The interviewees referred to both the informal and formal learning they had undertaken. How they had been learning was noted as well as what they said they were learning. There were many informal ways that the induction year teachers were learning, such as peer work and peer assessments, observing and shadowing, chatting to other staff and sharing ideas, and visiting other schools. It is not possible to say how effective this learning is but this is what the new teachers felt they were learning from. The teachers'' formal learning activities included central mentor meetings, training events in school, a university Masters programme and local authority probationer days. The informal learning referred to in the interviews was also noted in the GTCS profile documentation provided by the teachers (see below).

Observing others

In the second year's first questionnaire, 98.1% strongly agreed or agreed that they learnt from observing others with 1.9% neutral. In questionnaire two, all respondents agreed that they learnt from observing others. This shows the importance beginning teachers place on observing others teach and discussing issues with colleagues. This is a key advantage of the reduced teaching load for new teachers in Scotland. It gives them time to watch other teachers in their own school and in other schools where possible. They can see how teachers work with other pupils and also with their own pupils. The questionnaire responses suggested that observation was an important issue to raise with the interviewed teachers if they did not speak about it without being prompted.

Observations of other teachers and observations of the new teachers themselves appear to be a vitally important component in their learning. Some referred to being observed and implementing the feedback they had received. Others mentioned talking to colleagues and implementing new ideas. Some of the interviewees spoke of observing colleagues and then adapting the practices they had seen. There is a danger, of course, that if teachers are simply following their colleagues' practice, without reflecting on it or doing their own research, they will become enculturated into the current way of doing things rather than finding their own way or creating a new way of working with pupils. Although the ideas may be new to the novice teachers, they may in fact be the established practice in that and other schools.

The importance of colleagues

For both questionnaire respondents and interviewees, the importance of colleagues was a recurring theme, as well as the relationship with pupils and the learning environment of the school. The interviewed teachers understood they were learning from colleagues: one observed a colleague's lessons and "got some good ideas as to how I could do that with my own children". Another said they learnt "through the kids", finding out what worked and what didn't work. The new teachers said they learnt from their mentor, from their colleagues and from their pupils. In the new teachers' continuing professional development records, three of the interviewed teachers had recorded their "personal CPD" as learning from "professional discussion", "share ideas", "collaborative conversation", rather than just formal events or meetings. One of the new teachers' most important colleagues is their official mentor.

Mentors

The new teachers received different levels of support from their mentor; for example, in terms of the frequency they met, this is one way that the learning environments differed. One of the interviewed teachers struggled to meet with their mentor:

> ... what happened was we would go like sometimes a month, maybe two months without having a meeting, and it was, you were meant to have one every week ... I found that really difficult trying to find time to meet up with him, that was another quite a big problem that we were having.

Informal mentors

The mentor relationship can be an important part of the learning environment, but often, if the support was not provided by the official mentor, then it was found from informal sources around the new teacher. Colleagues in general played a more central role in the new teachers' learning. Just as the level of support of the mentor might differ, so did the level of support from colleagues. An expansive learning environment can amplify the effects of supportive colleagues and good mentoring while an individualistic one can reduce the mentor's influence on a new teacher (Williams et al. 2001). While quality mentoring supports teachers in their first teaching posts (Greenlee and Dedeugd 2002), informal activities, such as discussions and meeting outside the school day, are preferred over more formal mentoring support (Parker et al. 2009; Eraut 2004).

Learning environment

Antecedents for learning include a supportive learning environment; as Lave and Wenger (1991) indicated, what and how new entrants learn grows out of the environment in which they are situated. For new teachers, learning through peripheral participation occurs inside and outside the classroom while they carry out their work activities. This includes talking over problems with a colleague and reflecting on their experiences (Schön 1983). The teachers in this study had varying levels of access to other teachers to discuss issues and they had different opportunities to observe other teachers and to visit other schools.

The teachers' learning environment or school or workplace context has a profound impact on their first year of teaching (Johnson and Birkeland 2003). The learning environment can hold both expansive and restrictive practices, for example, there may be a close collaborative working culture or an isolated, individualist one. An example of an expansive learning environment came from a questionnaire respondent who was surprised by "how quickly I felt like a teacher and part of the school and the fact that other colleagues come to me for advice". While an example of a more restrictive practice was highlighted in a questionnaire respondent's comment "lack of support from the head teacher until late on in the year has affected my confidence the most". These practices highlight the differences that can be identified between schools with more or less expansive learning environments.

Expansive learning environment

The findings highlight how in an expansive learning environment new teachers have a wider range of learning opportunities and greater support from colleagues to help them in what is a very demanding year. The learning environment is a key antecedent to learning. In expansive learning environment, teachers' professional learning is not confined to off-the-job activities or specific events at work. When a teacher explains something to a colleague, for example, they are engaged in a learning relationship (Unwin and Fuller 2003). In schools with more expansive rather than restrictive practices, new teachers are treated as members of the community of practice of teachers who contribute ideas and share knowledge with colleagues.

Restrictive learning environment

Restrictive learning environments may be close to what Skruber (1987) described as bureaucratic or non-clarifying learning environments with expansive ones being similar to clarifying learning environments. Informal learning opportunities, and the organisational conditions within a school, play an important role in encouraging and supporting teacher learning and changes in practice (Mesler Parise and Spillane 2010). The presence or absence of learning affordances shapes the learning of new teachers. Not all are placed in expansive learning environments, for example one interviewed teacher explained that in their school there was "a big negative group and trying out new things is seen as a bad thing."

This did not set the new teacher back as there was another new teacher in the school who provided peer support. While peers can provide support to new teachers, head teachers play an even more pivotal role in new teachers' workplace learning.

Role of head teachers

The head teacher is a key figure in the transition process for new teachers (Tickle 2000) and likely to be in charge of access to learning opportunities and to decide how work is distributed and organised (Fuller and Unwin 2004a). If a manager pays greater attention to the allocation and structuring of appropriate work, then learning can be improved (Eraut 2007). The support of managers and the flow of information to employees have also been found to be important (Ashton, 2004). Hierarchical structures, leadership, cultural practices and personal relations in workplaces all influence access to knowledge and people's experiences, including how their learning is supported or restricted (Skår 2010, Skruber 1987). One of the interviewed teachers felt particularly undervalued by their head teacher, saying they were used only "as probationers" meaning treated as temporary induction year teachers, and that they were kept in their place and that they were "not quite the same value as others". This can be contrasted with the situation for two of the teachers who were asked by the head teacher which class they would prefer to teach.

Feedback

Feedback from superiors and management support for learning are two of the seven conditions that have been found to promote informal learning in the workplace (Skule 2004). Head teachers play a key role in encouraging teacher collaboration in their school (Flores 2001, Greenlee and Dedeugd 2002, Stanulis and Burrill 2004). New teachers in supportive environments are more likely to seek advice and overcome their doubts and difficulties more effectively (Greenlee and Dedeugd 2002). Head teachers who promote "a collaborative school culture and resource model", who answer questions and make themselves available for new teachers, more effectively support new teachers (Fantilli and McDougall 2009, p. 824). Those in charge of new teachers could do more to highlight what the new teachers contribute to their schools (Fox et al. 2011). Varying degrees of acceptance and support from head teachers and colleagues towards new teachers were linked to the antecedents for learning. For new teachers in restrictive learning environments, their circumstances may have changed little from before the implementation of Scotland's Teacher Induction Scheme (see Draper et al. 1997).

A school which appreciates its new teachers and uses their experiences is demonstrating expansive practice: "A key characteristic of an expansive learning environment is the belief that people at all levels across the organisation possess valuable skills and knowledge and have the capacity to learn" (Unwin and Fuller 2003, p. 19).

The learning environment is both the backdrop to new teachers' informal learning and factors within it can also trigger that learning. Antecedents and triggers are interrelated, as a teacher in a learning environment with support sees the benefit in trying out new ideas and has the confidence that they will be supported in this approach even if it does not go to plan immediately.

Triggers

There were several triggers to learning for the new teachers, such as close physical proximity to supportive colleagues, developing close interpersonal relationships with colleagues, the observation of other teachers' practice as well as collaboration and discussion with colleagues. Other triggers for learning were classroom experience, trial and error and learning from pupils. The new teachers' own individual learning dispositions and the interaction between their learning environment and their learning disposition were also catalysts for their learning.

Physical proximity to colleagues

Most questionnaire respondents at the end of the induction year indicated they were learning most in their own classroom. Physical proximity to colleagues is an important trigger for learning; as Hodkinson and Hodkinson (2005) pointed out, it allows teachers "to work closely together and spend non-teaching time together providing opportunities for positive learning and development" (p. 127). Most of the interviewed teachers were based beside colleagues teaching the same subject (in secondary schools) or the same stage (in primary schools). Having easy access to a mentor, in the same building or nearby and who has expertise in the new teacher's subject area can help new teachers (Barrera et al. 2010). Proximity to colleagues' work areas is a factor which influences teachers' engagement in informal learning activities, especially those at the beginning of their careers (Lohman 2006).

Interpersonal relationships

New teachers need good-quality interpersonal relationships in and around school so that they have the chance to ask for advice and talk over issues (Kelchtermans and Ballet 2002). New teachers themselves identify collegial interaction as an important working condition (Johnson and Birkeland 2003), just as nurses find it useful to follow and observe more experienced colleagues who are "good at something" (Skår 2010, p. 15). Similarly, hairdressers realised they would learn more effectively if, rather than working alone, they shared ideas with colleagues (Unwin et al. 2007). However, learning in and from social relations at work can be a double-edged sword as relationships can be both a source of pleasure and pain (Collin 2008).

At work, when people want to know something, they will, without thinking, move towards certain people whom they believe have the capacity (and perhaps goodwill) to help them (Unwin and Fuller 2003). However, these helpful colleagues, and their role in the induction of new teachers, are barely acknowledged in many schools. It takes time for new teachers to find out who they can go to for help and advice about different topics and who they should leave alone. Being able to "ask the silly questions" and to drop in whenever necessary was important for the interviewed teachers who were able to do this in their school and this practice was sorely missed by those who felt they could not do it where they worked.

Observation of colleagues

The observation of other teachers was another important learning activity for the new teachers in the study, for example, "I changed my whole style of, of doing art with the children. And that was from actually observing another class" and "I observed a few of her lessons and got some good ideas as to how I could do that with my own children."

Compared to more experienced teachers, new teachers are more likely to use observations and informal discussions with colleagues to learn (Richter et al. 2011). The reduced timetable provides time for observing other teachers and is an important antecedent for learning – having the time to do it and a trigger for learning – seeing a new way to practise activities and/or new ways of being a teacher. Time has been found to be a factor that influences teachers' engagement in informal workplace learning activities (Lohman 2006).

There are many ways that people learn through work: asking questions, locating useful people, listening and observing, learning from errors, giving and receiving feedback, and through mediating tools (Eraut 2007). Observing others in the classroom is an important way for new teachers to learn in the workplace. People need to be able to connect what they see others doing with their own practice so that by discussing what has been observed they are able to learn (Guile and Griffiths 2001). The new teachers considered observations as more important than being shown how to do things and all the formal professional development they took part in. The interviewees spoke of observing colleagues and then adapting those practices for use in their own classroom. Not only did they learn by observing others, in addition they referred to being observed and implementing the feedback they received from mentors and head teachers.

Collaboration with colleagues

Another trigger for learning was collaborating with other teachers. Through collaboration new teachers can explore uncertainties related to general teaching and learning issues as well as context-specific ones related to their school and classroom. Collaboration with other teachers is not intrinsically positive as it may reinforce existing beliefs, norms and values and so may not necessarily be an agency for change or enhanced professional practice. Two types of collaboration have been identified in relation to new teacher learning: spontaneous and structured (Williams et al. 2001). Spontaneous collaboration, being informal, unplanned and opportunistic, leads to the paradox that "the characteristics that take induction practice beyond the satisfactory and into the realms of excellence are, by their nature, not amenable to statute or external mandate" (p. 265).

While spontaneous or serendipitous collaboration is highly valued by new teachers and induction mentors it is "impossible to legislate for or to provide through formal imposition" (Williams et al. 2001, p. 263). The strongest predictor of teacher change in mathematics and English classroom practice in one study was collaborative discussion between teachers (Mesler Parise and Spillane 2010). Collaboration with experienced subject or stage colleagues, team teaching and informal mentoring are important ways that new teachers' development is supported (Fantilli and McDougall 2009). It has been found that teachers collaborate more at the start of their careers (Richter et al. 2011).

Discussions with colleagues

New teachers learnt from discussions with colleagues, including their designated mentor. These discussions were the backdrop to their overall learning and also a trigger for learning. Research participants understood that discussions with colleagues were very important for their learning.

Informal feedback is a key part of learning for new professionals (Eraut et al. 2000, Eraut 2007). Learning occurs while people are busy carrying out their work activities (Billett 2002a). Casual, incidental learning is seen as an inevitable way to learn (McNally 2006). New teachers want opportunities to share concerns with colleagues or discuss teaching and learning issues (Kelchtermans and Ballet 2002; Johnson and Birkeland 2003). Interactions with colleagues were very important to the new teachers. Interviewees and questionnaire respondents appreciated their discussions with colleagues about work and also being able to discuss "non-work" matters with colleagues, "switch off" from work and relax at break and lunch times.

Classroom experience

Most surveyed and interviewed teachers felt they were learning most often through working in the classroom. One way they learnt in the classroom was through trial and error. Interviewees said how important it was to take risks as well as responding to feedback from pupils. This is a type of personal learning (Eraut 2004). For learning to occur, there needs to be a trusting relationship between the learner and the workplace colleague providing knowledge and support. A good relationship means the learner having confidence to make mistakes, and have them corrected, or good practice identified, without losing face or feeling vulnerable (Ashton 2004). While there may be good relationships there can be tension if new teachers feel they do not have the opportunity to innovate and instead are expected to follow existing practice, for example, by keeping schools desks in rows rather than using a different seating structure, which was the case for one interviewed teacher.

Trial and error

The questionnaire respondents could see the importance of "trying out new ideas or taking risks" as part of their learning to be a teacher. In the second questionnaire, this was ranked second after "doing the job or classroom experience". One interviewee put it as "better to try and find a way of making it better than not to try it at all through being scared to try". Learning from trial and error and from taking risks is individualised learning that cannot be planned and is happening within a complex environment. The teachers may react immediately to what is happening in their classroom with reflection-in-action or through later reflection (Schön 1983 and 1987). Reflection-in-action was an important trigger for informal learning through trying out new things on the spur of the moment. The provision of opportunities to reflect on practice has been identified as a key factor in the journey from newcomer to mainstream participant (Fuller and Unwin 2003). For some of the study teachers, reflection on their own practice was an integral and significant part of their learning process. There were differences between the teachers about how often they would try out new ideas or take risks which may be explained by their different individual learning dispositions (see below).

Learning from pupils

Another trigger for learning was the pupils in the teachers' classrooms. Questionnaire respondents were asked whose needs were most important when planning their professional development, which elicited responses relating to themselves, their schools and their pupils. For example,

- "the pupils – it is for them you are driven to improve."
- "Ultimately, my current and future students – what do I need to develop to improve my delivery of teaching and learning, and promote their progress in the classroom."
- "The young people I learn and teach with."

The interviewed teachers were incentivised to learn because of their pupils, for example one said that what they had learnt from the pupils was how to give boys confidence in art, another that they were "learning loads of things from working with them. Learning what to do and what not to do!" and another said "working with a maths whizz. It was a learning curve." Other professionals have referred to their clients, patients and customers in relation to their workplace learning (Cheetham and Chivers 2001).

Individual learning disposition

Another trigger for learning centres round the individual themselves and their approach to learning. The term "individual learning disposition" is used to explain the differences between people's attitudes to learning (Shanks et al. 2012). It can be understood both as an antecedent or precursor to learning and as a trigger for learning, in being the reason why the teacher has sought out opportunities to learn. The individual's learning disposition consists of their attitude to learning, their aspirations and motivation for learning, their openness to learning opportunities and how they react to environmental learning factors (Hodkinson et al. 2008). It may enable or facilitate some learning while obstructing other types of learning.

In the second year of the study, eight of the ten interviewees appeared to have more expansive individual learning dispositions. For example, one was very open to new ideas and trying out new things in the classroom while another talked to others to solve problems. One interviewee was very keen to see everything as a positive learning opportunity; one sought to learn from people outside their own school in a teacher learning community. Other interviewees were very aware of learning all the time and being on the look-out for information that might be useful later on. However, a minority of the interviewed teachers had less expansive individual learning dispositions, for example, they did not seek out extra learning opportunities in the way that the other interviewees did.

Interaction between learning environment and individual learning dispositions

The interaction of learning environment and the individual's learning disposition results in a constantly changing situation. A school with more expansive practices may counteract the disadvantages of someone's restrictive individual learning disposition as the teacher will be exposed to more learning opportunities and support. Personal factors that have been found to influence teachers' motivation to take part in informal workplace learning include "initiative, self-efficacy, love of learning, interest in the profession, commitment to professional development, a nurturing personality and an outgoing personality" (Lohman 2006, p. 152).

Two difficulties have been identified when considering the level of importance of the individual in learning: overemphasising individual agency, and falling into organisational determinism (Hodkinson et al. 2004). The individual is important when considering workplace learning as it is not enough to only consider the learning/workplace environment. Informal learning will be different for each individual as each teacher will differ. Different people find different experiences formative (Cheetham and Chivers 2001), hence the emphasis on the teachers' individual learning disposition. Each person is unique with their own biography and individual learning disposition and differs according to their gender, race, nationality and class (Flores 2001; Johnson and Birkeland 2003). Within each of the schools, the interviewed teachers approached their learning and responded to learning opportunities in different ways. By considering the experiences of each individual teacher, it is possible to address one of the criticisms made of learning as participation theory, namely that not enough is made of the individual's personal identity changing as they move from novice to full participant (Hager and Hodkinson 2009).

New teacher learning is not a linear process from novice to expert, it is a dynamic process affected by the individual's level of effort and the responsiveness of the workplace (Fox et al. 2011). A person's individual learning disposition is not set in stone, as individuals' attitudes and aspirations towards work are not fixed from the outset of their careers: "Young people's vocational identities evolve during the course of their engagement with the learning opportunities (and barriers) afforded by the workplace" (Fuller and Unwin 2004b, p. 40).

Just as learning environments change over time, people's individual learning dispositions may alter. Dramatic changes in one of the interviewed teachers were traced in the four months between interviews. In the first interview, the teacher said it was necessary to "stamp down on them [the pupils]" as she was anxious about the responsibility of being a teacher and compared her own abilities to the children's, whereas in the second interview she referred to getting to know the pupils from actually speaking to them, including using a game-based learning activity. This teacher said they got help all the time from two other teachers who worked with the same age group of pupils in their primary school.

An individual's learning disposition may enable or facilitate some learning while obstructing other types of learning. It is both an antecedent and a trigger for learning – an antecedent as it relates to the individual's learning history and an important trigger for what learning opportunities they will look for and take part in. It is more than personal attitudes, motivations and interests; it includes a sense of what is possible and how to behave (Hodkinson et al. 2008). Someone's individual learning disposition develops through their life experiences and learning at home, at school, at work, in leisure activities and in their local communities (ibid.).

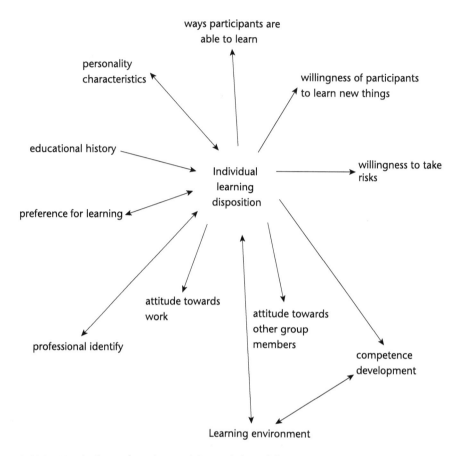

FIGURE 6.3 Active and passive participants (adapted from Gustavsson 2009, p. 249)

Individuals can choose how much they will engage in learning and how this response is affected by their personal life history, their education and their motivation or "learning territory" (Fuller and Unwin 2004a, p. 127). Seibert et al. referred to a self-directed learning orientation (2001, cited in Raemondonck et al. 2014, p. 192). The difference between people can also be understood in terms of how active or passive they are as participants in their learning (Gustavsson 2009). Figure 6.3 shows the different elements that influence an individual's learning disposition from their willingness to take risks to the ways they are able to enjoy learning.

Figure 6.3 shows the influences on individuals, and now we turn to the consequences of a new teacher's informal learning.

Consequences

The new teachers' informal learning resulted in several benefits such as a more expansive individual learning disposition, greater confidence in their practice as a teacher and collaborations with their colleagues.

Individual learning disposition

New teachers bring their skills, abilities and attitudes towards learning into their new job. People's past and ongoing experiences, in terms of education, family and work interact with each other and influence their attitudes to learning. An individual worker's dispositions will interact and influence the affordances of the workplace. There is an interdependence between individuals' intentional actions and their workplace practices (Evans et al. 2006; Skår 2010). People not only react to their workplace, they contribute to its construction as well.

Everyone has a different learning history (Eraut 2000) and an individual's motivation to learn may come from contributing to the work team, the work tasks, or the person's own need (Billett 2002b). This view contrasts with Lave and Wenger's (1991) emphasis on relations and practices in the social sphere without emphasis on the individual separately. The learning environment and the individual's learning disposition are both important and inter-reliant:

> On the one hand are the affordances of the workplace: its invitational qualities. On the other, is the degree by which individuals elect to participate in the work practice. Hence, there is an interdependence between the social practice and the individual acting in the social practice.
>
> *Billett 2001, p. 20*

While new teachers may have similar needs they may seek help and support in different ways (Ulvik et al. 2009). New teachers may take on the responsibility of using their own personal networks to gain support or help with a project (Fox et al. 2011). Of course, just as someone may exercise their free will by choosing to follow their colleagues' practice, they may decide not to take up those practices and to learn in a different way (Billett and Somerville 2004). Not all new teachers will be involved in transformational learning, for example, the novice may have a mentor with very different views on work and this has the potential to put the new entrant off that particular career completely (ibid.).

The teachers' individual learning dispositions can be seen as triggers for their own learning, whether they embrace every opportunity or affordance or whether they limit themselves to doing the bare minimum to satisfy requirements laid down by those above or around them. One way to understand what is going on in the induction year is to think of the way antecedents and triggers yield informal learning (see Figure 6.4).

Confidence

As teachers take part in informal learning their confidence increases, thus encouraging them to try out their ideas in the classroom. With a more expansive learning environment teachers also feel more confident and are happier to take risks, knowing that this is encouraged in their workplace. As observations, collaborations and

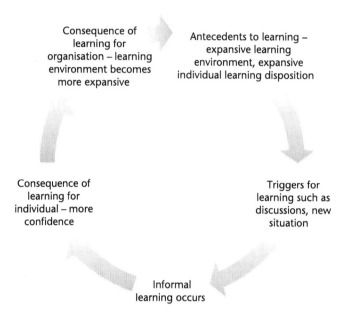

FIGURE 6.4 Antecedents, triggers and consequences of new teachers' informal learning at work

discussions take place new teachers learn and this also creates a more expansive learning environment.

The new teachers are working – they are reflecting on their actions, either at the time or later; in an expansive learning environment the new teachers are supported, they feel confident, they discuss their teaching with colleagues, they observe their colleagues and through the doing, the reflecting and the discussing they are learning and thus, they feel more confident.

Confidence, challenge and support are all important for new teachers (Eraut et al. 2000). If support is provided at crucial points, then this can lead to an increase in confidence. Confidence relates to being able to perform tasks or a role and also relates to confidence in the support and trust of colleagues. Increased confidence means that the individual can cope with more challenging work which in turn leads to further increases in confidence. Support and confidence are antecedents to learning and challenge can be a trigger for learning, with increased confidence being a consequence of that learning. In the teacher interviews towards the end of the induction year, the interviewees were able to look back on their learning during the induction year and see how their teaching practice had changed and also how their identity had changed as a result of their learning in the workplace. They had more confidence in their abilities and felt more comfortable with the responsibility of being in charge of children's learning. However, in one case, the first year of teaching had not gone well and the teacher took a break from teaching before returning to teaching in a part-time role some months later. The teacher's learning environment had not provided many expansive features and the teacher's confidence did not grow over the year. This highlights the different experiences and differing learning environments that the new teachers encountered.

Collaboration with colleagues

For the interviewed teachers the most important learning activities were all related to working with other teachers. This included talking with teachers to solve problems; being observed and receiving feedback; being part of a practice-based working group; observing other teachers; and meetings with other new teachers. For one teacher their involvement in Sports Day had made them realise that they wished to pursue a career in Physical Education. This shows how affordances to learn can widen teachers' horizons beyond their own classroom practice.

In summary, the antecedents to new teachers' learning were classroom experience, relationships with adults and children and some formal professional learning activities. Of particular importance were the new teachers' colleagues, in terms of observing them and discussing work, whether in the capacity of official mentor or not. The new teachers' learning environment and the support and feedback from head teachers were also important. The triggers for their learning were physical proximity to colleagues, their interpersonal relationships in and around school, their observations, collaborations and discussions with colleagues, and their classroom experience, including trying out new ideas and learning from pupils. Important triggers for learning were the new teachers' own individual learning dispositions and their learning environment. The consequences of this professional learning are that the new teachers' individual learning dispositions may develop alongside their confidence and the level of collaboration they take part in with colleagues.

Conclusion

With situated learning theory as a means to understand new teachers' learning, it is important to consider their communities of practice and to what extent they are accepted as novices and helped to move from peripheral participation into acceptance as a full member of the community. The antecedents, triggers and consequences of the new teachers' informal learning cannot be fully understood without keeping in mind the importance of other people in their learning. How the new teacher interacts with other people, adults, children and young people, and how they, in turn, interact with the new teacher play a major role in how and what the new teacher learns.

Teachers are responsible for the formal education of others and this may explain the over-emphasis on formal learning for teachers themselves. Administrators and professional bodies have been slow to recognise the importance of teachers' informal learning in the workplace. A possible explanation for the reticence in considering teachers' informal professional learning is that this may bring into question how children and young people learn, leading to an awkward examination of their own practices in schools and classrooms.

Factors affecting workplace learning do not operate in isolation from each other, but instead are interwoven, the individual with the social and vice versa (Warin and Muldoon 2009). Workplace learning needs to be understood as something that "both shapes and is shaped by the organisation itself rather than as a separately existing activity" (Fuller and Unwin 2004a, p. 128), providing both antecedents and triggers for learning. If school leaders (as employers) consider how they can provide environments for learning and opportunities to participate in communities of practice, they can maximise the organisation's learning potential for itself and for the individuals who work there (Guile and Griffiths 2001). The consequences of informal learning at work for new teachers are increased confidence and a willingness to try out new ideas and take risks.

It would be useful for schools with new teachers to assess the extent to which they have expansive or restrictive practices to support teacher learning. If new teachers were more aware of their own individual learning disposition and they could recognise the expansive and restrictive characteristics of their particular school workplace, it could help them to understand and address their professional learning at an earlier stage in their first year of teaching. New teachers and their mentors could discuss the new teachers' individual learning disposition and how best for them to take up affordances for learning. This "personal learning assessment could be used for performance coaching purposes to cultivate workers who are able to learn and grow continuously, even when adequate environmental resources are constrained" (Lohman 2006, p. 154). This can help them become "autonomous, self-directed learners who are skilled at getting the best out of all learning opportunities" (Cheetham and Chivers 2001, p. 285). School workplaces could invite participation from teachers and structure working conditions and arrangements so that their learning is explicitly supported (Billett 2002b).

This individualisation takes more time and there is also the problem with how to record, authenticate, recognise and value informal learning in the workplace (Skule 2004). A paradox of informal learning is that by recognising it, the experience is changed and may be lost, leading to a difficulty in distinguishing between informal learning that can be recognised and/or fostered and those that should not (Boud et al. 2009). However, it has been argued that rather than worrying about how to record or measure professional learning, it is more important that practitioners and researchers understand the realities of authentic professional learning so that new and useful ways of supporting professionals as they learn can be encouraged and become more widespread (Webster-Wright 2009).

New teachers in Scotland are in a particularly vulnerable position as they are temporary employees who are monitored and assessed by their mentor and head teacher and who rely on a satisfactory reference from their head teacher for their next post (see Shanks 2014). While the antecedents and triggers in relation to a new teacher's individual learning disposition cannot be immediately changed by a school, it is possible to provide triggers and an expansive learning environment for the new teacher, thus leading to teachers who are more likely to be lifelong learning professionals in the workplace.

Contributions to knowledge

The contributions to knowledge made by this research are that different fields of research have been brought together and the voices of new teachers have been heard in order to gain insight and understanding from their experiences and thus inform policy makers, administrators and other major stakeholders in education (Fantilli and McDougall 2009). Findings have shown that the emphasis on formal continuing professional development and professional standards leads to the neglect of new teachers' most vital learning.

The study highlights how new teachers learn from their colleagues in the workplace, predominantly through informal interactions about everyday practice. This builds on previous research showing the importance of informal learning and of expansive learning environments for learning in the workplace. New teachers need their own space to practise and learn in, they need opportunities to learn with colleagues and opportunities to learn on their own. While it has been highlighted that there is a shortfall in relation to Lave and Wenger's (1991) account of learning, in that it gives no consideration to the role of formal education institutions in a newcomer's learning process (Fuller and Unwin 2003), this research has shown the reverse is true in relation to teacher induction in Scotland, with little recognition given to informal learning. This informal learning is too vital to be neglected by administrators, ignored by policy makers, or excluded by researchers (McNally 2006). This research shows that even when formal professional learning is emphasised and privileged and the work of professionals is the formal learning of others, namely school pupils, people's most important learning at work occurs informally as they practise their profession, as they observe colleagues, as they discuss their work and as they become more engaged participants in their communities of practice. The notion of individual learning disposition of the person at work and how this interacts with and adapts to the learning environment is an attempt to address the criticism made of situated learning theory, in that the individual learner is not wholly subsumed in the focus on social practices and communities of practice. While the affordances being offered in the workplace are an important source of learning, whether learning will take place will still depend on a participant's individual learning disposition.

This study shows how new teachers learn from trial and error, from their classroom experience, from and with their pupils and colleagues and from some formal learning activities. Factors that are important in their learning are their individual learning dispositions, and the restrictive and expansive practices in their learning environment, including the level of support from their formal and informal mentors, from other colleagues and from their head teacher. Above all, the study found how colleagues affect the learning of new teachers.

Appendix 6.1 Coding glossary

Colleagues and school context

This code encompasses the interaction between the induction year teacher and their school and colleagues. For example, when an induction year teacher talks about their head teacher, their mentor or other staff. When they discuss the school, peer support, asking for help and advice. When they mention workplace/office politics it is included in this code.

Sub-codes: Asking for help and advice; Head teacher; Impact of school context; Mentors; Micro-political literacy; Other staff; Peer support.

Induction year

This code includes any item related to the induction year arrangements. For example, the organisation of the induction year, work-life balance during this year and the induction year teacher's self-belief.

Sub-codes: Issues in induction year; Work-life balance; Self-belief; Induction process.

Learning

This code encompasses references to learning made by the interviewees. This might be a reference to formal learning, ideas about learning, the impact of learning, informal learning, their learning needs and the spaces and places that learning takes place in. This also includes references to observations and the induction year teacher's attitude to observations. Sub-codes of formal learning and informal learning.

Sub-codes: Formal learning (spaces; physical places formal learning); Ideas about learning; Impact of learning (informal learning); Informal learning; Learning needs; Observations (attitude to observations).

Looking back to university course

This code is used to indicate when someone refers back to their initial teacher education course.

Organisation

This code encompasses the induction year teachers' views on their organisational skills.

Physical spaces

This code includes spaces the induction year teachers talk about and places where informal learning takes place and the response to the question "where does most of your learning take place?"

Sub-codes: Physical spaces informal learning; Most learning taken place; Spaces

Pupils

This code encompasses references to the induction year teachers' own pupils in their class/es and pupils in their school.

The job of teaching

This code includes references to the induction year teachers' reason for teaching, their expectations of the job and their job (in)security at the end of the induction year.

Sub-codes: Expectation of the job; Job (in)security; Reason for teaching.

Time

This code encompasses instances when time is referred to, for example the time it takes to prepare and plan for teaching, the 0.7/0.3 split in teaching time and CPD, the time to commute to school, what the induction year teachers do in their non-teaching time and their feelings about having or not having enough time.

Sub-code: Non-teaching time.

References

Ashton, DN, 2004, 'The impact of organisational structure and practices on learning in the workplace', *International Journal of Training and Development,* vol. 8, no. 1, pp. 43–53.

Barrera, A, Braley, RT & Slate, JR, 2010, 'Beginning teacher success: An investigation into the feedback from mentors of formal mentoring programs', *Mentoring & Tutoring: Partnership in Learning,* vol. 18, no. 1, pp. 61–74.

Billett, S, 2002a, 'Critiquing workplace learning discourses: Participation and continuity at work', *Studies in the Education of Adults,* vol. 34, no. 1, pp. 56–67.

Billett, S, 2002b, 'Workplace pedagogic practices: co-participation and learning', *British Journal of Educational Studies,* vol. 50, no. 4, pp. 457–481.

Billett, S, 2001, 'Learning throughout working life: Interdependencies at work', *Studies in Continuing Education,* vol. 23, no. 1, pp. 19–35.

Billett, S & Somerville, M, 2004, 'Transformations at work: Identity and learning', *Studies in Continuing Education,* vol. 26, no. 2, pp. 309–326.

Boud, D & Middleton, H, 2003, 'Learning from others at work: Communities of practice and informal learning', *Journal of Workplace Learning,* vol. 15, no. 5, pp. 194–202.

Boud, D, Rooney, D & Solomon, N, 2009, 'Talking up learning at work: Cautionary tales in co-opting everyday learning', *International Journal of Lifelong Education,* vol. 28, no. 3, pp. 323–334.

Burn, K, Hagger, H, Mutton, T & Everton, T, 2003, 'The complex development of student-teachers' thinking', *Teachers and Teaching,* vol. 9, no. 4, pp. 309–331.

Cairns, L, 2011, 'Learning in the workplace: Communities of practice and beyond', in M Malloch, L Cairns, K Evans and BN O'Connor (eds) *The SAGE Handbook of Workplace Learning,* SAGE, London, pp. 73–85.

Cheetham, G, & Chivers, G, 2001, 'How professionals learn in practice: An investigation of informal learning amongst people working in professions', *Journal of European Industrial Training,* vol. 25, no. 5, pp. 270–292.

Clarke, R, Matheson, I, Morris, P & Robson, D, 2007, 'Models of support in the Teacher Induction Scheme in Scotland', *32nd Annual Association for Teacher Education in Europe Conference, University of Wolverhampton,* 25–29 August 2007, ATEE.

Cohen, L, Manion, L and Morrison, K, 2007, *Research Methods in Education,* Routledge, Abingdon, Oxon.

Collin, K, 2008, 'Development engineers' work and learning as shared practice', *International Journal of Lifelong Education,* vol. 27, no. 4, pp. 379–397.

Curry, M, Jaxon, K, Russell, JL, Callahan, MA & Bicais, J, 2008, 'Examining the practice of beginning teachers' micropolitical literacy within professional inquiry communities', *Teaching and Teacher Education,* vol. 24, no. 3, pp. 660–673.

Draper, J, Fraser, H & Taylor, W, 1997, 'Teachers at work: Early experiences of professional development', *British Journal of In-service Education,* vol. 23, no. 2, pp. 283–295.

Edwards, A, 2005, 'Let's get beyond community and practice: the many meanings of learning by participating', *Curriculum Journal,* vol. 16, no. 1, pp. 49–65.

Eraut, M, 2007, 'Learning from other people in the workplace', *Oxford Review of Education,* vol. 33, no. 4, pp. 403–422.

Eraut, M, 2004, 'Informal learning in the workplace', *Studies in Continuing Education,* vol. 26, no. 2, pp. 247–273.

Eraut, M, 2000, 'Non-formal learning and tacit knowledge in professional work', *British Journal of Educational Psychology,* vol. 70, no. 1, pp. 113–136.

Eraut, M, Alderton, J, Cole, G & Senker, P, 2000, 'Development of knowledge and skills at work', In F Coffield (ed.), *Differing Visions of a Learning Society: Research findings,* Bristol, The Policy Press, pp. 231–262.

Evans, K, Hodkinson, P, Rainbird, H & Unwin, L, 2006, *Improving Workplace Learning*, Routledge, Abingdon, Oxon.

Fantilli, RD & McDougall, DE, 2009, 'A study of novice teachers: Challenges and supports in the first years', *Teaching and Teacher Education*, vol. 25, no. 6, pp. 814–825.

Felstead, A, Fuller, A, Unwin, L, Ashton, D, Butler, P & Lee, T, 2005, 'Surveying the scene: Learning metaphors, survey design and the workplace context', *Journal of Education and Work*, vol. 18, no. 4, pp. 359–383.

Flores, MA, 2001, 'Person and context in becoming a new teacher', *Journal of Education for Teaching*, vol. 27, no. 2, pp. 135–148.

Fox, A, Wilson, E & Deaney, R, 2011, 'Beginning teachers' workplace experiences: Perceptions of and use of support', *Vocations and Learning*, vol. 4, no. 1, pp. 1–24.

Fuller, A & Unwin, L, 2011, 'Workplace learning and the organisation', in M Malloch, L Cairns, K Evans and BN O'Connor (eds) *The SAGE Handbook of Workplace Learning*, London, SAGE, pp. 46–59.

Fuller, A & Unwin, L, 2004a, 'Expansive learning environments: integrating organizational and personal development', in H Rainbird, A Fuller and A Munro (eds) *Workplace Learning in Context*. London, Routledge, pp. 126–144.

Fuller, A & Unwin, L, 2004b, 'Young people as teachers and learners in the workplace: Challenging the novice-expert dichotomy', *International Journal of Training and Development*, vol. 8, no. 1, pp. 32–42.

Fuller, A & Unwin, L, 2003, 'Learning as apprentices in the contemporary UK workplace: Creating and managing expansive and restrictive participation', *Journal of Education and Work*, vol. 16, no. 4, pp. 407–426.

Greenlee, BJ & Dedeugd, IS, 2002, 'From hope to despair: the need for beginning teacher advocacy', *Teacher Development*, vol. 6, no. 1, pp. 63–74.

GTCS (General Teaching Council For Scotland), 2012, *The Standards for Registration: Mandatory requirements for registration with the General Teaching Council for Scotland*, Edinburgh, General Teaching Council for Scotland.

GTCS (General Teaching Council For Scotland), 2009, *Statistical Digest*, Edinburgh, General Teaching Council for Scotland.

Guile, D & Griffiths, T, 2001, 'Learning Through Work Experience', *Journal of Education and Work*, vol. 14, no. 1, pp. 113–131.

Gustavsson, M, 2009, 'Facilitating expansive learning in a public sector organization', *Studies in Continuing Education*, vol. 31, no. 3, pp. 245–259.

Hagger, H, Burn, K, Mutton, T & Brindley, S, 2008, 'Practice makes perfect? Learning to learn as a teacher', *Oxford Review of Education*, vol. 34, no. 2, pp. 159–178.

Hager, P & Hodkinson, P, 2009, 'Moving beyond the metaphor of transfer of learning', *British Educational Research Journal*, vol. 35, no. 4, pp. 619–638.

HMIE (Her Majesty's Inspectorate of Education), 2009, 'Learning together: Improving teaching, improving learning', Livingston, Scotland, HMIE.

Hodkinson, P & Hodkinson, H, 2003, 'Individuals, communities of practice and the policy context: school teachers' learning in their workplace', *Studies in Continuing Education*, vol. 25, no. 1, pp. 3–21.

Hodkinson, H & Hodkinson, P, 2005, 'Improving schoolteachers' workplace learning', *Research Papers in Education*, vol. 20, no. 2, pp.109–131.

Hodkinson, P, Biesta, G & James, D, 2008, 'Understanding learning culturally: Overcoming the dualism between social and individual views of learning', *Vocations and Learning*, vol. 1, no. 1, pp. 27–47.

Hodkinson, P, Hodkinson, H, Evans, K, Kersh, N, Fuller, A, Unwin, L & Senker, P, 2004, 'The significance of individual biography in workplace learning', *Studies in the Education of Adults*, vol. 36, no. 1, pp. 6–24.

Holton, JA, 2010, 'The coding process and its challenges', in A Bryant and K Charmaz (eds) *The SAGE Handbook of Grounded Theory*, London, SAGE Publications, pp. 265–289.

Ivankova, N, Creswell, JW and Stick, SL, 2006, 'Using mixed-methods sequential explanatory design: From theory to practice', *Field Method*, vol. 18, no. 1, pp. 3–20.

Jewson, N, Felstead, A, & Green, F, 2014, 'Training in the public sector in a period of austerity: The case of the UK', *Journal of Education and Work*, vol. 28, no. 3, pp. 1–22.

Johnson, SM & Birkeland, SE, 2003, 'Pursuing a "sense of success": New teachers explain their career decisions', *American Educational Research Journal*, vol. 40, no. 3, pp. 581–617.

Jones, M, 2002, 'Qualified to become good teachers: A case study of ten newly qualified teachers during their year of induction', *Journal of In-Service Education*, vol. 28, no. 3, pp. 509–526.

Kelchtermans, G & Ballet, K, 2002, 'The micropolitics of teacher induction. A narrative-biographical study on teacher socialisation', *Teaching and Teacher Education*, vol. 18, no. 1, pp. 105–120.

Kennedy, A, 2011, 'Collaborative continuing professional development (CPD) for teachers in Scotland: Aspirations, opportunities and barriers', *European Journal of Teacher Education*, vol. 34, no. 1, pp. 25–41.

Kinnear, PR & Gray, CD, 2009, *SPSS 16 Made Simple*, Hove, East Sussex, Psychology Press.

Kvale, S and Brinkmann, S, 2009, *InterViews, Learning the Craft of Qualitative Research Interviewing*, 2nd edn., London, Sage.

Lave, J & Wenger, E, 1991, *Situated Learning: Legitimate peripheral participation*, New York, Cambridge University Press.

Lohman, MC, 2006, 'Factors influencing teachers' engagement in informal learning activities', *Journal of Workplace Learning*, vol. 18, no. 3, pp. 141–156.

Marsick, VJ (ed.), 1987, *Learning in the Workplace*, Beckenham, Kent, Croom Helm.

Mcgregor, J, 2003, 'Making Spaces: Teacher workplace topologies', *Pedagogy, Culture & Society*, vol. 11, no. 3, pp. 353–378.

McNally, J, 2006, 'From informal learning to identity formation: A conceptual journey in early teacher development', *Scottish Educational Review*, vol. 37 (Special edition), pp. 79–89.

Meirink, JA, Meijer, PC, Verloop, N & Bergen, TCM, 2009, 'How do teachers learn in the workplace? An examination of teacher learning activities', *European Journal of Teacher Education*, vol. 32, no. 3, pp. 209–224.

Mesler Parise, L & Spillane, JP, 2010, 'Teacher learning and instructional change: How formal and on-the-job learning opportunities predict change in elementary school teachers' practice', *The Elementary School Journal*, vol. 110, no. 3, pp. 323–346.

Parker, MA, Ndoye, A & Imig, SR, 2009, 'Keeping our teachers! Investigating mentoring practices to support and retain novice educators', *Mentoring & Tutoring: Partnership in Learning*, vol. 17, no. 4, pp. 329–341.

Pearson, MA & Robson, D, 2005, *Experiences of the Teacher Induction Scheme: Operation, support and CPD*, Occasional Paper 6, Edinburgh, GTC Scotland.

Plano Clark, VL and Ivankova, NV, 2016, *Mixed Methods Research. A Guide to the Field.* London, Sage.

Raemdonck, I, Gijbels, D & Van Groen, W, 2014, 'The influence of job characteristics and self-directed learning orientation on workplace learning', *International Journal of Training and Development*, vol. 18, no. 3, pp. 188–203.

Richter, D, Kunter, M, Klusmann, U, Ludtke, O & Baumert, J, 2011, 'Professional development across the teaching career: Teachers' uptake of formal and informal learning opportunities' *Teaching and Teacher Education*, vol. 27, no. 1, pp. 116–126.

Sax, LJ, Gilmartin, SK & Bryant, AN, 2003, 'Assessing response rates and nonresponse bias in web and paper surveys', *Research in Higher Education*, vol. 44, no. 4, pp. 409–432. doi:10.1023/A:1024232915870

Schön, DA, 1987, *Educating the Reflective Practitioner*, San Francisco, CA, Jossey-Bass.

Schön, DA, 1983, *The Reflective Practitioner: How professionals think in action*, Aldershot, Basic Books Inc.

SERA (Scottish Educational Research Association), 2005, *Ethical Guidelines for Educational Research*, 2nd edn., Aberdeen, Scottish Educational Research Association.

Shanks, R, 2014, 'A study of learners' situational vulnerability: New teachers in Scotland', *Education in the North*, vol. 21 (Special Issue), pp. 2–20.

Shanks, R, Robson, D & Gray, D, 2012, 'New teachers' individual learning dispositions: A Scottish case study', *International Journal of Training and Development*, Special Issue on Continuing Professional Development, vol. 16, no. 3, pp.183–199.

Skår, R, 2010, 'How nurses experience their work as a learning environment', *Vocations and Learning*, vol. 3, no. 1, pp. 1–18.

Skruber, R, 1987, 'Organisations as clarifying learning environments', in VJ Marsick (ed.) *Learning in the Workplace*, Beckenham, Kent, Croom Helm, pp. 55–78.

Skule, S, 2004, 'Learning conditions at work: A framework to understand and assess informal learning in the workplace', *International Journal of Training and Development*, vol. 8, no. 1, pp. 8–20.

Stanulis, RN & Burrill, G, 2004, 'Preparing highly qualified teachers who keep content and context central: The Michigan State University Induction Program', *AERA Meeting*, San Diego, 12–16 April 2004, AERA.

Taylor-Powell, E & Renner, M, 2003, *Analyzing Qualitative Data*. G3658-12 edn. University of Wisconsin, Madison, WI.

Tickle, L, 2000, *Teacher Induction: The way ahead*, Buckingham, Open University Press.

Ulvik, M, Smith, K & Helleve, I, 2009, 'Novice in secondary school – the coin has two sides', *Teaching and Teacher Education*, vol. 25, no. 6, pp. 835–842.

Unwin, L & Fuller, A, 2003, *Expanding Learning in the Workplace. Making more of individual and organisational potential*, Leicester, NIACE.

Unwin, L, Felstead, A, Fuller, A, Bishop, D, Lee, T, Jewson, N & Butler, P, 2007, 'Looking inside the Russian doll: The interconnections between context, learning and pedagogy in the workplace', *Pedagogy, Culture & Society*, vol. 15, no. 3, pp. 333–348.

Warin, J & Muldoon, J, 2009, 'Wanting to be "known": Redefining self-awareness through an understanding of self-narration processes in educational transitions', *British Educational Research Journal*, vol. 35, no. 2, pp. 289–303.

Webster-Wright, A, 2009, 'Reframing professional development through understanding authentic professional learning', *Review of Educational Research*, vol. 79, no. 2, pp. 702–739.

Williams, A, 2003, 'Informal learning in the workplace: A case study of new teachers', *Educational Studies*, vol. 29, no. 2, pp. 207–219.

Williams, A, Prestage, S & Bedward, J, 2001, 'Individualism to collaboration: The significance of teacher culture to the induction of newly qualified teachers', *Journal of Education for Teaching*, vol. 27, no. 3, pp. 253–267.

7
THE POTENTIAL AND PARADOX OF INFORMAL LEARNING

David Boud[1] and Donna Rooney[2]

Introduction

Informal learning at work has attracted growing interest over the past two decades. Interest comes from multiple sources, including modern organizations that generally accept the promise of positive effects on productivity. Organizations have a vested interest in recognizing and harnessing informal learning – not least because of apparent cost efficiencies, for example, little or no training related costs, nor backfill costs to replace workers that are attending training.

Researchers coming from a range of disciplines are also attracted to informal learning at work (Fenwick 2008). Various researchers (ourselves included) seek to capture, name, and ultimately *understand* more about it. Interesting research questions arise when we understand that learning occurs without the infrastructure of curriculum, structured training activities, or the intervention of training personnel: what forms can it take and what are the effects on organizations? From our background in adult education research, our own concern is that in order to understand informal workplace learning, we need new and different perspectives to view it: perspectives that go beyond both conventional understandings of training derived from the vocational education and training literature, as well as from those arising from organizational theory. Informal learning in and for work is an important feature of working life, and as such requires a new set of understandings not located in either of these two areas.

To this end, this chapter makes use of practice-based theorizations. In particular, it draws on the work of Theodore Schatzki (2001, 2012) and Stephen Kemmis

---

1 Deakin University, Geelong, Australia; University of Technology Sydney, Australia, and Middlesex University, London, United Kingdom
2 University of Technology Sydney, Australia

Informal learning: potential and paradox **135**

(2000, 2005, 2010). This approach means that the activities or *practices* of workers, rather than individual workers, constitute the unit of analysis. This enables everyday work practices, undertaken with no thought to learning as such and often overlooked in other studies, to be examined in terms of learning. Understanding informal learning as embedded in practices differs from accounts of informal learning that see learning as 'a thing acquired by individuals' (Hager 2008), or as a phenomenon independent of the context in which it occurs, or as something that individuals do alone (ibid.). Through a practice approach, we understand learning as a phenomenon dependent on the activities, practices, and socio-material arrangements in which it is located.

Before continuing, however, we acknowledge that 'informal learning' is a contested term, subject to a number of definitions. To say that something is formal or informal is to oversimplify, as most practices that involve learning have features of formality or informality associated with them. To uncritically name learning as either formal or informal is to essentialize a complex combination of learning processes which have varying degrees of formality and informality (Colley, Hodkinson & Malcom 2003). For example, participation in a formal course may lead to little learning without the informal interactions among learners and between learners and teachers that typically occur. Conversely, informal learning among workplace peers may involve reference to formalized manuals or procedures. There are also issues about naming the learning of others when those others do not recognize it as learning (Eraut 2004; Boud and Solomon 2003). Therefore, in this chapter in the service of clarity, we take a broad view that understands informal learning as a phenomenon that is *not* the result of some planned and structured educational or training activity. In doing so, we acknowledge that some of the learning described here might also be categorized differently (for example, as incidental).

This chapter seeks to provide a fresh way of understanding informal learning at work through a secondary analysis of five published studies undertaken by researchers in our own institution in a broad range of Australian sites utilizing practice perspectives. The chapter is divided into three key parts. In the first part, by way of background, we outline developments in approaches taken in the study of informal learning and justify our approach and why it is a helpful framing for investigating informal workplace learning. The second part discusses a set of practices from across the studies, along with some examples, to give flavour to the range of practices identified. The third part turns attention to our analysis of the (learning rich) practices, and then to the learning *in* practices. It continues by drawing attention to the tensions of understanding learning as embedded in work, and the dilemma of seeking to influence informal learning through the examination of the potentially counterproductive effects of formalizing it.

Background

Approaching the study of informal learning

Interest in workplace learning has evolved over the past few decades, resulting in the development of a growing range of concepts that can be used to identify and understand it. To help make sense of the scope of these resources, there are useful synopses in contemporary literature. For instance, Hager (2011, 2012, 2014) has provided overviews of the development of approaches to the study of work-based learning that spans from early mentalist understandings, to socio-cultural, through to what he perhaps provocatively names postmodern theories. Similarly, in the introduction of a recent edited volume on the topic, Dochy (2011) provides an overview of various learning theories deployed in studies of workplace learning. Further overviews of workplace learning theories can be found in the work of Fenwick (2008), and others (for example, Malloch et al. 2011).

What is clear from discussions of this kind is that any approach, while illuminating some aspects of learning, also limits potential to notice others. For instance, some earlier cognitive approaches to researching learning have been recognized to be inadequate, given the assumptions of the individualistic nature of learning on which such approaches are based. Other limitations included a backgrounding of the material contexts in accounts of learning and the adoption of unproblematic static views of knowledge.

Many have responded by shifting their approach to one that focuses more on the social, or collective, nature of work. Lave and Wenger's (1991) well-cited 'communities of practice' (CoP) is a good example of approaching research in workplace learning in a manner attentive to the sociality of work. It focuses on informal learning without overemphasizing informality as such. While situated views like CoP have been well taken up by organizations, and may be helpful for describing how newcomers are inducted into a field, they are typically silent 'about how, in practice, members of a community *change* their practice or innovate' (Fox 2000, p. 860, emphasis added) – that is, processes through which ongoing learning occurs. Along with a silence on change and innovation, situated understandings of learning have been critiqued for various other reasons, including assumptions about homogeneous 'communities' and the limiting of 'situatedness' to the social context alone (see for example, Gherardi, Nicolini & Odella 1998; Roberts 2006).

To this end, there are more recent approaches that attend to the physical, social and political contexts of work. For these sorts of approaches, learning (and *not* learning for that matter) is not simply a matter dependent on individuals and their interactions, but also on the physical, social, cultural and political contexts in which work is carried out. Billett's (2001) significant attempt to bring together the individual *and* the work context – with context offering affordances for, or inhibiting, workplace learning – provides an early example of this approach. His later work expanded on these ideas (Billet 2011; Billett 2004). Further examples of approaches alert to the social, organizational and political context, with a less central focus on learning as such, include complexity and activity theories. These provide more complex understandings of non-homogeneous workers' learning in socio-political contexts and their constructivist understandings of learning leave open possibilities for innovation (cf. Engeström 2009; Engeström, Engeström & Vahaaho 1999).

A practice approach (and why we adopt it)

While we appreciate the insights made available through this emerging body of work, and in particular the more recent developments, we take a 'practice approach' to our discussion here. Practice based theories represent an emerging tranche of contemporary research offering new and different understandings for those interested in work and learning (Hager, Lee & Reich 2012). Practice theory is not a unitary approach and nuances are seen amongst its central proponents (Gherardi 2000, 2009; Kemmis 2000, 2005; Kemmis et al. 2014; Nerland & Jenson 2012; Schatzki 2001, 2012). While a full discussion of differences between practice scholars is beyond the scope of this chapter, some shared features are relevant to our discussion.

Practices are a collective pursuit. Understanding practices as a common enterprise has important implications for understanding informal learning – not least of all in avoiding inappropriately individualized accounts of informal learning. A practice approach takes the connected activities of work, rather than attributes of individuals, as the unit of analysis. A practice is the 'organized constellation of different peoples' activities' (Schatzki 2012, p. 13), and as such it has a shared understanding among those who practice them. Practices are not the 'possessions' of individual practitioners' but are 'the collective 'property' of groups (Kemmis 2005, p. 393). In other words, a practice approach is more cognizant of the collective and integrated nature of work because a practice is a shared enterprise that extends beyond any individual person or discrete set of work processes.

A practice has '*extra-individual* features' (Kemmis 2005, p. 393). Not only do humans shape practice, but non-human features of practice are also afforded agency, for instance, history, materiality and the socio-political influence practices. A practice approach is attentive to the context (not as a stage or background) but as implicated in, and/or shaping, practice. Fenwick et al. (2011) have been among the key proponents in this regard, in particular drawing attention to the socio-material aspects of work and learning and the value in research of pursuing the everyday objects of work.

A practice is ever emergent. However, it typically has a history that precedes those who practice it (Schatzki 2012). Given the significance of ever-changing contexts in which they are enacted, each enactment or iteration of a practice leaves open the potential for it to be done differently. A practice approach, then, not only recognizes how practices persist, but also how they change over time. This understanding is especially helpful when considering learning. Silvia Gheradi's work on innovation (2000, 2009) is a key resource here as she notes how small-scale innovations, as a result of practices being undertaken in always unique circumstances, are daily occurrences in organizations.

Finally, understanding practices in this way invites drawing on different and more useful metaphors for learning. Many point to the limitations of traditional metaphors for learning. While Sfard (1998) provided an important contrast in learning metaphors (acquisition versus participation) in the late 1990s, others have since acknowledged and worked with and extended her ideas (Boud & Hager 2011;

Hager 2008; Rooney & Solomon 2006). In particular Hager (2004, 2008, 2014, 2012) consistently argues the limitations of the common 'transfer' and 'acquisition' metaphors that have static views of knowledge. Practice based approaches employ different metaphors, including the metaphors of 'participation' or 'becoming'. These metaphors invite epistemological questioning – how is knowledge enacted, co-produced – as well as a focus on collective, coordinated and *in situ* activities of workers. Whereas 'becoming' metaphors invite consideration of not only how worker and organizational identities are produced through practice, but also acknowledge and exemplify the importance of recurrent learning (Hager & Hodkinson 2011).

While these are not the only features of practice as seen in literature, for present purposes they provide a useful basis for discussion.

Method

This chapter undertakes a secondary analysis of five published studies. Secondary analysis involves using data from previous studies to ask new questions or provide new insights into some phenomena (Heaton 2008). In the present case, key papers published in international journals from a series of qualitative studies undertaken within our own research group over a 15-year period were chosen as the data set. These met a quality standard, having all been peer-reviewed, involved existing workgroups at different levels of the organisations concerned, and represented a very wide range of workplace contexts. All included a focus on what is here described as informal learning, though this label was not often used in the original studies. While secondary analysis of quantitative data is a common strategy, the same cannot be said of qualitative data. However, its popularity is growing due to its capacity to make better use of large amounts of data (among other things). In our own case, the data sets are compatible though not quantitatively commensurate (see below). Furthermore, because one or both of us undertook most of the original fieldwork, we are familiar with the specificities of the studies. These facts address many of the key methodological concerns of secondary analysis. Another concern of secondary analysis we consider here is that of ethics, and in particular the informed consent of participants to participate in secondary studies (Heaton 2008). Across the studies, all participants gave informed consent for interview and focus group data to be included in publications. In two of the five studies' informed consent forms, the use of data is limited to the original study alone (i.e. the context, judgement and informal learning, neighbourhood centre studies). In these instances, we only reuse passages from existing publications in addition to citing their sources.

We take a two-step approach to our analysis. First, we look across each study to identify work activities that involve learning. The following criteria are used to warrant relevance:

- The practices are ones where learning of some sort has been identified.
- The practices are independent of any formal training programs or initiatives explicitly intended to bring about learning.

- The practices primarily serve some function other than bringing about learning. This means that mentoring and coaching (which have some deliberate pedagogical intent) are excluded.
- The practices, when intentionally deployed, do not involve people who occupy a learning function within the organization (e.g. trainers and HR personnel).
- As in the source studies, practices were identified that were typically commonplace in the work unit and were not outliers.

This strategy generates a list of practices from across the multiple and very diverse sites of five separate studies: a wider range of contemporary work than any single study alone. Second, we look across the list and frame these activities as practices before focusing specifically on the contingencies of informal learning within these practices. This focus also leads to identifying some tensions between effective learning and those who seek to actively promote it, which we illustrate with further empirical examples. The aim of this analysis, shared with the original studies, is not to seek the ability to generalize to other contexts, but to portray issues that arise in such studies that may have resonance elsewhere.

The studies

We draw from five Australian studies (see below) undertaken since the early 2000s. The studies represent the work of at least 15 researchers (including six doctoral students attached to the studies). One or both of the current authors, or their immediate colleagues, were involved in each study (which explains the regrettable abundance of self-citation here!). The studies are:

1. Uncovering learning at work in a public sector organization
2. Context, judgement and informal learning: an investigation of factors crucial for enhancing performance
3. Beyond training: integrated development practices in organizations
4. Neighbourhoods: centres of learning
5. Identifying and developing capability in engineers' continuing professional learning.

Each study identifies and analyses *inter alia* forms of informal learning typical of the work of the organizations or contexts in which they were conducted. As the studies' names suggest, the foci differed considerably (see Table 7.1). However, despite differences they share three important features. The first is that all studies are broadly interested in learning in work. While workplace learning can occur in structured learning activities that might be described as 'formal', the foci of these studies were on learning that ensues as people go about their everyday activities (not learning as result of structured educational events). Hence, a first unifying feature of the studies is that each can be said to explore aspects of 'informal' learning.

A second similarity among the studies is that all are richly qualitative in nature. They employed a combination of ethnographic data collection methods including semi-structured interviews and focus groups where participants were invited to talk at length about their ordinary work and to give examples of their daily work practices. Data collection also included non-participant observations and, in some cases, member feedback sessions. Not only do comparable methods across studies result in data sets that are more readily suited to the analysis (Heaton 2008), but they are also appropriate methods for the practice approach taken here: "There is no alternative to hanging out with, joining in with, talking to and watching, and getting together the people concerned" (Schatzki 2012, p. 25).

In its original form, the qualitative data of each study was typically subject to thematic analysis drawing out key themes concerning learning. Some made use of spatial, identity and discourse theories in their analysis, whereas others made explicit use of socio-material and practice based theorizations. While exact figures are near impossible to ascertain, the combined studies accrued hundreds of hours of qualitative data, represent the experiences and input of several hundred participants, and prompted numerous published accounts of learning (of which we draw upon here).

A third similarity is that the studies were each undertaken in one or more Australian sites. While varying in size and type, the sites included: a further education college, a winery, a community college, a public utility, a local council, a large engineering firm, an orchestra, a commercial kitchen, a corrective services unit, and community/neighbourhood centres. They thus share a very broad socio-cultural context, though it must be recognized that the Australian working population is very diverse in terms of ethnicity, country of origin and educational background.

Learning practices from across the studies

What were the practices identified in the studies that involved learning? In identifying these practices, we follow Schatzki's point about noticing how people name their activities (2012, p. 24), as this helps confirm a shared meaning. The names given to the practices identified below could easily be given as the answer to the question, "*What are you doing?*"

While not exhaustive, the examples below provide good illustrations of the range of practices identified across the various studies. In addition to these are other well-documented practices, including: *performance appraisals* (Chappell et al. 2009), *coming into the office* (Solomon, Boud & Rooney 2008), and *work design* (Price, Scheeres & Boud 2009).

The identified practices are presented in four main groups. First are practices germane to the particular nature of the occupations involved. The second group includes practices that are seen in multiple types of work. Third are responses to 'out of the ordinary' events. The final group includes common practices that happen in all kinds of workplaces, but are not necessarily part of the essential business of the organization. In each group, brief examples give flavour. The practice and illustrations of it are then drawn on in following parts of the chapter.

TABLE 7.1 Identification of practices that generate learning informally

Identification of practices that generate learning informally 1

Practice	Organization	Studies practices seen in	Examples of learning	Learning features							Practice features		
				Potential for change as result	Realized through chat/talk	Social: others involved	Collective learning	Learner faced some difference	Involved significant change	Learning not main object of practice	Practice germane to profession or work type	Common in many forms of work
Meetings • Design reviews • Faculty meeting • Toolbox meetings	• Further Education college • Public utility • Winery • Local Council • Engineering firm • Public utility	1, 3, 5	Engineers learned about aspects of others work that and how it impacts their own job (e.g. construction engineers from estimators). Toolbox meetings at Council, Public Utility and Engineering supported worker learning around safe work practices.	✓	✓	✓	✓	✓		✓		✓
Performance appraisals	• Local Council • Engineering firm • Public utility	1, 3, 5	Performance appraisal unfolded as both accountability and mentoring. The later featuring advice from their managers enabling them to learn to do their jobs differently.	✓	✓	✓						✓
Acting up	• Local Council	3	Council worker acting in a more senior position learned not only about the acting job, but also their own job from a new perspective	✓	✓			✓	✓	✓		✓

(continued)

TABLE 7.1 Identification of practices that generate learning informally *(continued)*

Identification of practices that generate learning informally 2

Practice	Organization	Studies practices seen in	Examples of learning	Learning features							Practice features		
				Potential for change as result	Realized through chat/talk	Social: others involved	Collective learning	Learner faced some difference	Involved significant change	Learning not main object of practice	Practice germane to profession or work type	Common in many forms of work
Unplanned radical change	• Local Council	3	A major fire resulted in most workers learning to carry out their work the morning after in a new environment under new conditions.	✓		✓	✓	✓	✓	✓		✓
Rehearsals	• Orchestra	2	Practice for performance	✓	✓	✓	✓			✓	✓	
Work design teams	• Local Council	3	Leading up to a restructure, council workers participated in teams to redefined their own and others' jobs	✓	✓	✓	✓	✓	✓	✓		
Site walk	• Engineering firm	5	Undertaking a site walk together with others enabled engineers to learn from others site walkers and the context.	✓		✓	✓	✓		✓	✓	✓

Practices germane to the occupations involved

Some practices are unique to the occupation or professions involved. Several practices were identified that fit this category. For instance, Hager and Johnsson (2012) identified rehearsals as a practice that supported learning among orchestral musicians. They also identified chefs and kitchen staff learning in the delivering an à *la carte* dining service (2012). In another study, the site-walk practice undertaken in engineering work was a practice involving learning (Rooney et al. 2015a; Rooney et al. 2015b), and this constitutes a first example.

A site-walk generally involves the purposeful inspection of aspects of a particular work site. Engineers along with other relevant people typically undertake the site walk. For instance, an environmental scientist, client, or proxy for a client and/or the *foreman*[*sic*] may accompany the engineer. Despite being an everyday practice for engineers, these site walks are shown to be 'complex and potentially learning-rich practices' (Rooney et al. 2015b). The engineers talked about how their work has changed since environmental matters became more prominent – and how they think differently about their work now that undertaking site-walks sometimes involves environmental scientists (ibid.). They also added how the emergent interest in environmental matters is reshaping how they currently undertake their site-walks and other aspects of their work. They note how two decades ago, a similar reshaping took place, along with much associated learning, when matters of safety became prominent.

Practices seen in multiple types of work

Unlike, say, site walks and rehearsals (germane to the work of engineers and musicians), there are practices that are more dispersed and are common in multiple types of work. A good example of this is meetings, and these were identified in several of the studies as practices where learning occurred (Reich et al. 2015; Rooney et al. 2015a; Scheeres et al. 2010). Another example is safety practices, and both the *Beyond Training* as well as the *Engineers' Professional Learning* studies identified these as practices involving learning.

While most organizations have in place general procedures around worker safety, they are perhaps more pronounced in work involving hazardous conditions. This was the case for winemakers and utility workers in the *Beyond Training* study. An example from this study includes the observation of a team leader. The organization had implemented safety audits as part of larger initiative to reduce worker injuries. The organizational expectation is that *all* workers share the responsibility of keeping themselves *and* their fellow workers safe. During such an audit, a manager observed a team leader with his sleeves rolled up (Australian weather conditions result in very high incidences of melanomas—outdoor workers are advised to wear long sleeves to prevent them). The manager describes how the observation unfolded:

> [He said] "You're dealing with apprentices a lot of the time, how do they feel, don't you think it'd be good if you could set the example and therefore they won't have melanomas like you've got if they have their sleeves rolled

down" and you could see the brain tick and he thought about it, and the next minute he rolled his sleeve down.

Price et al. 2012

A different example is that of reception work. Many types of organizations include reception work, and in the *Neighbourhood Centre* study, the work of a volunteer receptionist provides a helpful example. Reception work in the centre brought the receptionist in contact with a variety of others and in particular with prisoners' families (the centre involved was located in a regional town that had a jail). Learning is identified as he describes how he came to challenge his previous understandings of offenders:

> I thought that was just something that happened to other people – it happened in the news, and then all of a sudden you have contact with these people. It's not just the person in jail that suffer – you have the family and it's not their fault either [it] makes you ask why they did it. There's always two sides to every story [but] you only ever get [the] news – the criminal – the police side.
>
> *Rooney 2011, p. 218*

Practices responding to 'out of the ordinary' work

So far the practices are part of the seemingly ordinary work of those involved. However, there were also examples across the studies where the impetus of learning came from responding to the challenges of 'out of the ordinary', or to some sort of significant change. These challenges or changes could be either planned or unplanned. Learning was prominent in responding to planned change, such as implementing a restructure, as seen in two *Beyond Training* study sites (a public utility and a local council). However, learning was also intensified in responding to unexpected events. A good example here is the learning by council workers as the result of a fire that burnt down the council chambers. In these examples, the workers spoke about intense periods of learning as they responded to the challenges presented.

A less dramatic example of learning in 'out of the ordinary work', albeit a more prolific one, is identified in the practice of 'acting up'. Acting up is the name given to a common practice in many organizations where one worker temporarily takes on the work of another due to illness, leave, or some other circumstance. Given the unfamiliarity of the work involved, those who acted up talked explicitly about the excitement and fear involved in taking on these temporary roles, and 'learning by the seat of their pants' (Price, Scheeres & Boud 2009).

Common practices **at** *work, but not key part* **of** *work itself*

While the practices (site walks, acting up, reception work, and rehearsals) are sanctioned organizational practices, other mundane and less job-related activities involving learning were also identified across the studies' published accounts. Some of these included taking a break and/or eating together (Rooney & Solomon 2006), smoking or drinking (Rooney, Manidis & Scheeres 2016), and moving between work sites (Solomon, Boud & Rooney 2008).

Our example here involves local council field workers (e.g. dog catchers, parking attendants and rangers) who would meet in a local park for lunch. They told the researchers how they would chat about all sorts of things, and while much of this was non-work related, there was also general chat about aspects of an individual's work that would impact on another's (Rooney & Solomon 2006).

Influencing contingencies of informal learning

From our reading across the source studies, we turn first to reiterating some key features of everyday (learning) practices, before turning attention explicitly to learning (in practices).

Key features of everyday (learning) practices

The practices discussed above are independent of any formal training programs that exist within the organizations studied. Given that they all involve learning of some kind, they are also presented as examples of informal learning. Additionally, they are not understood as primarily serving a learning function. Rather, they serve a substantive organizational purpose. When intentionally deployed, those who deploy them do not see themselves as enacting a learning function within the organization involved, they are simply 'doing their work'.

The various examples also illustrate how practices proliferate in work. Practices are ubiquitous and are part of the day-to-day happenings of the sites involved. While they might respond to massive change (such as a fire, or a restructure), they are also a response to the everyday challenges of the jobs involved (e.g. site walks and rehearsals). Any single set of workers may undertake a number of these practices in any given day. Say, engineers might attend a meeting, have lunch, and then carry out a site walk. Understanding the ubiquitous nature of practices has profound implications for understanding informal learning.

Informal learning is entwined in these everyday practices of work. It cannot be understood independent of the practices in which it occurs: for example, the volunteer's learning about offenders' circumstances or the engineer's learning about environmental matters cannot be understood without also appreciating the practices of reception work and site walks. The practices listed above demonstrate the ubiquitous nature of informal learning. Learning is not something that happens occasionally by *some* workers in some situations, but can proliferate in the work practices of *all* forms of workers in a multitude of practices. This is not to say that *all* workers *always* learn through undertaking a practice. To make such a claim would not only be unhelpful, but would also dismiss occasions where learning does not occur, such as in the repetition of a standard response to a common problem. Rather, our point is that work consists of multiple practices and these practices have potential for informal learning.

Key features of everyday learning (in practices)

Informal learning, like practices, is profoundly situated. It is not enough to say context matters. Rather, what we might call 'context' is implicated in learning. For instance, temporal implications impact the learning of engineers as they respond to the contemporary focus on the environment, just as they did two decades ago when safety matters were prominent in other groups. Australia's geographical location is implicated in outdoor workers' learning about sun-safety, just as the location of a jail near the neighbourhood centre provided impetus for the volunteer receptionist's learning about the lives of offenders and their families. Furthermore, the socio-political climate has invitational qualities when it comes to learning; take, for example, the new public management discourses which shape organizational restructures, which in turn shape learning.

Informal learning is in between, or at the intersection of, the practice and the immediate circumstances in which a given practice is practised in a given context (Solomon, Boud & Rooney 2008). Workers learn informally as result of meeting the contingencies of everyday work. While the practices have a history beyond that of the individual, there is always some element of uncertainty (same practice, which can be different with each iteration). The emergent nature of practice points to the necessity of informal learning. Workers also learn informally in response to unforeseen events. Challenges (e.g. fire, restructure, critical incidents) present intensified periods of uncertainty, requiring historical practices to be intensified or redefined.

An associated feature of informal learning is that, like the practices it is embedded in, it is relational. Learning involves others. While this itself is not new, what *is* worth stressing is the heterogeneous relationships involved. In many of the examples above, the (learning) practices involved non-homogeneous workers – that is, those involved in the practices were not necessarily employed to undertake the same sort of work, nor in any type of supervisory relationship with others. For instance; site walks involved engineers, environmental scientists, clients; reception work involved volunteers as well as members of the local community; safety practices involved managers and outdoor workers. This means that everyone has the potential to be involved in others' learning and to learn from others. Interestingly, these others are not 'teachers' or 'trainers': environmental scientists, centre users and managers are not normally regarded as 'teachers' or 'facilitators', yet in our studies they were necessary implicated in the engineer's, receptionist's and outdoor worker's learning.

What also becomes obvious, is how learning is mediated through talk or chat (Boud, Rooney & Solomon 2009). For instance, it is through talking to centre users that the receptionist learned, or the chat between field workers that enabled informal learning. Again we point out that the unlikelihood that interlocutors involved would normally consider themselves as teachers or learners, yet they 'teach' each other all the same, without this being a conscious part of what they see themselves as doing.

Tensions and dilemmas

The understandings of informal learning above present a paradox. On the one hand, the discussion and examples in the previous part of this chapter point to the ubiquitous nature of informal learning itself. Informal learning is embedded in the practices of everyday work and is intrinsic to that work. It is not a separate object of attention in the way that training might be. On the other hand, and perhaps *because* of its ubiquitous nature, it is (most often) invisible to those involved, as well as to observers of work (e.g. managers and researchers alike). While learning may be embedded in work practices and more prolific than first thought, we add that this has both positive and negative consequences and, in this final part, we outline some tensions and illustrate these with further examples from the studies.

The nomenclature surrounding learning presents an associated dilemma. The naming of 'invisible' learning as learning has consequences for those involved. In some cases, it may be 'safe' for those who learn to acknowledge their learning, and to identify as a learner. For instance, it is reasonable to assume that someone who is temporarily 'acting up' may not know all there is to know about the role they are acting in, whereas the same might not apply to a highly experienced engineer working on a multi-billion-dollar construction. There are consequences for one's identity and one's perception in the eyes of others for naming oneself or being named a learner, and for framing what is done in a learning discourse. It is little wonder then that, in some cases, there can be resistance to naming one's learning and to naming oneself as a learner (Boud & Solomon 2003). For example, how can one justify to oneself or to others drawing a full salary when only being 'a learner'? Learners are commonly seen as junior or subordinate, and traditionally, learning is seen as what is needed at early stages of a career. Why name everyday working practices as learning, with the consequences to self and others that such identification brings, when they are a necessary and intrinsic part of work itself? A lifelong learning discourse may have pervaded the domain of education and training policy, but that does not mean that it is widely accepted in workplaces.

But it is not only the learners who engage in the naming and framing of practices in particular ways. Indeed, this very chapter has renamed the work practices of workers as learning practices. The consequences of this may also have consequences. For instance, our intention of saying something about informal learning may impact a manager's decision to seek an intervention impacting on future workers and, through extension, may result in further worker resistance. Likewise, in many organizations, there are various discourses of learning in circulation that espouse, if not celebrate, the value of workers' learning; for example, the learning company or the learning organization. Some of these may be codified in policy documents and vision statements, yet there is potential for tension when these exist alongside workers' perceived consequences of 'being a learner' within the organization.

We began this chapter by talking about employer organizations' interest in informal learning, driven by the promise of organizations harnessing the potential of informal learning. It is not unreasonable for managers to seek interventions that potentially maximize opportunities for informal learning in their organization. However, there are associated dilemmas of seeking to influence informal learning, as well as potentially counterproductive effects of formalizing it. Like resistance to naming learning, there can also be resistance to interventions that seek to promote it. To best illustrate this point we return to the council field workers, and offer one last example.

For many years, council field workers met informally for lunch and in so doing exchanged information about aspects of their work that had implications for their workmates' work. In all, field workers utilized these informal events as valued opportunities for networking (Boud, Rooney & Solomon, 2009, p. 329). Building on this example, their manager had also recognized the potential of this practice for networking and sought an intervention in the form of scheduled, compulsory morning teas. However, field workers voiced their resistance to the intervention:

> We have a compulsory morning tea, believe it or not – to make people talk to each other, and it's really strange because all these people in the office that you don't know and you can't really talk to them because you're only sort of may talk to them once a month [. . . and] we just stand around and stare at each other.
>
> *Boud, Rooney & Solomon, 2009, pp. 330–31*

What had been an organic practice that fostered informal learning and was motivated by a desire of colleagues to share their experiences of doing a similar and sometimes challenging job was eroded by a well-intentioned management intervention meant to foster it. The movement of the practice from the informal to the formal domain of work-life fundamentally changed its character. It was perceived differently by the workers and led to their alienation from it. As decisions about it moved up the hierarchy, its ownership shifted away from the workers to managers. Ultimately, despite well-meaning attempts to foster learning, the implementation of the morning tea did not appear to deliver what those who initiated it expected – perhaps even undermining the desired effects.

We should be careful though not to over-interpret this phenomenon. There is of course a place for management-initiated learning interventions, and they may be prompted by observations of what appears to be effective in the informal domain. We do not advocate a hands-off approach, but for extremely careful consideration in thinking through the implications of interventions. As in this case, good intentions can lead to bad outcomes. When attempting to influence informal learning, the introduction of formality can effectively eliminate or occlude the very phenomenon it is seeking to foster. To this end, Schatzki adds the following: 'The best that designers of lives and institutions can do is create contexts that, as experience and thought show, make certain activities very or more likely' (Schatzki 2012, p. 22).

The paradox of informal learning is that it can be readily undermined by the good intentions of those who seek to identify, name and/or foster it. It is important not to view workplace practices solely through the lens of education and training. These practices do many things and to extract a 'learning method' from a complex set of social relations and expect it to operate independently from the networks and expectations that hold it in place is naïve. We therefore need to conceptualize informal learning quite differently than hitherto. It is no longer a kind of workplace learning event characterized by a lack of deliberate intervention by those who oversee training and development that is unchanged when systematized by those in authority. It should be regarded as sets of learning practices initiated and constructed by learners themselves to pursue ends they believe to be mutually worthwhile. Such informal learning may also pursue the goals of managers and trainers, but this is not necessarily the case and it must never be assumed to be so. In some cases, informal learning can help workers meet challenges not yet articulated by managers; in others, workers may pursue directions or means counter to those desired by those who manage.

This points to the need to develop a more discriminating discourse in workplace learning that goes beyond formality and informality to recognize whose interests are being pursued, to what ends, in which context and according to whose strategies and processes. Learning cannot be extracted as a distinct entity from the multiple sets of expectations, relationships and purposes of work, nor indeed from the exigencies of work itself. It is not possible to assume that there are shared intentions for learning between or among different parties. Research on workplace learning in general and informal learning at work in particular must take this centrally into account in research studies.

Conclusion

This chapter has reframed informal learning through the use of a practice lens. It has used practice theory to locate informal learning as an intrinsic feature of everyday work. Learning is not positioned in relation to formal educational or training programs but as an everyday workplace phenomenon in its own right.

It is necessary to understand informal learning as a phenomenon dependent on the activities, practices and socio-material arrangements in which it is embedded. The concept of practices enables everyday work activities, often overlooked in other studies, to be examined in terms of learning. This leads us to suggest that practices should be units of analysis in future studies of informal learning and that frameworks which privilege the socio-cultural and socio-material elements of work itself and shared interests, rather than notions of curriculum and pedagogy, be taken as a starting point for the discussion of learning.

References

Billett, S. 2001, 'Learning through work: workplace affordances and individual engagement', *Journal of Workplace Learning*, vol. 13, no. 5, pp. 209–14.

Billett, S. 2004, 'Workplace participatory practices: conceptualising workplaces as learning environments', *Journal of Workplace Learning*, vol. 16, no. 6, pp. 312–24.

Billett, S. 2011, 'Workplace curriculum: practice and propositions', in F. Dochy, M. Gijbels & P. van den Bossche (eds), *Theories of learning for the workplace: building blocks for training and professional development programs*, Routledge, London, pp. 17–36.

Boud, D. & Hager, P. 2011, 'Re-thinking continuing professional development through changing metaphors and location in professional practice', *Studies in Continuing Education*, vol. 34, no. 1, pp. 17–30.

Boud, D. & Solomon, N. 2003, '"I don't think I am a learner": acts of naming learners at work', *Journal of Workplace Learning*, vol. 15, no. 7/8, pp. 326–31.

Boud, D., Rooney, D. & Solomon, N. 2009, 'Talking up learning at work: cautionary tales in co-opting learning', *International Journal of Lifelong Education*, vol. 28, no. 3, pp. 323–34.

Chappell, C., Scheeres, H., Boud, D. & Rooney, D. 2009, 'Working out work: integrated development practices in organisations', in J. Field, J. Gallacher & R. Ingram (eds), *Researching transitions in lifelong learning*, Routledge, London, pp. 175–88.

Colley, H., Hodkinson, P. & Malcom, J. 2003, *Informality and formality in learning: a report for the Learning and Skills Research Centre*, Report, Learning and Skills Research Centre, London.

Dochy, F. 2011, 'Introduction: building training and development programmes on recent theories of learning', in F. Dochy, M. Gijbels & P. van den Bossche (eds), *Theories of learning for the workplace: building blocks for training and professional development programs*, Routledge, London.

Engeström, Y. 2009, 'Expansive learning: toward an activity-theoretical reconception', in K. Illeris (ed.), *Contemporary theories of learning: learning theorists . . . in their own words*, Routledge, London, pp. 53–73.

Engeström, Y., Engeström, R. & Vahaaho, T. 1999, 'When the centre does not hold: the importance of knotworking', in S. Chaiklin, M. Hedegaard & U.J. Jensen (eds), *Activity theory and social practice: cultural-historical approaches*, Aarhus University Press, Aarhus, pp. 345–74.

Eraut, M. 2004, 'Informal learning in the workplace', *Studies in Continuing Education*, vol. 26, no. 2, pp. 247–73.

Fenwick, T. 2008, 'Workplace learning: emerging trends and new perspectives', in S. Merriam (ed.), *New directions for adult and continuing education: third update on adult learning theory*, Jossey-Bass, San Francisco, CA.

Fenwick, T., Edwards, R. & Sawchuck, P. 2011, *Emerging approaches to educational research: tracing the socio-material*, Routledge, London.

Fox, S. 2000, 'Communities of practice, Foucault and actor-network theory', *Journal of Management Studies*, vol. 37, no. 6, pp. 853–67.

Gherardi, S. 2000, 'Practice-based theorizing on learning and knowing in organizations', *Organization*, vol. 7, no. 2, pp. 211–23.

Gherardi, S. 2009, 'Communities of practice or practices of communities', in C. Fukami (ed.), *The SAGE handbook of manaement learning, education and development*, SAGE, Los Angeles, CA, pp. 414–530.

Gherardi, S., Nicolini, D. & Odella, F. 1998, 'Toward a social understanding of how people learn in organizations', *Management Learning*, vol. 29, no. 3, pp. 273–97.

Hager, P. 2004, 'Lifelong learning in the workplace? Challenges and issues', *Journal of Workplace Learning*, vol. 16, no. 1/2, pp. 22–32.

Hager, P. 2008, 'Learning and metaphors', *Medical Teacher*, no. 30, pp. 679–86.

Hager, P. 2011, 'Historical Tracing of the development of theory in the field of workplace learning', in M. Malloch, L. Cairns, K. Evans & B. O'Connor (eds), *The SAGE handbook of workplace learning*, Sage, pp. 17–32.

Hager, P. 2012, 'Theories of practice and their connections with learning: a continuum of more and less inclusive accounts', in P. Hager, A. Lee & A. Reich (eds), *Practice, learning and change: practice-theory perspectives on professional learning*, Springer, Dordrecht, pp. 17–32.

Hager, P. 2014, 'Practice as a key idea in understanding work-based learning', in P. Gibbs (ed.), *Learning, work and practice: new understandings*, Springer, Dordrecht, pp. 85–106.
Hager, P. & Hodkinson, P. 2011, 'Becoming as an appropriate metaphor for understanding professional learning', in L. Scanion (ed.), *"Becoming" a professional: an interdisciplinary analysis of professional learning*, Springer, Dordrecht, pp. 33–56.
Hager, P. & Johnsson, M. 2012, 'Collective learning practice', in P. Hager, A. Lee & A. Reich (eds), *Practice, learning and change: practice-theory perspectives on professional learning* Springer, Dordrecht, pp. 249–65.
Hager, P., Lee, A. & Reich, A. (eds) 2012, *Practice, learning and change: practice-theory perspectives on professional learning*, Springer, Dordrecht.
Heaton, J. 2008, 'Secondary analysis of qualitative data', in P. Alasuutari, L. Bickman & J. Brannen (eds), *The handbook of social research methods*, Sage, London, pp. 506–19.
Kemmis, S. 2000, 'Five traditions in the study of practice', in S. Kemmis & R. McTaggart (eds), 'Participatory action research', Chapter 22 in Denzin, N. and Lincoln, Y. (eds), *Handbook of Qualitative Research*, 2nd edn, Sage Publications, Thousand Oaks, CA, pp. 1–18.
Kemmis, S. 2005, 'Knowing practice: searching for saliences', *Pedagogy, Culture and Society*, vol. 13, no. 3, pp. 391–426.
Kemmis, S. 2010, 'What is professional practice? Recognising and respecting diversity in understandings of practice', in C. Kanes (ed.), *Elaborating professionalism, innovation and change in professional education*, Springer, Dordrecht, pp. 139–66.
Kemmis, S., Wilkinson, J., Edwards-Groves, C., Hardy, I., Grootenboer, P. & Bristol, L. 2014, *Changing practices, changing education*, Springer, Singapore.
Lave J, & Wenger E. 1991 *Situated learning: legitimate peripheral participation*. Cambridge University Press, Cambridge/
Malloch, M., Cairns, L., Evans, K. & O'Connor, B.N. (eds) 2011, *The SAGE handbook of workplace learning*, SAGE Publications Ltd., London.
Nerland, M. & Jenson, K. 2012, 'Epistemic practices and object relations in professional work', *Journal of Education and Work*, vol. 25, no. 1, pp. 101–20.
Price, O., Scheeres, H. & Boud, D. 2009, 'Re-making jobs: enacting and learning work practices', *Vocations and Learning*, vol. 2, no. 3, pp. 217–34.
Price, O., Johnsson, M., Scheeres, H., Boud, D. & Solomon, N. 2012, 'Learning organizational practices that persist perpetuate and change: a Schatzkian view', in P. Hager, A. Lee & A. Reich (eds), *Practice, learning and change: practice-theory perspectives on professional learning* Springer, Dordrecht, pp. 233–48.
Reich, A., Rooney, D., Gardner, A., Willey, K., Boud, D. & Fitzgerald, T. 2015, 'Engineer's professional learning: a practice-theory perspective', *European Journal of Engineering Education*, vol. 40, no. 4, 366–79.
Roberts, J. 2006, 'Limits to communities of practice', *Journal of Management Studies*, vol. 43, no. 3, pp. 623–39.
Rooney, D. 2011, 'Centres "down under": mapping Australia's neighbourhood centres', *Australian Journal of Adult Learning*, vol. 51, no. 2, pp. 203–25.
Rooney, D. & Solomon, N. 2006, 'Consuming metaphors: stimulating questions for everyday learning', *Studies in the Education of Adults*, vol. 38, no. 1, pp. 64–73.
Rooney, D., Manidis, M. & Scheeres, H. 2016, 'Making space for consuming practices', *Vocations and Learning*, vol. 9, no. 2, pp. 167–84.
Rooney, D., Willey, K., Gardner, A., Boud, D., Reich, A. & Fitzgerald, T. 2015a, 'Engineers' professional learning: through the lens of practice', in B. Williams, J. Figueiredo & J. Trevelyan (eds), *Engineering practice in a global context: understanding the technical and the social*, CRC Press, Leiden, The Netherlands, pp. 265–83.

Rooney, D., Gardner, A., Willey, K., Reich, A., Boud, D. & Fitzgerald, T. 2015b, 'Reimagining site-walks: sites for rich learning', *Australasian Journal of Engineering Education*, vol. 20, no. 1, pp. 19–30.

Schatzki, T. 2001, 'Introduction: practice theory', in T. Schatzki, K. Centina & E. von Savigny (eds), *The practice turn in contemporary theory*, Routledge, New York.

Schatzki, T. 2012, 'A primer on practices', in J. Higgs, R. Barnett, S. Billett, M. Hutchings & F. Trede (eds), *Practice-based education: perspectives and strategies*, Sense Publishers, Rotterdam, pp. 13–26.

Scheeres, H., Solomon, N., Boud, D. & Rooney, D. 2010. 'When is it okay to learn at work? The learning work of organisational practices', *Journal of Workplace Learning*, vol. 22, nos 1 & 2, pp. 13–26.

Sfard, A. 1998, 'On two metaphors for learning and the dangers of choosing just one', *Educational Researcher*, vol. 27, no. 2, pp. 4–13.

Solomon, N., Boud, D. & Rooney, D. (2008). The in-between: exposing everyday learning at work, *International Journal of Lifelong Education*, vol. 25, no. 1, pp. 3–13.

8
INFORMAL LEARNING AT WORK
What do we know more and understand better?

Herman Baert[1]

Introduction

Both in the practices of Human Resource Development and in the research into the training and professional development of staff for and in work environments, much attention and effort has been given over the past few decades to informal learning in the workplace. This comes to expression once again in this book with a meta-synthesis of research (Kyndt et al., Ch. 2) and the results of recent research.

HRD practices

Various motives and considerations are at the basis of managers' and HRD professionals' interest in workplace learning. One of these is the popular conviction that a person can only fully learn a profession and how to do certain functions or jobs through hands-on experience. Immersion in the reality on the work floor, confrontation with "real-life" questions and problems, and focusing specifically on solutions for which one has to immediately search and process relevant information and knowledge and find appropriate alternatives and solutions through experimentation are tantamount to learning while working. Those who believe in this view are eager to refer to John Dewey's concept of "*learning by doing*".

But there's more. Motives related to the limitations and criticism of formal off-the-job courses and training also play a role. Formal courses in the context of education can indeed provide a basis, but are often not able to respond promptly to developments that are well under way in innovative businesses and organisations. Various factors constitute constraints and obstacles, such as long-term procedures for education and educational reforms, an institute of education's financial limitations when it comes to investing in the latest technologies and tools, or the time necessary for the extra training or retraining of teachers. It is thus telling that, in particular,

1 KU Leuven, Belgium

large companies and powerful sectors on the labour market set up their own training centres and corporate universities which are very directly attuned to job performance and also concentrate on learning in the workplace in more formal or more informal ways. Furthermore, the impact or the transfer of formal training courses in terms of behavioural change of employees and teams is not on the whole considered significant. Figures circulate, whether or not based on research, of off-the-job-training as having an effective and lasting impact of just 10–40 per cent. On top of this there are the financial costs involved, not only for the programme development, the trainers, the venues, the travel and accommodation expenses, but also for employee absence on the work floor and the possible substitution of employees who are attending a training course. If employees can learn in the workplace, there is no problem – it is thought – of having to transfer what has been learned in the formal learning environment to the working environment, and the abovementioned costs can be reduced if not eliminated: this is the widely accepted line of reasoning. This is the thinking of practitioners who like to appeal to the concept of the *"learning organisation"* put forward by Chris Argyris (e.g. Argyris & Schön, 1996) among others. It also appeals to young professionals who want to learn a great deal while working in order to optimise their employability and their career opportunities. "Learning while working" is almost as important for them as "working while learning", with learning in the workplace being seen as a driving force for professional development. In times of the so-called "war for talent", offering learning opportunities becomes a means of attracting and retaining employees, in particular employees in the knowledge-intensive and innovative sectors.

Research on learning in the workplace

Researchers' still-increasing interest in learning in the workplace is without doubt stimulated by HRD practices and the need that they have for more clarity and more insight into the impressionability and efficiency of this phenomenon. In this regard, programmes and subsidies for practical and policy-oriented research have made and still make it possible to set up research projects. (See, for example, some of our own research projects: Baert, H., De Witte, K. & Sterck, G. (2000); Baert, H., De Rick, K. & Van Valckenborgh, K. (2006); Baert, H., Clauwaert, L., & Van Bree, L. (2008).) However, the research interest extends further than the desire to serve practice and policy and, at least as far as scientific institutes and academic researchers are concerned, also has the aim of contributing to the appropriate development of theory. (See, for example, some of our own projects: Baert, H. & Govaerts, N. (2012); Kyndt, E., Govaerts, N., Dochy, F. & Baert, H. (2011); Kyndt, E. & Baert, H. (2013) and also the theoretical work by, for example, Marsick, V. J. & Volpe, M. (red.) (1999); Eraut, M. (2004); Tannenbaum, S. I., Beard, R. L., McNall, L. A. & Salas, E. (2009); Marsick, V. J. & Watkins, K. (2015).) Indeed, in the most frequently used didactic models and frameworks for instructional design and the learning theories on which they are based, they concern intentionally planned, systematic and targeted forms of learning in specifically organised environments and specific delivery modes such as courses, seminars, computer-aided learning, handbooks and distance learning. Informal learning in the workplace differs fundamentally from this because it takes place in an environment that has been in the first place intentionally organised for working, and because in this context learning, with programmatically established learning objectives and didactic methods, is neither the primary nor the explicit reason. In order to conceptualise informal workplace learning, to describe it and to explain it, and also to be able to effectively influence and optimise it, it is necessary to have one's own theoretical framework.

Questions and approach

The questions that we wish to discuss in this concluding article are therefore the following:

- Do the contributions of the researchers in this publication lead to conceptual clarity with respect to the concept of "informal learning at work"?
- Is it possible, on the basis of the articles, to develop one single universal and empirically founded theoretical framework or model?[2]

Conceptual clarity refers to the definition of a phenomenon in an unequivocal way so that it allows for a valid description and analysis, which subsequently permits researchers to make statements about one and the same reality on the basis of measurements of operational variables. This is a primary condition necessary in order to be able to compare research results.

A theoretical framework means a model that includes, in a universal way, the most powerful factors[3] and relevant variables which encourage, or on the contrary discourage, informal workplace learning and where the relations between these factors and variables are empirically defined. Model building can fulfil an essential role in the creation of a refined description and imaging, in the articulation of research hypotheses and the development of activities intended to bring about improvement, as well as in the realisation of such activities. A theoretical framework or model has necessarily to be a simplified image of a complex reality. The advantage of this abstracting reduction is the clarity it provides of what is essential in order to understand a phenomenon and to intervene forcefully. The limitation is that certain factors and/or variables can escape attention in specific situations, with a distorted understanding and inadequate intervention as a result.

Taking this into account, when considering the second question we must ask ourselves whether one single model of the complex reality of informal learning in the workplace is actually possible. This will logically depend on an unequivocal definition of learning in the workplace, but will be just as dependent on the possible and decisive differences with respect to target populations and types of organisations/workforce units, and/or work environment and task characteristics of the staff (see Kyndt et al., Ch. 2). The state of the research must prompt us to be cautious when attempting to develop one single universal model. Indeed, Kyndt et al. determine in their review study that "during the last decade, a substantial amount of research on the factors that influence informal workplace learning has appeared [... *but* ...] despite these endeavours, there is a lack of overarching theoretical frameworks combining the results of the individual studies." What is then possible on the basis of the contributions compiled in this book?

Being aware that scientific knowledge is established progressively and is continually evolving, the questions as they are formulated above sound absolute and ambitious. It is therefore more realistic to put the questions in relative terms, namely as follows. Has more conceptual clarity been established with these recent publications than before, and can a more developed and empirically based theoretical framework or model be developed?

Putting things into perspective like this raises the need for points of reference in order to determine possible progress. To which state of affairs does one revert in order to then measure the progression that the chapters in this book might provide? And to what extent does this book offer a reliable point of reference when it comes to the state of the knowledge in this area? Regarding this latter reference point – the current state of the art – a strength and a limitation immediately become apparent. Kyndt et al.'s Chapter 2, a review study with a fairly broad exploration of the international literature and with the ambition of making a meta-synthesis, is a valuable contribution. The fact that a limited number of authors present their most recent research results is a limitation.

We have chosen the results of our own research, carried out between 1997 and 2010, as a point of reference for a previous phase of the current research and the recent knowledge development. This is a pretentious and disputable choice, for which the following justification – which is open to discussion – is given. We discuss two paths of research and what they signify in terms of material for a first point of reference.

In 1997, we – Baert, De Witte and Sterck – began a three-year research project about HRD policy in social profit organisations in Flanders, which has 6 million inhabitants and is one of the Regions that make up the Federal State of Belgium. It was comprised of three phases: (1) a large-scale and extremely extensive survey on the extent to which HRD policy in these organisations had been developed, (2) an action research phase with 40 organisations to jointly improve certain aspects of their HRD policy and practices, and (3) a phase to develop a handbook to design and carry out a high-quality HRD in social profit organisations. In each of these phases, attention was given to informal learning as one of the aspects of the HRD. In other words, the international literature was in all phases explored and used for conceptualising, operationalising and optimising workplace learning (see Baert, De Witte, & Sterck, 2000).[4] Subsequent research and, by no means least, multiple contacts with practical experience (such as post-academic courses with the handbook as a guide and advisory meetings with HRD professionals) led, in 2010, to a thoroughly revised edition of the abovementioned handbook (Baert et al., 2011). In view of the increased interest in the policy and practice of workplace learning and the stream of publications, the chapter on workplace learning has as a result received a substantial update and a more prominent place in the second version. Definitions and theoretical frameworks from these studies and publications will be used below.

During the 2005–08 period, two research projects were carried out that specifically dealt with workplace learning. One project sought indicators of high-quality workplace learning (Gielen & Lauwers, 2007), and a second research project developed a cartography of the conditions for workplace learning in labour organisations (Baert, Clauwaert & Van Bree, 2008). In these projects, use was also made of the available international literature at that time (see ibid., fns 4 and 7, and the list of references) and of numerous interviews with HRD-professionals and employees on the work floor. These results will also be used to help answer the main questions in this chapter.

Do the chapters provide (more) conceptual clarity?

Work and the workplace

It is striking that in the chapters in this book, no definition is given of the general concepts of "at work" and "the workplace", although a specific explanation is indeed given throughout of what sort of work is meant in the study presented (for example, innovative jobs in IT, engineering work, chefs and kitchen staff, radiologists, auditors, social workers in community centres, teachers in schools having pupils with additional support needs . . .). We refer here to the conclusion we formulated on the basis of our previous research in order to come to a definition of workplace learning in what follows. We have not found any indications in the chapters for adapting the following definition.

We understand by the concept "workplace", different work situations in which an employee repeatedly finds himself or herself, and the work processes that take place there. Examples of these are: conducting a sales meeting with clients, examining and treating patients, starting up and implementing an innovative digital communication project, assembling cars, cleaning offices, carrying out security operations, keeping the books, flying an aircraft, etc.

The various work situations simultaneously refer to physical places, where work processes are undertaken by people on their own, but in general in virtual contact with others, or together with colleagues, or where people meet colleagues in the margins of work. Examples of these are: the meeting room during a work-related discussion, the assembly hall where cars are built with robots, the computer desk in the office of a bank, the coffee corner or staff restaurant where people talk (about work or otherwise) with colleagues; the home of the customer or patient who is being visited, the reception desk of a hotel where the receptionist serves guests, the operating theatre of a hospital, the room in one's own home from where one teleworks, the office of the boss with whom a performance review is taking place, etc. (Baert et al., 2008, p. 10.)

What we want to indicate with these numerous examples is that the very great diversity of work and workplaces must make us alert when we wish to attempt to develop one single universal theoretical framework for informal learning at work. However, before discussing this, we will first examine more closely the concept of "workplace learning" or "learning at work."

Learning at work

Partly on the basis of the available literature at the time from the most authoritative authors, and on the basis of numerous conversations with researchers and practitioners with whom we worked together, we formulated the following definition of workplace learning:

> Workplace learning is a process of continual change in the competences, knowledge, skills and attitudes respectively of employees and teams of employees, in situations in or near the workplace that have the high-quality execution and work progress as primary objective. "What" (learning content), "how" (learning process) and "when" (learning period) is learned lies in the first instance in the hands of the learning employee and the work processes in which he or she plays a role. Key people and employees in the labour organisation can facilitate and encourage this learning by creating, more or less as policy, favourable conditions and conditions in the employee's environment (including work environment), that can be used to learn. Depending on the readiness to learn and the learning ability of the employee, and the extent to which he or she is aware of the opportunities for using the workplace conditions to learn, the competency development will take place less or more intentionally or incidentally and be less or more extensive.
>
> *Baert et al., 2008, p. 20; Baert et al., 2011, pp. 198–199*

Which elements from the contributions published here can lead to a reformulation of this definition? We review these elements and then use them for an adapted definition.

The qualification "*informal*" does not occur in the "learning at work" terminology or in the abovementioned definition, and this is a conscious choice. There were two arguments for this. A first argument is related to the, in our opinion, proliferation of terminology. In UNESCO's authoritative and frequently quoted publications from the 1960s onward, there was a continual reference to formal, non-formal and informal education.[5] All three of these concepts refer to the environment in which the learning takes place. In brief, this refers to:

(a) Formal: an environment that is intentionally and specifically created with the intention of acquiring knowledge and expertise and that leads to an officially recognised diploma or certificate;
(b) Non-formal: an environment in which learning does indeed take a central place, together with social networking and recreation for example, but that does not lead to a diploma, but possibly does lead to a recognition of the acquired skills, and

(c) Informal: environments with a different main objective than learning and developing skills (such as producing, providing services, practising sport, creating art, etc.), but where, *in the process* and *on reflection*, a person can learn, individually as well as jointly with others.

Learning in the three environments is always a process of change in the knowledge, attitudes and/or skills of a person or a group of people, a team. It is therefore not the learning itself that is formal, non-formal, or informal, but the environment in which it takes place. It is for this reason that "informal" is not included in the concept definition.

A second argument – that moreover has more weight – relates to the difficulty of making a radical distinction between formal and informal learning. Both the literature (see e.g. Doornbos et al., 2008, quoted in Kyndt et al., Ch. 2) and our own research indicated strongly that it is here a question of a continuum or a "sliding scale of formality". In other words, the environment in which learning takes place and the way in which people learn can be or become less or more formal. Figure 8.1 demonstrates this by way of a number of examples.

Are both arguments still valid in 2018? If we stick to terminological purism, the answer is yes. If, however, we take the widespread linguistic usage into consideration – in the everyday speech of practitioners and policy makers as well as in the scientific literature – then we must accept that the terminology of "formal and informal learning" has become widely used. This is in our opinion difficult to deny any more. Nevertheless, Boud and Rooney begin their chapter with: "We acknowledge that 'informal learning' is a contested term subject to a number of definitions" (Ch. 7, p. 135). On the one hand, they take a broad perspective that "understands informal learning as a phenomenon that is *not* the result of some planned and structured educational or training activity". On the other hand, they emphasise that

> . . . understanding informal learning as embedded in practices differs from accounts of informal learning that see learning as "a thing acquired by individuals" [...], or as a phenomenon independent of the context in which it occurs, or as something that individuals do alone.
>
> *Ibid., p. 135*

Through a practice approach, they understand learning "as phenomena dependent on the activities, practices, and socio-material arrangements in which it is located" (Ch. 7, p. 135). I can endorse this line of reasoning inasmuch as no negative definitions have crept into my first definition either, and because this is not only a question of learning as an individual, but also of teams in the sense of "the collective 'property' of groups" (Kemmis, 2005, p. 393, quoted in Boud & Rooney, Ch. 7, p. 137). Moreover, work processes, work situations and physical places are included in the definition of a workplace, and the relationships or interconnectedness with work processes and conditions in work situations and places are also indicated in the concept of "workplace learning". All the same, Boud and Rooney's chapter, and their reference (that we also previously used) to the work of Billett and the "social

Informal workplace learning	*Formal workplace learning – on the job learning*		*Training – off the job learning*
Learning by doing • Practising routines and procedures • Solving problems that occur during the working situation • Performing difficult tasks with assistance • Job rotation **Learning through looking up information** • Looking up information in manuals, handbooks or work instructions • Searching by following computer instructions **Learning from colleagues** • Asking for advice and assistance • Talking about work experience together • Working together with a more experienced colleague **Learning from others** • Learning from customers, patients, users, suppliers, etc. • Networking (including in learning networks)	**Learning through coaching and instruction** • Consulting and discussing with a coach • Getting explanation or instructions from your colleague or manager **Learning through giving training** • Learning through helping, showing someone the ropes, or training colleagues **Learning through self-analysis and reflection** • (Narrative) journal • Portfolio **Learning through evaluation and feedback** • Performance review • Assessment interview • Competency assessment **Godfather/ Godmother/ mentoring** **Peer consultation**	**Workplace training** • Leittext-method • Attending demos (demonstration video or PC demo) • CAL (Computer Aided Learning) **Introduction programme for newcomers** • Introductory course • Initiation course **Supervised work placement/ internships** **Project groups** • Study groups as part of a learning programme • Quality circles	**Formal education** • Secondary education • Adult education • Higher education • Post-graduates **Specific professional training and supplementary training from** • Labour market training agencies • Professional associations • Commercial training providers • Suppliers of equipment **E-learning & web based training and correspondence courses** **Professional in-house training** **Congresses, conferences, seminars, trade fairs**

FIGURE 8.1 The sliding scale of informal and formal learning (Baert, 2014, p. 187)

informal learning activities" indicated by Gerken et al., and the distinction "learning from oneself and learning from others" (Gerken et al., Ch. 5, p. 82) do encourage me to give the social or interactive dimension – which they call the "sociality of work" – and the changes or innovation of/in teams in a labour context a nevertheless slightly more prominent place in a reformulation. But, according to Boud and Rooney, "This is not to say that *all* workers *always* learn through undertaking a practice" (Ch. 7, p. 145).

Their request for consideration of even broader approaches to "the physical, social and political contexts of work" is already partially included in the above definition of the workplace and of workplace learning, but should in our opinion receive explicit (or more explicit anyway) attention in the construction and reconstruction of a theoretical framework.

The nature of informal or everyday learning at work can be a little more accurately defined than "the process" used in our definition. In Chapter 5 by Gerken et al. and in the reference to Mulder (2013), there are multiple references to informal learning activities (that) are defined as cognitive and physical learning activities (that lead to cognitive activities), with the interesting addition: that can be implicit, deliberate or reactive (see also Eraut, 2004). Adding to this that the specified activities imply the gaining of experience and reflection on this experience (see also the reference to Dewey in the review by Kyndt et al., Ch. 2) may describe even more substantially the singularity of learning in the workplace.

I have objections to the addition of the frequently occurring characterisation of informal learning (see also the review by Kyndt et al., Ch. 2) that "informal workplace learning can be defined as spontaneous, unplanned learning that occurs at any time in work contexts". Here too the definition is negative ("unplanned"). But, above all, I do not believe the so-called "spontaneity" of that learning. People only learn when they are triggered to do so (see below) and have a learning readiness, develop learning attitudes and learning intentions, and see activities and conditions (see below) in the workplace as opportunities they can make use of to learn and therefore also make efforts to learn (through reflection). Furthermore, this learning can be facilitated by the creation, more or less as policy, of favourable conditions for learning. It therefore seems to me more appropriate to define it as more or less intentional and more or less incidental, respectively continuous, rather than speaking of "spontaneous learning". Taking this argumentation further, it is not appropriate to include in a definition, as does occur frequently, that informal learning occurs in contexts that are not explicitly created to evoke learning (see also the review by Kyndt and Baert 2013). Here too, the definition is negative, and here too, the fact that conscious intentional favourable conditions can be created for informal workplace learning is ignored.

This latter comment must not be misunderstood. The favourable conditions for learning at work are not the learning stimuli that are offered in formal and non-formal learning environments such as an instruction, an exercise, or a case study. Those favourable conditions, which we will discuss more fully below, are for example a positive learning climate or a management leadership style that is focused on development. Employees' learning at work is namely elicited through problems, questions, changes, challenges, etc. in the work itself, or in the work processes. It is for this reason that the addition to the definition of the factor "triggers" warrants recommendation. That happened already in the definition and the list of six characteristics of informal learning provided by Watkins and Marsick (1992) and Marsick and Volpe (1999) and confirmed by Kyndt et al. who cited "triggered by a jolt that can be internally or externally situated" (Ch. 2, p. 13). Grohnert et al. (Ch. 4, p. 66) refer in this respect to the research stream that has demonstrated the value of critical incidents for learning and future performance improvement.

In addition to the question of what lies at the start of the learning process – the triggers which have just been mentioned – the question also arises of what the end point or the objective of workplace learning is. Posing that question is somewhat unusual because in previous articles, one also reads that learning at work is "something *unstructured* in terms of learning objectives". The formulation of the question can be contested for two reasons. Goal-orientation presumes namely "knowing what precedes learning and what achievement is desired" and subsequently intentional, focused and organised efforts to reach objectives, as is intended in educational settings and – generally at least in part – brought about. Learning in the working environment differs fundamentally from this because working is focused on the (high-quality) production of products or services. As stressed by Hirschmann and Mulder (Ch. 3, p. 1) and Grohnert et al. (Ch. 4, p. 65), the aim of behaviour at work is to solve a problem, find a solution, etc. In other words, it is to improve work; learning as such is not the aim of behaviour at work and it occurs as a by-product of work activities and tasks. Boud and Rooney also posit that "those who deploy them do not see themselves as enacting a learning function within the organization involved, they are simply 'doing their work'" (Ch. 7, p. 145). We established similar conclusions in our research into learning patterns in organisations and teams (Baert & Govaerts, 2012). The additional comment of Boud and Rooney on activities at the workplace is interesting, however: "Additionally, they are not understood as primarily serving a learning function. Rather, they serve a substantive organizational purpose." (Ch. 7, p. 145) It is indeed likely that learning at work benefits the organisation, but matters may also be learned that are not of importance for the strategic goals of the organisation or are even in conflict with them. In relation to the former, we have in mind the learning results that can be important for an employee's career (as well) and that help him or her to find work in another organisation and realise his or her ambitions. In the second case, it can relate to finding personal "informal" solutions for example, for quality norms and procedures that deviate from the "formal requirements and rules" set by the organisation and its monitoring bodies. Bearing these considerations in mind, the addition may be made to the definition of (the outcomes) of workplace learning that it may be of benefit to the organisation and to the career of the employee.

Making use of the above elements, drawn from the preceding chapters in this book, we seek to redefine and better conceptualise respectively the phenomenon of learning at work.

Learning at work is a process of change in the competences, knowledge, skills and attitudes respectively of employees and teams of employees that comes about embedded in situations in or in close proximity to the workplace. The change is triggered by disturbances such as critical incidents, errors and challenges in the work processes in which the employees complete tasks together, with the high-quality execution and innovation of the work as the primary objective. The cognitive and physical learning activities (that lead to cognitive activities) can be implicit, deliberate, or reactive. The employee is the initial and main agent for "what" (learning content), "how" (forms of learning) and "when" (learning period) learning takes place. Managers, HRD professionals and colleagues in the labour organisation can facilitate and encourage this learning by creating favourable organisational conditions as well as conditions in the employee's work environment that can be used to learn. Depending on the readiness to learn, the learning intentions and the learning ability of the employee, and the extent to which he or she is aware of the opportunities for using the workplace conditions to learn, the competency development will take place less or more intentionally or consciously and less or more incidentally or continually. It can be both to the benefit of the organisation and its teams as well as to the individual benefit of the employee's career.

Elements of this definition that have not previously been discussed will be explained as part of the presentation of the theoretical framework.

The development of our initial theoretical framework

In order to be able to describe and elucidate learning at work and to be able to effectively influence and optimise it, more is needed than a definition of the concept as developed above. A theoretical framework or model is indispensable for this. What we mean by a theoretical framework in this article is not only an ordered list of factors and/or variables that are intended to map out the main aspects of a phenomenon, but also a definition of those factors and measurable variables and the presumed relationships between them (Miles & Huberman, 1994). With a model, a further step is taken by empirically examining the impact of the variables and their effective mutual relationships. According to this understanding, a model is an advanced form of scientific knowledge development.

Is it possible to develop a single universal and empirically more founded theoretical framework or model on the basis of the chapters in this book than we have up to now presented and employed in subsequent research and in interventions in practice between 1997 and 2010? In the "Questions and approach" section, we have already indicated that – for several reasons – there is some doubt as to whether establishing a single theoretical framework or model is possible, and that, at the very least, caution is called for in the attempt to do so. We will therefore first present the conceptual framework that we developed previously and explain the reasoning or underlying theoretical approach. We will then do the same for the frameworks discussed in the chapters, at least insofar as they were submitted to empirical research or were the result of such. It will become apparent that establishing a single universal and comprehensive model is (as yet) not possible, but that an improvement of the scientific quality of our framework is. In that sense, this "theoretical framework synthesizes existing theories and related concepts and empirical research, to develop a foundation of a new theory" (Rocco & Plakhotnik, 2009, p. 9) and to provide a reference point for the interpretation of new findings (Merriam & Simpson, 2000, cit. in Rocco & Plakhotnik, 2009, p. 4).

A theoretical framework at the start

As was indicated in the "Questions and approach" section, between 1997 and 2010 we developed and revised a theoretical framework of learning at work in a number of studies, making use in that process of the international literature and our own research results. We are presenting this framework here as a relative reference point in order to subsequently be able to situate progress in the knowledge development.

Figure 8.2 gives a general picture of the results at the time. It gives an overview of the relevant factors that are to be made operational, using variables in terms of organisational and behavioural indicators. We explain this and refer selectively to a few sources from which we drew inspiration without, however, covering the whole literature review again.

For the construction of this model, above all, shorter or longer lists of influential factors were found in the literature, but only a few conceptual or theoretical frameworks that also mapped out the relationships between the factors or variables of the phenomenon of learning at work. Examples of these are Sambrook's "Holistic framework of factors influencing work-related learning" (2005, p. 2) and Eraut's conceptual framework (2004, p. 268). They group together – each in their own way – a number of variables under "context factors" (such as organisation culture, managerial support, work structure, social relationships, etc.) and "learning factors" (staff characteristics such as motivation, confidence and commitment, etc.) We also

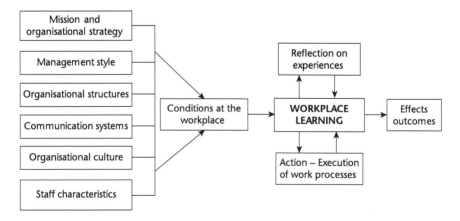

FIGURE 8.2 Influencing factors for learning at work (Baert et al., 2000, p. 175; Baert et al., 2011, p. 210)

wanted to include the process character of workplace learning (more) explicitly in the conceptual framework that we developed. To this end we made use of the CIPO base model (Context – Input – Process – Output) that is used in many fields and the decision-making process that forms its dynamic.

As far as that is concerned, the context factors or (stimulating or inhibiting) conditions for learning are given in six groups on the left in Figure 8.2. The conditions are the job-related activities, available tools and forms of interaction in the work environment which employees can use to learn to the extent that they feel triggered to learn. The learning process itself comes about through the interaction between working and reflecting on what takes place during that work in terms of critical incidents and errors, problems and questions, or challenges to approach (or to learn to approach) matters in a better or different way. When competencies are developed through the learning process and knowledge is generated and shared, this leads to effects or outcomes that can be beneficial for the functioning of the employees, their teams and the organisation and/or for their career.

Factors and variables with an impact on learning at work

As mentioned, we found various lists of factors and variables in the literature that can influence learning in the workplace. Some have been used (deductively) in or have arisen (inductively) from empirical research, both quantitative and qualitative. Examples of those lists that inspired us back then are: the Canadian Survey of Informal Learning Practices (Livingstone, 2001), research on "Learning intensive jobs" and the "Learning conditions" of the Norwegian Institute for Labour and Social Research (Skule, 2004; Skule & Reichbron, 2002). Also the Canadian research "Learning at work – workplace appraisal of informal learning" (CEW, 2007) and the subsequent research "The Workplace Informal Learning Matrix" (CEW, 2007)[6] assessed skills acquired on the work floor ("Working with others", "Oral communication", "Problem solving", "Decision making", "Learning skills"). The research carried out on behalf of the United States Department of Labor in which "work-related activities with the greatest chance of informal learning" were assessed (EDC, 1998) correlated closely with the approach to workplace learning that we examined at the time.

In Table 8.1, we give an overview of the relevant originally selected variables, supplemented with the additional variables (in italics) that are provided by the chapters in this book. For the "conditions at the workplace" factor, the unaltered list which we verified on the basis of a literature review and via a research questionnaire (Baert et al., 2008, p. 87–92) and was also applied in subsequent research (Kyndt, Dochy & Nijs, 2009) follows here first. The list of conditions in Table 8.1 reflects not only all those things that actually happen or can happen on the work floor, but is also an expression of a choice of activities and facilities that one wishes to take into account on the sliding scale of formal–informal learning. That this is an optional choice is apparent, for example, from the choice that Boud and Rooney make in terms of the multiple forms of informal learning. They posit: "The practices primarily serve some function other than bringing about learning. This means that mentoring and coaching (which have some deliberate pedagogical intent) are excluded" (Ch. 7, p. 139). They do mention – without compiling a quasi-exhaustive list – site walks by engineers, rehearsals, meetings, safety practices/audits, reception work, acting up, council workers as result of a fire, taking a break and/or eating together (Ch. 7).

We defined "conditions at the workplace" as activities and facilities created in the social, material and informational environment of the workplace by agents of the organisation (e.g. managers, HRD professionals, supervisors) and by the employees themselves, so that they and other employees can use them for learning and not just for work and job-related purposes (Baert, et al., 2008). We prefer "conditions" above "resources", because these conditions also include the "learning practices" that Boud and Rooney identify in their studies in this book and those to which they refer in other studies: performance appraisals, coming into the office and work design (Boud & Rooney, Ch. 7, p. 140). These conditions also concern the activities that link different innovation tasks and the corresponding work activities employees carry out in the innovation process, such as acting upon feedback, proactively seeking information and seeking for help (Gerken et al., Ch. 5, p. 83). Similar activities used by teachers in their CPD (Continuing Professional Development) are "professional discussion", "collaborative conversation" and "being observed and receiving feedback" (Shanks, Ch. 6, p. 125). The six specific categories that we distinguished were later on grouped in three general categories by Kyndt, Dochy and Nijs (2009, p. 373).

An overview now follows of the specification and operationalisation of the context factors or conditions for learning that are given in six groups in Figure 8.2. Table 8.2 gives an overview not only of the factors and originally selected variables that influence learning at work, but also of the most influential additional variables and of the original variables (in italics and with an additional reference) that are confirmed on the basis of empirical research reported in the articles in this book. In this table, we do not make a distinction between triggers and antecedents, because sometimes a factor can be a trigger in one case and an antecedent in another case. For example the factor "employability": the need to keep up one's employability can be a trigger, but a well-developed and sustainable employability can be a helpful disposition for (informal) learning. Please note in this regard that some variables can have both a facilitating and an inhibiting impact. For example, the factor "strategy of the organisation": a strong involvement in determining the strategy of an organisation and making it operational can provoke and influence learning, but an intensive participatory approach with a lack of final and shared decisions can inhibit the commitment and the motivation to learn.

Outcomes or consequences of informal learning at the workplace

When we conceive the output of informal learning processes as sustainable changes in the behaviour of the worker, due to acquiring new competences, knowledge,

TABLE 8.1 Learning conditions: categories and items

General learning conditions	Specific learning conditions	Items
Communication, interaction, cooperation and participation	Work organisation	Consult other departments Results of inquiries Trade union meetings Internal job openings Job rotation Common breaks
	Internal learning networks	Work groups Intervision Debriefings Project teams Self-directing teams Common rooms
	External learning networks	External colleagues Visit other organisations Demonstrations Guest speakers Community of practice
Feedback, evaluation, coaching and reflection	Individual learning coaching	Personal development plan Job controls Walk along with colleague Contact person Coach Internship Buddy system Godfather/godmother Trial period Mentor Complex assignments
	Individual work coaching	Feedback on functioning Coach Functioning consultation Career consultation
Information	Information systems	Knowledge of decisions Job aids Databases Newsletter Internet Work e-mail address Phone Library Log TV CD-ROMs Idea box Quality manual Reports, files Radio

TABLE 8.2 Context factors and variables that influence informal learning at work

Factors	Original variables[1]	Additional variables
Mission and organisational strategy	• The presence and consciousness of an explicit mission and (long-term) strategic vision of the organisation • Participation and commitment to the determining of strategy • Citing learning as a source of dynamic in the strategy of the organisation to be(come) a learning organisation	
Management style	• *Creating time for analysis and reflection* (Kyndt et al., Ch. 2) (Grohnert et al., Ch. 4) • Being oneself an example of learning while working *Communicating their own challenges and mistakes*, Grohnert et al., Ch. 4) • *Giving constructive feedback* (Kyndt et al., Ch. 2) (Grohnert et al., Ch. 4) • Stimulating innovation initiatives • Facilitating collaborative decision making • Promoting working together • *Appreciation and support of efforts to learn* (Kyndt et al., Ch. 2) Superior feedback: rewards for proficiency (Skule, in Kyndt et al., Ch. 2)	• Democratic leadership and people having some control (Skule in Kyndt et al., Ch. 2) • Intensification of jobs reduces the time for learning (Hirschmann & Mulder, Ch. 3)
Organisational structures	• *Autonomy and room for manoeuvre in the individual execution of a job* (Kyndt et al. Ch. 2) • *Task complexity and challenge* (Kyndt et al., Ch. 2) ("*More engagement in – especially social-cognitive – learning activities while accomplishing a complex work task*" Hirschmann & Mulder, Ch. 3) • *Variety in the job* (Kyndt et al., Ch. 2) • Learning potential of a job • Diversity and complementarity in teams • Self-directing teams • Availability of learning conditions/ resources	• Workload (Kyndt et al., Ch. 2) • High amount of information processing (Hirschmann & Mulder, Ch. 3) • Management position (Gerken et al., Ch. 5)
Communication systems	• *Promotion of the circulation of knowledge* (Kyndt et al., Ch. 2) • Openness towards information and knowledge from inside and outside the organisation • Communication between all units of the organisations • Introduction courses for new employees • *Time and space for social contact among employees* (Kyndt et al., Ch. 2)	• Proximity/distance to work of colleagues (Kyndt et al., Ch. 2)

Factors	Original variables[1]	Additional variables
Organisational culture	• *Open learning climate* (Grohnert et al., Ch. 4) (Watkins & Dirani, 2013) • *Mutual trust* (Kyndt et al., Ch. 2) • Encouragement to take well-reasoned risks • Openness to learn from mistakes • Appreciation of critical questions • Minimal regulatory guidance and control, maximal dialogue and initiative • Command of time pressure	• Receiving collegial support (Kyndt et al., Ch. 2) (Shanks, Ch. 6)
Staff characteristics	• Readiness and motivation to learn • Learning competences for self-directed learning • Self-efficacy (Hirschmann & Mulder, Ch. 3) • Competences for teamwork and team learning • *Openness to give and receive feedback* (Gerken et al., Ch. 5) (Grohnert et al., Ch. 4) • The will to innovate • *Tolerance for unpredictability and uncertainty – skills for coping with change* (Kyndt et al., Ch. 2)	• Tenure (Kyndt et al., Ch. 2) and the number of different job functions taken up in an organisation (Gerken et al., Ch. 5) • Amount of task experience, including critical experiences (Grohnert et al., Ch. 4) • Age and preference for individual/social learning (Kyndt et al., Ch. 2) • Hierarchical position and support for learning (Kyndt et al., Ch. 2) • Meta-cognition: knowing about one's knowledge, judgement processes and one's actual performance (Grohnert et al., Ch. 4) • Initiative (Lohman, Skule in Kyndt et al., Ch. 2) • Workload and job demands (Skule in Kyndt et al., Ch. 2) • Outgoing or nurturing personality (Kyndt et al., Ch. 2)

Note:
1 See the list of literature with, in addition to our own research and publications, the following as primary sources: Bandura (1997); Education Development Center (1998); Ellinger (2005); Ellström (2001); Eraut (1994); Marsick & Watkins (2015); Onstenk (1994); Sambrook (2005); Skule (2004); Sterck (2004); Straka (2004); Tjepkema (2003); Van Biesen (1989); Van Woerkom (2003).

skills and/or attitudes or renewing or updating them, the question of the outcomes or consequences is: what are the ultimate benefits for the employees and managers individually and for the organization as a whole?

Important to consider is that outcomes or consequences of informal learning can be expected or even intended, but they are different from formal learning: they cannot be defined at the start of the process of learning in terms of reaching clear-cut objectives. The ways of measuring or assessing the learning outcomes will be discussed later. Here, we present an overview of the outcomes or consequences as we identified them earlier and we add the outcomes reported in the studies published in this book (see italics), irrespective the rigour of the assessment, the methods and techniques used and the specific context and the timeframe in which they are reached. Some of the outcomes can be at the same time operating as antecedents for learning. For instance, a learning culture and improving a learning culture in an organisation are both an antecedent or a condition and an outcome for (informal) learning. And benefits can be mirrored and conceived as mutual benefits. Also important is to keep in mind that many of the outcomes listed in Table 8.3 can also be produced by formal learning activities and that it cannot be concluded that informal learning is best suited for obtaining these results.

TABLE 8.3 Possible outcomes or consequences of informal workplace learning (adapted from Baert et al., 2011)

For the individual workers	*For the team(s) and the organization as a whole*
Innovative work behaviour (Gerken et al., Ch. 5)	Innovation and continuous renewal (Gerken et al., Ch. 5)
Job satisfaction	Consumer or client satisfaction
Flexibility	Commitment and corporate sense
Keeping their job and maintaining viability	Retention of workers
Employability for changing his job during the career	Capacity to deal with strategic changes
Job mastery, Performing high-quality judgements (Grohnert et al., Ch. 4)	Quality gains
Promotion/advance career	Improved team and organisational performance
Financial rewards	Monetary benefits and savings
Trust	Trust
Love and joy of learning	Improve the learning culture

Towards a theoretical framework revisited

Before starting with an exercise of further model development, we are taking a moment to ask whether it is possible to develop and empirically substantiate one single comprehensive and universal framework. The fact that none of the contributors to this book makes any attempt to do so, or had that intention, could already be an indication of the hopelessness of pursuing this. What has been done until now? Also with Kyndt et al. (Ch. 2, p. 12), it can be established that "During the last decade, a substantial amount of research on the factors that influence informal workplace learning has appeared. However up to now, no effort has been made to review these findings in a systematic manner", possibly leading to the construction of a new theoretical model. They do however indicate that "some theoretical studies do exist" and they briefly discuss the studies carried out by Brooks and Supina, (1992), Billett (1995) and Kwakman (2003), and they also make use – as we previously have done – of the authoritative work of Marsick and Volpe (1999). These authors continued their efforts to develop a more mature model called "the social interaction version of triggers, antecedents and consequences of informal and incidental learning at work". Kyndt et al. (Ch. 2) make no mention of the model of Tannenbaum et al. (2009), although it involves a design with the characteristics of a similar comprehensive theoretical framework with similar components that we included in our first model. So what can our ambition be, taking into account the research reported in this book?

As emphasised by many authors, the phenomenon of learning at work is a complex one, in which a very great number of factors and variables play a role. This means that summarising the whole reality in a single model must necessarily involve a reduction, given the current knowledge and the manageability of the framework in research and publications. The question arises of what the guiding principles will be for such a reduction. Part of the answer relates to the purpose of the model development. This purpose may involve on the one hand being able to describe and explain the phenomenon (see also Boud & Rooney, Ch. 7), and "ultimately *understand* more about it" and on the other hand, being able to influence it. This can lead to differences between an explanatory and an influential model, knowing that it may not be possible to influence or manipulate all factors and variables that have a facilitating or inhibiting role and are therefore not all relevant for the inclusion in a framework or model. For example, when the age of an employee plays a role in informal learning, this is an established piece of data, good to know and explain, but with little or no significance for an intervention because it cannot be changed. The learning climate in an organisation for example can, however, change through conscious interventions and unplanned stimuli. Another part of the answer involves the process of model construction, which may take place in a deductive or inductive manner. Deductive construction means that an existing theory is used, for example, a learning theory or a social change theory, in order to make an application and realisation for the phenomenon of "learning at work". This focuses the researcher's attention and is in this way inevitably selective. Basically, an inductive way of working involves the identification, on the basis of empirical-analytical research, of factors and variables and their impact and the identification of relationships by way of statistical techniques and analyses. It is however naive to think that an inductive approach could grasp the complete reality, even after extensive research. Indeed, for the construction of a certain measuring instrument or even for the most open observation possible, an appeal will have to be made, consciously or unconsciously, to conceptual categories which inevitably focus the attention in a selective way and make observations and measurements feasible.

Instead of exclusively choosing one of the two development tracks, we want to keep, following the approach of the grounded theory, to the adductive track which goes to and fro between deduction and induction (Glaser & Strauss, 1967; Strauss & Corbin, 1994) that we already followed in constructing an initial theoretical framework. This means taking a theory of learning and change as a departure point and using this to select and define a number of relevant concepts and then test them against and complete them with variables that have been empirically shown to be influential. This is what Soulliere et al. (2001) mean with conceptual modelling as "the three simultaneous, explicit, continuing respecification dialogues: the nature and dimensionalization of concepts, the relative importance of concepts, and the nature of relationships among concepts." Subsequent research must then demonstrate whether the presumed relationships between the factors and variables actually arise and to what extent they have an impact.

The abovementioned criteria that a theoretical framework must meet are: it must give an albeit reduced, but still valid picture of the reality, and provide a selection of relevant factors and variables that are research-based and manageable in optimisation practice terms and which are empirically measurable and tested and of which the mutual relations can be or have been mapped out. We add to this that we focus our attention specially on factors and variables that can be influenced, without falling into the trap that influencing is optimally possible without first understanding or giving the impression that intensively descriptive and explanatory research as well as action-research in relation to the effectiveness of the interventions would be unnecessary.

Reframing the initial theoretical framework

None of the chapters in this book puts forward a (new) more or less comprehensive model for learning at work. Most of them – and especially the empirical studies by Gerken et al. (Ch. 5) and Grohnert et al. (Ch. 4) – do however include variables and (empirically verified) relationships that are stimulating for a reframing of the model that is presented in Figure 8.2. We make use of these elements and also of a reflection on earlier contributions we have made to the development and partial empirical testing of a theoretical framework. Inspired by Marsick and Watkins (2015), special attention will be given to the process of learning itself, as a Dewey-influenced problem-framing/problem-solving cycle and depicted by Stephenson (2015) as a spirograph. We first discuss the factors and the variables that we want to include and subsequently organise them in a framework.

The influential factors and variables for learning at work - revisited

Since we wish to illustrate the dynamic of learning at work as an individually driven and by context and social interaction triggered and nurtured process, we are opting

Informal learning at work: new insights? **173**

to retain the CIPO base model with its process rationale that we previously used. To conceptualise both the context (C) and the process of input, process and output that the individual goes through (I-P-O) for this choice, we found support in Tynjälä's view (quoted in: Kyndt et al., Ch. 2, p. 14):

> It is important to notice that both the individual and the environment deserve attention . . . While the organisation of work sets the context and conditions for learning, it continues to be the reciprocal interaction between the individual and the workplace that determines learning.
>
> *Tynjälä, 2008, p. 141*

The learning process (P) as a process of change can however be even better conceptualised then the "reflection on action" as depicted in Figure 8.2, when it is presented as a (implicit and/or explicit) decision-making process with a succession of triggers (critical incidents and errors, problems and questions, unexpected results, challenges to approach matters better or differently[7]), that provokes disturbances (see also Hirschmann & Mulder, Ch. 3),[8] and possibly also a learning need, that subsequently can lead to a learning intention,[9] and to the undertaking of learning activities that can lead to a (sustainable) change of competences and knowledge (with effects for the organisation and/or the career of employees – see also Dochy et al., 2011). This process scheme is analogous to the theoretical frameworks developed by Baert, De Rick and Van Valckenborgh (2006) and Boeren, Nicaise and Baert (2010) with respect to learning in organisations and in adult education. It has been co-inspired by Fishbein and Ajzen's theory of the reasoned action (1980 and the review of the research relating to the antecedents of employees' involvement in work-related learning by Kyndt & Baert, 2013). We will take up this process chain – visualised in Figure 8.3 – further on as a central part of the theoretical framework.

The relationship between working and learning or work activities and learning activities can be even more correctly depicted when we emphasise their interconnectedness. In this regard, we want to answer Boud and Rooney's plea to position discussion of informal learning as part of everyday working life (Boud & Rooney, Ch. 7). This is made possible by not placing the learning activities in

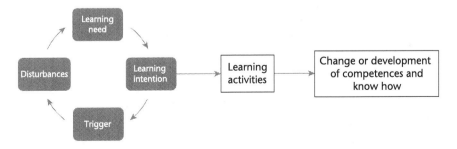

FIGURE 8.3 Process factors of learning at work

the workplace – the learning practices – separately, as we did with the "conditions at the workplace" – but to situate them in the activities in the workplace taken in their entirety (as we have defined them above). By the embedded learning activities of the work-related learning activities we mean making use while learning of the work activities and facilities created in the social, material and informational environment of the workplace by agents of the organisation (e.g. managers, HRD professionals, supervisors) and by the employees themselves, so that they and other employees can use them for learning and not only for work and job-related purposes.

By putting extra emphasis on the embedded character of the learning activities, we align ourselves with Fenwick et al. (2011) and Boud and Rooney who "understand learning as phenomena dependent on the activities, practices, and socio-material arrangements in which it is located" and with Kemmis (2005) (quoted in Boud & Rooney, Ch. 7, p. 137), who suggests that "Practices are not the 'possessions' of individual practitioners" but are "the collective 'property' of groups." In other words, a practice approach is more cognisant of the collective and integrated nature of work because a practice is a shared enterprise that extends beyond any individual person or discrete set of work processes (ibid.).

For the work-embedded activities to be actual learning activities, they must, in addition to an active component, also include a reflective component. This has to do with action and reflection as dimensions of learning while working and working while learning. We take up both of these components once again, certainly in light of the literature review of Kyndt et al. in Chapter 2, which reveals reflection as a crucial factor as well as the numerous times that the other contributors in this book also specifically refer to it. See for example, the definitions of informal learning as "learner initiated behaviour that involves action and reflection" (Gerken et al., Ch. 5, p. 82) and of reflection as "the engagement in thoughtful consideration about one's experience to uncover insights and see connections and consequences" (ibid., p. 84). Boud and Rooney add to this: "What also becomes obvious, is how learning is mediated through talk or chat" (Boud & Rooney, Ch. 7, p. 146). Figure 8.4 gives a visual presentation of this.

What Figure 8.4 indeed shows is that informal learning is by essence embedded in work activities and that reflection is crucial, but it doesn't clarify the dynamics of the

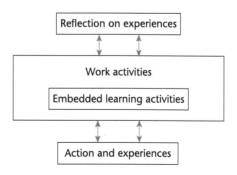

FIGURE 8.4 Working and learning: embedded activities

learning process itself. The research findings by Gerken et al. in Chapter 5 are already more detailed and at the same time more specific with respect to the context and the focus on innovation. Their Figures 5.1 and 5.2 represent the empirically observed dynamics of reflection and innovative work behaviour connected to the process from the opportunity of exploring new ideas to the realisation of these ideas. When compared with the Marsick and Watkins model of informal and incidental learning as a socially constructed process (Marsick & Watkins, 2015), the first one seems to be compatible but the second one offers a more general and advanced solution to revisit this part of our initial theoretical model. For this reason it will be integrated in Figure 8.6.[10]

Kyndt et al. (Ch.2, p.16) conclude from their meta-synthetic literature review that by using the content analysis method they identified thirteen themes that could be brought under three broad categories: personal characteristics, work environment factors, and job characteristics. We are regrouping the six context factors that we initially distinguished in three main groups, since this was more logical and consistent, as shown in Figure 8.5. We are making no further subdivision except for the work environment, and the content overlaps with the thirteen themes that Kyndt et al. distinguish, but is limited to a selection of variables which have been shown to be or are accepted to be crucial.

However, this rearrangement has as a consequence that the content of the three factors presented in Table 8.2 – namely organisational structures, organisational culture and staff characteristics – also need to be regrouped. This gives the following picture in Table 8.4. The original and the additional variables are combined here.

A comprehensive theoretical framework revisited

We now bring all the elements discussed above in a synthetic overview with an indication of the main relationships between the factors (see Figure 8.6). It is beyond the scope of this chapter, insofar as the impact of and all interaction between the variables is conceived and has already been empirically established, to visualise

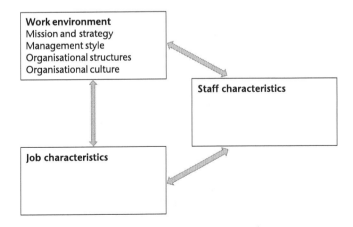

FIGURE 8.5 Context factors that influence learning at work

TABLE 8.4 Factors and variables with an impact on learning at work - revisited

Factors	Variables
Mission & organisational strategy	• The presence and consciousness of an explicit mission and (long-term) strategic vision of the organisation • Participation & commitment to the determining of strategy • Citing learning as a source of dynamic in the strategy of the organisation to be(come) a learning organisation that is open to support continuous renewal
Management style	• *Creating time for analysis and reflection* (Kyndt et al., Ch. 2) (Grohnert et al., Ch. 4) • Being oneself an example of learning while working • *Communicating their own critical experiences*, Grohnert et al., Ch. 4) • *Giving constructive feedback* (Kyndt et al., Ch. 2) (Grohnert et al., Ch. 4) • Stimulating innovation initiatives • Facilitating collaborative decision-making • Promoting working together • *Appreciation and support of efforts to learn* (Kyndt et al., Ch. 2) • Superior feedback: rewards for proficiency (Skule, in Kyndt et al., Ch. 2) • Democratic leadership and people having some control (Skule in Kyndt et al., Ch. 2) • Intensification of jobs reduces the time for learning (Hirschmann & Mulder, Ch. 3)
Organisational structures	• Diversity and complementarity in teams • Self-directing teams • Availability of learning conditions/resources • Management position (Gerken et al., Ch. 5)
Communication systems	• *Promotion of the circulation of knowledge* (Kyndt et al., Ch. 2) • Openness toward information and knowledge from inside and outside the organisation • Communication between all units of the organisations • Introduction courses for new employees • *Time and space for social contact among employees* (Kyndt et al., Ch. 2) • Proximity/distance to work of colleagues (Kyndt et al., Ch. 2)
Organisational culture	• *Open learning climate* (Grohnert et al., Ch. 4) • *Mutual trust* (Kyndt et al., Ch. 2) • The encouragement to take well-reasoned risks • Openness to learn from mistakes • Appreciation of critical questions • Minimal regulatory guidance and control, maximal dialogue and initiative • Command of time pressure • Receiving collegial support (Kyndt et al., Ch. 2) (Shanks, Ch. 6)
Job characteristics	• *Autonomy and room for manoeuvre in the individual execution of a job* (Kyndt et al., Ch. 2) • Task complexity and challenge (Kyndt et al., Ch. 2) ("*More engagement in – especially social-cognitive – learning activities while accomplishing a complex work task*" Hirschmann & Mulder, Ch. 3)

Factors	Variables
	• High exposure to demands (Skule in Kyndt et al., Ch. 2) • *Variety in the job* (Kyndt et al., Ch. 2) • Learning potential *and intensity* of a job (Skule in Kyndt et al., Ch. 2) • Workload and job demands (Skule in Kyndt et al., Ch. 2) • High amount of information processing (Hirschmann & Mulder, Ch. 3)
Staff characteristics	• Readiness and motivation to learn • Prior learning; competences for self-directed learning; self-efficacy (Hirschmann & Mulder, Ch. 3) • Competences in teamwork and team learning • *Openness to give and receive feedback* (Gerken et al., Ch. 5, Grohnert et al., Ch. 4) • The will to innovate • *Tolerance to unpredictability and uncertainty – skills for coping with change – skills for coping with change* (Kyndt et al., Ch. 2) • Tenure (Kyndt et al., Ch. 2) and the number of different job functions taken up in an organisation (Gerken et al., Ch. 5) • Amount of task experience, including critical experiences (Grohnert et al., Ch. 4) • Meta-cognition: knowing about one's knowledge, judgment processes and one's actual performance (Grohnert et al., Ch. 4) • Initiative (Lohman, Skule in Kyndt et al., Ch. 2) • Age and preference for individual/social learning (Kyndt et al., Ch. 2) • Hierarchical position and support for learning (Kyndt et al., Ch. 2) • Outgoing or nurturing personality (Kyndt et al., Ch. 2) • The task experience within a specific domain and its validity (Grohnert et al., Ch. 4)

Note:
1 We separated in this table the category 'job characteristics' from the category "staff characteristics".

and discuss all of them in detail. The chapters in this book give a more refined picture of a selection of variables.

We will however take up one element – namely, the results – that we did not discuss (anew) above. In the presentation of our initial theoretical framework we put forward that when competences are developed through the learning process and knowledge is generated and shared, this leads to effects or outcomes that can be beneficial for the functioning of the employees, their teams and the organisation and/ or for their career. With the arrows in Figure 8.6, which link effects with work environment, with staff characteristics and with job characteristics, we suggest that the dynamic can take place in two directions. Three possible examples: successful learning experiences demand not only an open learning climate, but achieving this can, within the organisation, extend the learning climate to more employees and teams and/or strengthen it. The ability to process a certain amount of information is without a

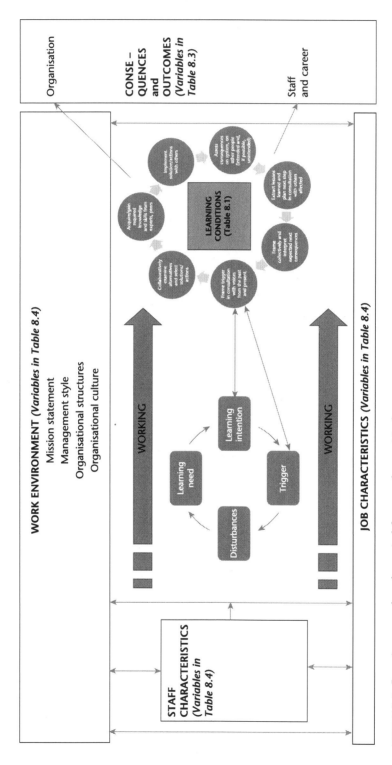

FIGURE 8.6 Learning at work: a theoretical framework – revisited

doubt a condition for being able to learn from action and experience. However, the fact that informal learning processes also do succeed will more than likely increase the processing capacity of individuals and teams. Competences for teamwork and team learning are to a certain extent necessary for informal learning in embedded activities, but at the same time, it may be accepted that positive learning experiences also contribute to the further development and spreading of these competences.

Although the examples given here formulate the likely mutual effect relations, they still maintain a hypothetical character. The chapters in this book do not offer too much in the way of empirical support in this regard. The research of Grohnert et al. (Ch. 4) shows that – under certain conditions – learning at work can lead to high-quality judgements by professionals. Gerken et al. (Ch. 5) demonstrate that informal learning can result in the idea realisation and the acceptance of innovations. Boud and Rooney (Ch. 7) mention in the studies effects on the safety of employees and on the mutual understanding between employees and clients. Hirschmann and Mulder (Ch. 3) refer to a possible improvement of problem solving with IT professionals. But in the majority of these chapters, effects and the reciprocal relations are not the focus of the contribution.

Conclusion and discussion

Taking the initial theoretical framework that we developed in the 1997–2010 period as our point of reference, and what the articles in this book currently offer, we asked two questions:

- Do the contributions of the researchers in this publication lead to (more) conceptual clarity with respect to the concept of "informal learning at work"?
- Is it possible, on the basis of the articles, to develop one single universal and empirically founded theoretical framework or model?

The answer to the first question is, in our opinion, convincingly positive, in the sense that, with the help of elements that many researchers brought to the fore, we were able to define learning at work with precision. In our opinion, this revised definition makes it possible to come to (more) valid and comparable research questions and designs. The decisiveness of this statement can at the same time be put in perspective, first because we take our initial definition as the overriding point of reference, and subsequently because in this domain of science and research, only seldom does a definition succeed in being generally accepted and used.

The second question must be answered in a nuanced manner. The chapters and our reflection on the basis of our reading of them have made it possible for us to revise and improve our initial theoretical framework. The revision gives a clear (or clearer) insight into the underlying theories about learning and change and has in all respects a comprehensive character, also through the – still manageable – multiplicity of factors and variables for which the empirical basis has been shown.

At the same time, it must be recognised that the relationship between the many factors and variables relies above all on conceptual assumptions and has only been empirically tested for certain sets of factors and variables. Moreover, it must be recognised that the theoretical framework is a reduction of the complexity of the phenomenon, a reduction that is substantially driven by a certain view of learning and change. If other views and other selections of – at least in part – other factors and variables are taken, the development of theory or model building will lead to other results. It is as a result not possible to conclude that the revised framework is universal, although it may be for many and various organisations, teams and employees and significant contexts and may promote targeted research. However, even then, caution is still called for in making generalised conclusions, since empirical verification of factors, variables and their mutual relations is still fully underway.

Further research

The setting-up of further research is therefore recommended in order to examine whether the presumed relationships between the factors and variables do indeed occur, in extremely diverse contexts (industrial and service sectors, small and large organisations, routine and innovative work environments and jobs etc. and for diverse types of employees and careers) and to what extent they have an impact.

In setting up that research, the following suggestions deserve to be taken to heart:

- Although we could design a comprehensive theoretical framework of informal learning at the workplace mapping the most influential variables, the reality of how informal learning is taking place and what outcomes are attained is very diverse. A better understanding of this type of learning requires complementary research based on learning histories and individual biographies of learning. Narrative approaches of learning histories of a variety of employees in a variety of regions, organisations and career paths must be encouraged. See, for example, Hodkinson et al.'s "Learning lives project" (2004).
- Boud and Rooney (Ch. 7, p. 149) recommend that "practices should be units of analysis in future studies of informal learning and that frameworks which privilege the socio-cultural elements of work itself, rather than notions of curriculum and pedagogy, be taken as a starting point for the discussion of learning."
- Much research makes use of self-reporting by way of written questionnaires. It is worth recommending making use of mixed methods (combinations of qualitative and quantitative research) with, for example, case studies with observation followed by questionnaires (see e.g. Grohnert et al., Ch. 4) or the Vignette Technique (see Hirschmann & Mulder, Ch. 3). This is especially so when it comes to assessing the outcomes of informal learning alternatives for the traditional ways of measuring outputs and outcomes of formal learning are needed. The use, for example, of the critical incident technique and of approaches like the theory-of-change evaluation and the theory-of-action analysis, the Strategic Leverage through Learning© and the Learning Network theory could be alternatives.

- Although a variety of staff and managers is covered by all the studies reviewed and reported in this book and by some of the studies with mixed samples, it remains unclear how important the differences among these categories could be and if these differences hold constraints for developing a universal, comprehensive theoretical framework of informal learning at the workplace. For instance, the idea by Eraut (2004) that the contextual factors trigger informal learning in particular for knowledge workers, professionals and managers, all of whom bring intrinsic motivation, critical thinking and problem-solving skills to the task at hand, raises questions. Are workers in routine jobs on the shop floor, with restricted responsibilities and low(er) literacy levels and education, less triggered or triggered in a different way compared to others? Are the need, the motivation, the degree of self-directedness, the modes of learning, the amount and/or the benefits of informal learning for them, compared to knowledge workers, professionals and managers, different, less relevant or in one way or another compensatory for their confined formal training records? And what about the ethnic and cultural differences of the employees and managers in local and international companies and enterprises? More systematic comparative research could be helpful to better depict and understand the variety and the complex reality of informal and incidental learning according to the actors involved.
- (More combined) account should be taken in research designs of the subjective approach of experiences and perceptions and also of the objective approach of diverse aspects. A specific application of this is the recommendation of Hirschmann and Mulder (Ch. 3, p. 58): "Thus, in future research, the perceived complexity of work tasks should be taken into account, in addition to the objectively measured complexity of work task, in order to be able to control if the objective complexity is interpreted as intended."
- While in this book much attention goes to process aspects and context variables, it is striking that the measurement of (specific) effects, their relevance and sustainability and the empirical establishing of the outcomes or added value hardly receives any discussion. The belief in the (added) value of informal learning at work or "everyday learning" can benefit from more empirical substantiation.
- Longitudinal research with multiple measurements over a longer period seldom occurs. The suggestion made by Grohnert et al. (Ch. 4) thus deserves the necessary attention and efforts: "In environments where professionals change employers, tasks or fields more often, measures need to be included that capture the different kinds of experiences in their respective learning contexts."
- The focus in this book and in the revisited theoretical framework is on informal learning at the workplace. First of all, we must keep in mind, as Shanks stresses in relation to teachers (Ch. 6), that most employees are involved in different and changing groups at their workplace and that they have varying levels of access to other colleagues. Deepening our insight in informal learning as a differentiated and evolving reality requires multiple case studies. Moreover, informal learning is

also taking place in other social networks and communities of practice such as families, sports clubs, trade unions, political parties, grass-roots groups, and so on. It would be interesting to explore if and how the informal learning of an individual in different contexts is complementary, supportive, mutually beneficial or not, and if the same or different variables – with the same or different impact – are influential.

Promoting and facilitating informal workplace learning

Although attention in this article has primarily been given to the conceptualising of learning at work and the development of a theoretical framework, with empirical substantiation, in the direction of a model, we finally wish to reflect very briefly on the possible interventions for the optimisation of learning at work.

While we started this chapter with the observation that over the past decades much attention and effort has been given to informal learning at the workplace, we notice at the same time that valuing informal learning and its outcomes is still not evident in all sectors. Where diplomas and certificates are decisive eligibility criteria for recruitment and promotion, informal learning is not fully in the picture. For instance, in Shanks's chapter on teachers in school environments (Ch. 6), a reference is made to the statement by Eraut, Alderton, Cole and Senker (2000) that, compared to formal learning, informal learning is undervalued and that research by Kennedy (2011) is showing that current policies on teacher learning in Scotland still favour more formal types of CPD over informal or incidental learning. A precondition for valuing informal workplace learning is of course the recognition and the validation of what is learned. Methodologies and instruments like assessment centres and portfolios are more and more implemented, although differences among countries (e.g., the USA versus Belgium) and sectors (e.g., public administration and health care versus ICT and financial branches) remain strong. These differences also exist when it comes to rewarding informal learning outcomes in terms of a better position in the labour market, more flexible access to jobs and (financial and/or "social") promotion in one's career. The issue of the valuing of informal learning – that was mentioned but not elaborated on in the chapters – is given special attention in the context of a future-oriented policy of lifelong learning and the creation of a learning climate in society (Baert, 2014).

When writing our handbook for a strategic VTO policy (*Vorming, Training, Opleiding* – Formation, Training, Education) back in 2000 and 2011, we emphasised that informal or workplace learning may not be formalised in the way that educational programmes, courses and training off-the job are formalised. Formalisation is destructive for the nature and possibilities of informal learning in embedded activities at the workplace. It is by influencing and changing the context factors and variables that informal learning, which is initiated and directed by the employees and their teams, can be optimised. It is precisely for this reason that we have given preference in the theoretical framework to variables that can be influenced or manipulated. A few examples should be sufficient to clarify this. An expansion of the possibilities for contact between employees and the stimulation of trust and psychological safety will have a positive influence on the development of a learning need and a learning intention. Managers who encourage the taking of well-reasoned risks, who are open to mistakes being made and appreciate critical questions will certainly come across learning employees. In giving employees the opportunity and the time to think along with them regarding the strategy of the organisation, they will not only be able to expect more commitment, they will also challenge their employees to prepare themselves more for the future by acquiring other new competencies. Or as Gerken et al. (Ch. 5, p. 95) write

> ... organisations should illustrate how employees can use reflection as a powerful tool to smoothen the accomplishment of work tasks during innovation processes. For instance, supervisors may encourage employees to examine their performance and underlying assumptions during and after work tasks. This could be done by supporting their ideas through feedback but also by providing on-demand support for their questions.

A similar idea from the perspective of leadership is launched by Grohnert et al. (Ch. 4): leaders can develop an open climate and communicate values supportive of learning by "communicating their own critical experiences, asking for honest input from different levels of the hierarchy, and publicly rewarding learning of colleagues." Managers also can discuss the processes and the outcomes of learning in the workplace during appraisal interviews (see e.g., Hirschmann & Mulder, Ch. 3).

This belief in optimisation may not hinder a critical stance to the promotion of informal learning at work. Boud and Rooney (Ch. 7) point out that promoting informal learning can effectively inhibit it and seeking to influence informal learning holds potentially counterproductive effects. Too much emphatic promotion can give workplace learning an obligatory character and in this way replace the intrinsic or autonomous motivation with an extrinsic and controlled motivation that may elicit a resistance to learning. At the same time, it should not be overlooked – something that frequently happens, in our opinion – that promoting learning in the workplace also involves financial investments and expertise with respect to the dynamics of learning.

Notes

1 KU Leuven, Belgium
2 The terms "conceptual framework", "theoretical framework" and "model" are often used interchangeably in the literature. See for example, Rocco and Plakhotnik (2009). In this article, when speaking of a conceptual framework we mean an ordered set of factors and/or variables that are intended to delineate the primary facets of a phenomenon. A theoretical framework goes a step further and makes the recordable or measurable variables and the assumed relationships between them more explicit. A model goes another step further, in particular by specifying the impact of the variables and their mutual relationship and by empirically substantiating this. A model is in this sense an advanced form of scientific knowledge-development.

3 We use "factor" as an umbrella concept for a cluster of variables that are interconnected.
4 The list of references contains among others a selection taken from the leading sources that were consulted at the time.
5 See for example, UNESCO (1972).
6 In the first research, questionnaires, observations and interviews were used as research instruments to assess the job skills. Both managers and employees were included in the sample. The "Workplace Informal Learning Matrix" was developed on the basis of these results. Skills relating to the following domains were studied through this research instrument: "Working with others", "Oral communication", "Problem solving", "Decision making", "Learning skills". This matrix additionally accessed the workplace culture, leadership skills and diversity and culture. It was used with a hundred "supervisors and middle managers".
7 Examples of triggers are: rapid changes in the global, technologically-driven environment characterized by knowledge work, collaborative and innovative work structures, flatter organizations that are decentralized, strong relationships with customers who increasingly seek input into design of products and services, and flexible partnerships with suppliers for rapid, lean, just-in-time production and delivery and initial performance.
8 Hirschmann and Mulder (Ch. 3) refer to Piaget for conceiving disturbances as perceived as errors, unexpected results of actions, or knowledge gaps.
9 The formulation of a learning intention takes up a central role within the decision-making process with respect to an engagement in learning activities. The intention to participate in learning activities is a robust predictor of actual participation in learning activities (Baert et al. (2006), Kyndt et al. (2011), Kyndt & Baert (2013)).
10 The exploration of opportunities for improvement, generating new ideas and strategies and implementing these in the organization mentioned in the framework of Gerken et al. (Ch. 5) are covered respectively the learning spirograph of Stephenson (2015) and by the process of "fram[ing] the trigger in consultation with voices from the past & present, collaboratively examin[ing] alternatives and select[ing] solutions/actions and implement[ing] solution/actions with others" in Marsick and Watkins's Model of Informal and Incidental Learning (2015). See figure on: https://www.researchgate.net/publication/273343428_Promoting_Assessing_Recognizing_and_Certifying_Lifelong_Learning/figures.

Bibliography

Note: the chapters in this book are used as a primary source. Except for exceptional cases due to the originality or specificity of a quote, reference is not always made to the authors to which the primary sources refer; see the references in the articles themselves in this regard.

Argyris, C. & Schön, D. (1996). *Organizational Learning II: Theory, method and practice*. Reading, MA: Addison-Wesley.
Baert, H., De Witte, K. and Sterck, G. (2000). *Vorming, training en opleiding. Handboek voor een kwaliteitsvol VTO-beleid in welzijnsvoorzieningen* (Instruction, Training and Education = ITE). Handbook for a High Quality ITE policy in Welfare Services). Leuven: Garant.
Baert, H., De Rick, K. & Van Valckenborgh, K. (2006). Towards the conceptualization of "learning climate". In R. Vieira de Castro, A. Vitoria Sancho & P. Guimaraes (Eds.), *Adult Education, New Routes in a New Landscape*. Braga, Portugal: University of Minho, Unit for Adult Education.
Baert, H., Clauwaert, L. & Van Bree, L. (2008). *Naar een cartografie van condities voor werkplekleren in arbeidsorganisaties in Vlaanderen* (Workplace learning: towards a cartography of conditions

for informal and non-formal workplace learning. Research report Policy Research Centre Work and Social Economy) Leuven: Steunpunt Werk en Sociale Economie.

Baert, H. De Witte, K., Govaerts, N. & Sterck, G. (2011). *Werk maken van leren. Strategisch vormings-, trainings- en opleidingsbeleid in organisaties* (Making work of learning. Strategic formation, training and educational policy in organisations). Leuven: Garant.

Baert, H. & Govaerts, N. (2012). Learning patterns of teams at the workplace. *Journal of Workplace Learning. 24*(7–8), 538–550.

Baert, H. (2014) Blijven leren: de toekomst. Volwassenen stimuleren om te leren. Een strategische verkenning (Continuing to learn: The future. Encouraging adults to learn. A strategic exploration). Leuven-Brussels: Acco – Vlaamse Onderwijsraad.

Bandura, A. (1997). *Self-efficacy: The exercise of control*. New York: Worth Publishers.

Billett, S. (1995). Workplace learning: Its potential and limitations. *Education & Training, 37*(5), 20–27.

Billett, S. (2002). Towards a workplace pedagogy: Guidance, participation and engagement. *Adult Education Quarterly, 53*(1), 27–43.

Bjornavold, J. & Colardyn, D. (2005). *The Learning Continuity: European inventory on validating non-formal and informal learning. National policies and practices in validating non-formal and informal learning.* CEDEFOP Panorama series, 117. Luxembourg: Office for Official Publications of the European communities.

Bjornavold, J. & Colardyn, D. (2004). Validation of formal, non-formal and informal learning: Policy and practices in EU Member States. *European Journal of Education, 39*(1), 69–89.

Boeren, E., Nicaise, I. & Baert, H. (2010). Theoretical models of participation in adult education: The need for an integrated model, *International Journal of Lifelong Education, 29*(1), 45–61.

Brooks, A. & Supina, J. (1992). Reframing HRD: Insights from research on the development of exemplary managers. *Studies in Continuing Education, 14*(1), 156–165.

CEW (Centre for Education and Work) (2007). *The Workplace Informal Learning Matrix* [WILM]. Accessed 3 October 2007: http://www.wilm.ca/en/research.html

Dochy, F., Gijbels, D., Segers, M. & Van den Bossche, P. (2011). *Theories of Learning at the Workplace: Building blocks for training and professional development programs.* London & New York: Routledge.

EDC (Education Development Center) (1998). *The Teaching Firm: Where productive work and learning converge.* Newton, MA: Education Development Center, Inc.

Ellinger, A. D. (2005). Contextual factors influencing informal learning in a workplace setting: The case of "reinventing itself company". *Human Resource Development Quarterly, 16*(3), 389–415.

Ellström, P.-E. (2001). Integrating learning and work: Problems and prospects. *Human Resource Development Quarterly, 12*(4), 421–435.

Enos, M. D., Kehrhahn, M.T. & Bell, A. (2003). Informal learning and the transfer of learning. How managers develop proficiency. *Human Resource Development Quarterly, 14*(4), pp. 369–387.

Eraut, M. (1994). *Developing Professional Knowledge and Competence.* London: Falmer Press.

Eraut, M. (2004). Informal learning in the workplace. *Studies in Continuing Education, 26*(2), 247–273.

Eraut, M., Alderton, J., Cole, G. & Senker, P. (2000). Development of knowledge and skills at work. In: F. Coffield, (ed.), *Differing Visions of a Learning Society: Research findings.* Bristol: Policy Press, pp. 231–262.

Fenwick, T., Edwards, R. & Sawchuck, P. (2011). *Emerging Approaches to Educational Research: Tracing the socio-material.* London: Routledge.

Fishbein, M. & Ajzen, I. (1980). *Understanding Attitudes and Predicting Social Behavior.* Englewood Cliffs, NJ: Prentice-Hall.

Fordham, P. (1993). *Informal, Non-Formal and Formal Education Programmes*. London: YMCA.

Gielen, H. & Lauwers, B. (Ed.) (2007). *Europees Sociaal Fonds-project. Indicatoren voor kwaliteitsvol werkplekleren* (European Social Fund Project. Indicators for high-quality workplace learning). Berchem: VOV-Lerend netwerk.

Glaser, B. & Strauss, A. (1967). *The Discovery of Grounded Theory: Strategies for qualitative research*. New York: Aldine.

Govaerts, N., Kyndt, E., Dochy, F., & Baert, H. (2011). Influence of learning and working climate on the retention of talented employees. *Journal of Workplace Learning, 23*(1), 35–55.

Groot, W. & Van den Brink, H. (2000). Education, training and employability. *Applied Economics, 32*, 573–581. doi:10.1177/1745691612459060

Hager, P. (1998). Understanding workplace learning: General perspectives. In: Boud, D. (ed.), *Current Issues and New Agendas in Workplace Learning*. Springfield, VA: NCVER, pp. 30–42.

Hodkinson, P., Hodkinson, H., Evans, K., Kersh, N., Fuller, A., Unwin, L. & Senker, P. (2004). The significance of individual biography in workplace learning, *Studies in the Education of Adults, 36*(1), 6–24. Cit. in: Shanks (Ch. 6)

Kennedy, A. (2011). Collaborative continuing professional development (CPD) for teachers in Scotland: Aspirations, opportunities and barriers. *European Journal of Teacher Education, 34*(1), 25–41. Cit. in: Shanks (C. 6)

Kwakman, K. (2003). Factors affecting teachers' participation in professional learning activities. *Teaching and Teacher Education, 19*, 149–170.

Kyndt, E. & Baert, H. (2013). Antecedents of employees' involvement in work-related learning: A systematic review. *Review of Educational Research, 82*(3), 273–313.

Kyndt, E., Dochy, F. & Nijs, H. (2009). Learning conditions for non-formal and informal workplace learning. *Journal of Workplace Learning, 21*(5), 369–383.

Kyndt, E., Govaerts, N., Dochy, F. & Baert, H. (2011). The learning intention of low-qualified employees: A key for participation in lifelong learning and continuous training. *Vocations and Learning, 4*, 211–229.

Livingstone, D. W. (2001). *Adults' Informal Learning: Definitions, findings, gaps and future research*. Toronto: Ontario Institute for Studies in Education.

Marsick, V. J. & Volpe, M. (eds.) (1999). Informal learning on the job. In R.A. Swanson (ed.), *Advances in Developing Human Resources*. Minneapolis: University of Minnesota Press.

Marsick, V. J. & Watkins, K. (2015). *Informal and Incidental Learning in the Workplace*. New York: Routledge.

Merriam, S. B. & Simpson, E. L. (2000). *A Guide to Research for Educators and Trainers of Adults*, updated 2nd ed. Malabar, FL: Krieger.

Miles, M. B. & Huberman, A. M. (1994). Qualitative Data Analysis: An expanded sourcebook, 2nd ed. Thousand Oaks, CA: Sage.

Mulder, R. (2013). Exploring feedback incidents, their characteristics and the informal learning activities that emanate from them. *European Journal of Training and Development, 37*(1) 49–71.

Onstenk, J. (1994). *Leren en opleiden op de werkplek; een verkenning in zes landen. Adviescentrum Opleidingsvraagstukken*. (Learning and instruction in the workplace; an exploration in six countries. Advice Centre Educational Issues) Amsterdam: RVE/A&O.

Onstenk, J. (2001). Epiloog: Van opleiden op de werkplek naar leren op de werkplek. (Epilogue: From instruction in the workplace to learning in the workplace.) *Pedagogische Studiën, 78*(2), 134–140.

Ouarter, J. & Midha, H. (2001). *Informal Learning Processes in a Worker Co-operative*. Nall Working Paper no. 45. Toronto: Centre for the Study of Education and Work.

Rocco, T. S. & Plakhotnik, M. S. (2009). Literature Reviews, Conceptual Frameworks, and Theoretical Frameworks: Terms, functions, and distinctions. *Human Resource Development Review*, 8(1), 120–130.

Rutten, L. (2005). *Buitengewoon geleerd: Hoe bouwwerknemers zich hun vakbekwaamheid eigen maken* (Exceptionally Educated: How construction workers pick up professional skills). 's-Hertogenbosch: CINOP.

Sambrook, S. (2005). Factors influencing the context and process of work-related learning: Synthesizing findings from two research projects. *Human Resource Development International*, 8(1), 101–119.

Skule, S. (2004). Learning at work: A framework to understand and assess informal learning in the workplace. *International Journal of Training and Development*, 8(1), 8–20.

Skule, S. & A. N. Reichbron (2002). *Learning Conducive Work: A survey of learning conditions in Norwegian workplaces*. Thessaloniki: CEDEFOP.

Soulliere, D., Britt, D. W. & Maines, D. R. (2001). Conceptual modeling as a toolbox for grounded theorists. *The Sociological Quarterly*, 42(2), 253–269.

Sousa, J. & Quarter, J. (2003). *Informal and Non-formal learning in Non-profit Organisations*. Nall Working Paper. Toronto: Centre for the Study of Education and Work.

Stephenson, W. Todd. (2015). Midnight running: How international human resource managers make meaning of expatriate adjustment. Unpublished doctoral dissertation. Athens, GA: The University of Georgia.

Sterck, G. (2004). *Leerbeleid en leerpatronen in kennisintensieve arbeidsorganisaties: concepten en praktijken*. Doctoraatsverhandeling. Katholieke Universiteit Leuven, Faculteit Psychologie en Pedagogische wetenschappen, Centrum voor permanente vorming in beroepen en organisaties (Learning policy and learning patterns in knowledge-intensive labour organisations: concepts and practices. PhD thesis. Katholieke Universiteit Leuven, Faculty of Psychology and Educational Sciences, Centre for continuous education in occupations and organisations).

Straka, G. A. (2004). *Informal Learning: Genealogy, concepts, antagonisms and questions*. Bremen: Universität Bremen, Institut Technik und Bildung [ITB].

Strauss, A. & Corbin, J. (1994). Grounded theory methodology. An overview. In: Denzin, N. K. & Lincon, Y.S. (eds.) *Handbook of Qualitative Research*. Thousand Oaks, CA: Sage.

Tannenbaum, S. I., Beard, R. L., McNall, L. A. & Salas, E. (2009). Informal learning and development in organizations. In S. W. J. Kozlowski & E. Salas (eds.), *Learning, Training and Development in Organizations*. New York: Routledge, pp. 303–333.

Tjepkema, S. (2003). *The Learning Infrastructure of Self Managing Work Teams*. Published doctoral dissertation. Twente: University Press Twente.

Tjepkema, S., Stewart, J., Sambrook, S., Mulder, M., ter Horst, H. & Scheerens, J. (2002). *HRD and Learning Organisations in Europe*. London: Routledge.

Tynjälä, P. (2008). Perspectives into learning at the workplace, *Educational Research Review*, 3(2), 130–154.

UNESCO (1972). *Learning to Be* (eds. Faure, E. et al.). Paris: UNESCO.

Van Biesen, C. F. (1989). Alledaags leren in arbeidsorganisaties (Everyday learning in organisations). In *Ontwerp: tijdschrift voor volwasseneneducatie, 1,* Leiden: SMD, pp. 4–11.

Van Woerkom, M. (2003). *Critical Reflection at Work. Bridging individual and organizational learning*. Published doctoral dissertation. Enschede: Printpartners Ipskamp.

Watkins, K. E. & Dirani, K. M. (2013). A meta-analysis of the dimensions of a learning organization questionnaire: Looking across cultures, ranks, and industries. *Advances in Developing Human Resources*, 15(2), 148–162. doi:10.1177/1523422313475991

Watkins, K. E. & Marsick, V. J. (1992). Towards a theory of informal and incidental learning in organizations. *International Journal of Lifelong Education*, 11(4), 287–300.

INDEX

access to experts 48–49
access to information 23
accommodation 45
accurate judgements 65
acquisition: feedback 21; formal learning 158; informal learning 135; knowledge 4, 21; master's degrees 19; metaphors 137–138; non-formal learning 158; skills 165; task experience 67
"acting up" 144, 147
action theory (Frese & Zapf) 41, 45, 46
active participants 122
activities, as learning 29
activity perspective on learning 5
Adaptive Control of Thought (Anderson) 4
age 18–19
Ajzen, I. 173
Alderton, J. 182
amount of change 27 *see also* participation
"analysing the situation" learning activities 56–57
Anderson, J. R. 4
Anseel, F. 76
antecedents for learning 9; empirical research study 12–36; explaining 29; learning as 29; learning dispositions 120; learning environments 114–115; macro-environment 26; new teachers 100–101, 110–116, 124–125; organising 29; support and confidence 124
apprenticeships 1
architectural structure of organisations 23
Argyris, C. 4, 154

Ashton, D. T. 21, 23
"asking silly questions" 117
assessing work task complexity 46
assimilation 45
auditing profession study 68–76; deliberate practice 70–71; implications for practice 76; judgement quality 69–70; limitations 75–76; methods 68–69; results 71–74
Australian studies 139–140, 146
automotive supply study 90–92
autonomy 27–28
Aveyard, H. 16

Baert, H. 3, 156, 158, 173
Baldwin, T. T. 5
barriers of informal learning *35–36*
Berg, S. A. 19, 21, 26
Beyond Training study 143, 144
Billett, S. 14, 29, 102–103, 123, 136, 171
Boeren, E. 173
Boud, D.: employee safety 179; everyday working life 162, 173, 174; future research 180; informal learning as a contested term 159; informal meetings 148; inhibiting factors 183; reflection 3
Brooks, A. 171
Brown, T. M. 47
budgets 24, 101
bureaucratic learning environments 115

Canadian Survey of Informal Learning Practices (Livingstone) 165
case-based reasoning (Kolodner) 4

Centre for Education and Work (CEW) 165
characteristics of work tasks *see* work task characteristics
Cheetham, G. 126
Chi squared analyses 106, 108
Chivers, G. 126
Chyung, S.Y. 19, 21, 26
CIPO base model 165, 173
classroom experience 101, 119
Clauwaert, L. 158
coaching 18
coding 107
Coetzer, A. 26, 28
cognition 47
cognitive expertise research 68
cognitive informal learning 81
cognitive learning activities 4, 8, 43–44, 163 *see also* physical learning activities
cognitive processes 5, 47–48
cognitive theories of information processing 4
Cole, G. 182
collaboration 18, 118, 125
collaborative activities 21
colleagues (coding) 128
collegial support 24
common practices at work 144–145
communication *167*
communication systems *168*, *176*
"communities of practice" (CoP, Lave and Wenger) 102, 136
competences 2–3, 177
complementarity 5–6
complexity of work tasks 40–59; defining 46–47; effects 47–49; employee performance 41; future research 58; IT-domain 47; learning activities 54–56; research designs 49–51; vignettes 52–53 *see also* performance; work task characteristics
comprehensive theoretical frameworks 170–181
computers 23–24 *see also* Internet searches
conceptual clarity 155, 179
conceptualisation of resources (Hobfoll) 29
conceptual modelling 172
"conditions at the workplace" 166
confidence 123–125
connectivity 93
consequences of learning 9–10, *124*, 170
conservation of resources theory (Hobfoll) 29, 30
constraints and obstacles 153

context 6, 42–43, 146
context factors 165, 166, *168–169*
contextual factors 41, 181
continua of learning 6–8
continuing professional development (CPD) 101, 102, 110, 127
continuous feedback 67
control of learning 7
Cope, J. 66
corporate universities 154
cost-effective informal learning 14
cover teachers 24
Critical Appraisal Skills Programme (CASP) 16
critical experience 66, 70, 71–73, 75, 76
critical incidents 66
Croskerry, P. 64, 65
cultural differences 181
Curry, M, 102

daily activities 13, 41, 42, 65, 145–149
deductive construction 171
deliberate learning 8, 43
deliberate practice 4, 63–76; continuous feedback 67; determinant of performance 63–64, 66; elements 66–68; environments with limited validity 65–66; learning mechanisms 75; and task experience 73–75
democratic and shared leadership 28
De Rick, K. 173
determinants of informal learning 41
developing expertise 44 *see also* software developers
Dewey, J. 13, 153
De Witte, K. 156, 158
diagnostic reasoning model (Croskerry) 64
didactic models and frameworks 154–155
discontinuous change 2
discussions with colleagues 110–111, 118–119
disturbances (Piaget) 41, 44–45, 46
diversity of experience(19
Dochy, F. 4, 136
Doornbos, A. J. 14, 20, 27
dynamic of learning at work 172

educational backgrounds 19
effects *see* outcomes
Ellinger, A. D. 22, 25–26
Elmore, J. 63
embedded learning activities 174
empirically observed dynamics of reflection *89*, *92*, 175

"employability" 166
employees 1–2 *see also* personal characteristics
engagement in work tasks 4
Engeström, Y. 4
Engineers' Professional Learning studies 143
English-language proficiency 19
environmental inhibitors 22
environmental validity (Kahneman and Klein) 64
environments with limited validity 65–66
equilibration 45
Eraut, M.: antecedents 29; intention to learn 8, 43; mentoring 101; triggers 181; unconscious/conscious learning 67; undervalued informal learning 182; workplace studies 25
Ericsson, K. A. 4, 63–64, 66, 75
ethnic differences 181
ethnographic studies 25
everyday learning practices *see* daily activities
expansive learning environments 115
expansive learning theory (Engeström) 4
expansive practices 126
experience: complexity of work tasks 46; cyclical model 6; and expertise 63; high judgement quality 65; and informal learning 13; learning from 6
experience-based knowledge 48
experience concentration 19
experiential learning theory (Kolb) 3
expertise 63
experts, access to 23
explanatory models 171
explicit learning 8

facilitators of informal learning *35–36*
factors, and variables 172–177, 180–182
feasibility of collaborative activities 21
feasibility of innovative activities 21
feedback: acting on 83; deliberate practice 67; learning conditions *167*; studies 93; of supervisors 93; teachers 118–119; teaching 116; triggers for learning 76
Fenwick, T. 136, 174
Fishbein, M. 173
Flanders (Belgium) 156
Ford, J. K. 5
formalisation 182–183
formal learning: changing work context 14; continua 6–8; CPD documentation 110; and informal learning 6, 135, 158–159; on the job learning *160*;

off-the-job-training 101, 153–154; work-related learning 5
Frese, M. 41, 45, 46
Freund, L. 48
Fuller, A. 122

game-based learning activities 121
games 64
gender 19, 49
geographical locations 146
Gerken, M. 161, 174–175, 179, 183
goal-oriented behaviour 45, 162
Granath, J. Å. 103
Gray, C. D. 106
Grohnert, T. 162, 179, 181, 183
grounded theory 172
Gustavsson, M. 122

Hager, P. 136, 138, 143
Hambrick, D. Z. 64, 75
hands-on experience 153
Hayes, A. F. 70–71
head teachers 115–116
help seeking behaviour 83–84, 93
Hicks, E. 23
hierarchical structures 26–27, 115–116
high cognitive effort 67–68
High Impact Learning that lasts (HILL, Dochy & Segers) 4
high-quality connectivity 84
high-quality judgements 64–65, 66, 67
Hirschmann, K. 162, 179, 181
Hobfoll, S. E. 29
Hodkinson, H. 117
Hodkinson, P. 117
Human Resource Development (HRD) 1; policy study 156–157; practices 153–154; resources 24; trial-and-error learning 25
human resource (HR) 1
human resource management (HRM) 2–3

idea generation 94
idea promotion 82, 94
idea realisation 82, 93, 94
implicit learning 8, 43
individual and organisational *consequences* 9
"individual-cognitive learning activities" 54
individual informal learning 8–9, 81
individualisation 126
individual learning 103 *see also* participation
individual learning dispositions 120–121, 123, 126 *see also* personal characteristics
individual learning results 44

"individual-physical learning activities" 54
induction year (coding) 128
inductive working 171
influencing factors 164–165, 172–175
informal contacts 22
informal information exchanges 148
informal learning: approaches to 135–136; contested term 135, 161–162; defining 6–8, 12–14, 42, 44, 81, 82; inhibiting and promoting factors *17–18*; investing in 14; not organised and structured 41; paradox 126, 147–149; relational 146; search terms 30; social interaction 8–9, 81; types 8–9
information processing 48
information search 64–65, 71–72
information seeking 84
information systems *167*
inhibiting factors *17–18*; interactions 22; isolation 23; job characteristics 26–29; learning resources 22–24; organisational features 21; rewards 21–22; social support 24–26 *see also* personal characteristics
innovation 80, 81–82, 93
innovation-specific reflection 85, 91–92, 94, 95
innovative activities 21
innovative work behaviour 80–95; context-bound construct 94; defining 82; innovation-specific reflection *92*; interdependent innovation tasks 83; learning from others 84; measuring 90; stimulating 81
intention to learn 8, 13, 43
interaction partners 49
interactions 4, 22–23
International Forum of International Audit Regulators (IFIAR) 63
Internet searches 8, 18, 23 *see also* computers
interpersonal relationships 117
"invisible" learning 147
Ioannou, G. 2
isolation 23
IT-domain study 40–59; complexity of work tasks 47; gender distribution 49; individual learning results 44; learning activities 53–56; problem-driven learning 40–41; research design 49–53; Vignette Technique 58
IWB scale (Messmann & Mulder) 90

Jerusalem, M. 53
job-based HRM systems 2–3

job challenge 28
job characteristics 26–29, *176–177*, 177
job control 27–29
job demands 27, 28–29
job functions 93–94
job of teaching (coding) 129
job satisfaction 21
job variety 28
Johnson, E. 69
Johnsson, M. 143
judgement accuracy 70–72
judgement quality 64–65, 67, 69–70

Kahneman, D. 64, 65, 74–75
Kemmis, S. 134–135, 174
Kennedy, A. 182
Khaddage, F. 84
Kinnear, P. R. 106
Klein, G. 64, 65, 74–75
Kleine, B. 75
Knezek, G. 84
knowledge 2
knowledge gaps 47
"knowledge workers" 49
Knowles, M. 13
Kolb, D. A. 3
Kolodner, J. L. 4
Krampe, R. T. 4, 63–64, 66, 75
Kwakman, K. 18, 21, 25, 27, 29, 171
Kyndt, E.: literature review 174, 175; research on influential factors 156, 171; size and learning conditions 21; spontaneous and unplanned learning 161; triggers 162; work-related learning 3

Lave, J. 3, 102, 114, 123, 127, 136
leadership 183
learners 147
learning: as changes in social practices 101; favourable conditions 161–162; nomenclature 147; non-interpersonal sources 81; through talking 146
learning ability 163
learning activities 43
Learning and Development 1–3
learning at work 158–183; defining 158, 163; factors and variables 165–166, 172–175; optimisation 182; research 154–155; theoretical foundations 3–6; theoretical frameworks 163–164, 177–179; use of "*informal*" 158–159
"Learning at work – workplace appraisal of informal learning" (CEW) 165

"learning by doing" (Dewey) 153
"learning by the seat of their pants" 144
"learning-by-walking-around" (Granath) 103
learning climate 70, 171
learning (coding) 128
learning-committed orientation 25
learning conditions 165–166, *167*
learning culture 25–26
learning environments 114–115, 120–122
learning from oneself 81, 82–83
learning from others 81, 82–83, 84, 93
learning from others and innovative work behaviour study 85–90
learning from pupils 119–120
learning histories 123
"learning intensive jobs" 165
learning intentions 163 *see also* personal characteristics
Learning Network theory 180
learning opportunities, and gender 19
"*learning organisation*" (Argyris) 154
learning-oriented organisations 26
learning practices 140–145, 166
learning process (P) 43, 173
learning resources 22–23
"learning territory" (Fuller and Unwin) 122
"learning while working" 154
"legitimate peripheral participation" (Lave and Wenger) 102
less complex work task vignette 52
Lievens, F. 76
lifelong learning 40
Likert-type "Inquiry & Dialogue" scale 70
limited validity environments 64–65, 66
literature review 15–18, *32*
Livingstone, D. W. 18, 24, 165
Lohman, M. C. 13, 19–20, 22, 24, 25, 126
longitudinal research 181
looking back to university course (coding) 128
lunches 148

Macnamara, B. N. 64, 75
macro-environments 26
mammograms 63
management-initiated learning interventions 148
management style factor *168*, *176*
managers: accessibility 23; hierarchical structures 26–27; learning-committed orientation 25; qualitative research 25
Manuti, A. 3
marital status 19

Marsick, V. J.: action-reflection-action cycles 8; everyday encounters 83; informal learning characteristics 162; informal learning definition 13; informal learning model 6, 45, 46, 175; informal workplace learning 66; learning climate 67, 70; social interaction model 171
master's degrees 19
mental activities 43
mentoring 18
mentors 23, 110, 114
Messmann, G. 90
meta-cognition processes 67–68, 76 *see also* performance; reflection
metaphors 137–138
meta-synthesis: literature review 15–18, *32*; strengths and limitations 30–31
Mezirow, J. 3
Miller, C. E. 47
Mills, L. 84
mission and organisational strategy factors *168*, *176*
Mitchell, L. 24
mixed-method research studies 16, 103–108, 180
model building 155, 180 *see also* theoretical frameworks
motivation 22, 43, 121
MouselabWEB (Willemsen and Johnson) 69
Mulder, R. H. 8, 90, 161, 162, 179, 181
music 64
mutual effect relations 179

National Institute for Health and Clinical Excellence (NICE) 16
Nawab, A. 22
Neighbourhood Centre study 144
networking 19, 22
new teacher learning 100–129; antecedents 100–101, 110–116, *124*; classroom experience 119; collaboration 118–119; communities of practice 102–103; confidence 123–125; consequences 122–125, *124*; CPD 101, 110, 182; discussions with colleagues 110–111; dynamic process 121; feedback 116, 118–119; induction year 110; interpersonal relationships 117; learning activities 111–112; learning disposition 120, 123; learning environments 114–115; learning from pupils 119–120; legitimate peripheral participation 102; mentors 110, 113–114; observation of

colleagues 117–118; observing others 113; temporary employees 126; trial and error 119; triggers 100–101, 116–122, *124 see also* teaching
Nicaise, I. 173
Nieuwenhuis, L.F.M. 18
Nijhof, W.J. 18
Noe, R. A. 9, 81, 82
nomenclature of learning 147–148
non-clarifying learning environments 115
non-complex activities 54
non-formal learning 158–159
non-interpersonal sources 9
non-profit organisations 21
non-teaching time 101 *see also* teaching
non-western cultures 26
Norwegian Institute for Labour and Social Research 165
novel challenges 6
nurturing personalities 20
NVivo (qualitative data analysis software) 106

observing behaviour 8, 117–118
obsolescence 2
off-the-job-training 154
older people 18
"on-the-job learning" 30, *160*
open-mindedness 20
operationalisation of context factors 166, *168–169*
opportunities to experiment 28
opportunity exploration 82, 93, 94
organisational culture 25–26, *169, 176*
organisational learning theory (Argyris and Schön) 4
organisational structures 21, *168, 176*
organisation (coding) 128
Oswald, F. L. 64, 75
outcomes 29, 42, 170, 177
outgoing personalities 20
"out of the ordinary" challenges 144
Ouweneel, A.P.E. 28
overt activities 43

Pakistan 26
Papalexandris, A. 2
paradox of informal learning 126, 147–149
participation: amount of change 27; formal learning 24; metaphors 138; in networks 22; organisational decision making 28
part-time workers 27
passive participants 122
payment systems 21

performance: complexity of work tasks 41, 46–47; self-efficacy 58 *see also* complexity of work tasks
personal characteristics 43, 58; attitudes towards learning 20; engagement in informal learning 18–21; motivation 121; participation 29; personality 19–20 *see also* inhibiting factors; self-efficacy
physical learning activities 4, 43–44, 59, 163 *see also* cognitive learning activities
physical places 7, 157
physical proximity to colleagues 116–117
physical spaces (coding) 129
Piaget, J. 41, 44–45, 46
post-industrial society 2
practice-based approaches 136–137, 159
Prastacos, G. 2
precursor to learning *see* antecedents for learning
predictors for informal learning 41
Price, O. 143–144
proactive employees 20
problem-driven learning 40–41
problem solving 47–48, 59
process factors of learning *173*
PROCESS macros (Hayes) 70–71
professional learning 65
professional literature 18, 19, 20, 57
progressive learning 156
project-teams 22
promoting factors of informal learning *17–18*
psychological characteristics 19–20
pupils (coding) 129

qualitative studies: critical appraisal 16, *33*; managers facilitating learning 25; meta-synthesis 30; secondary analysis 138–140
quantitative research 16, 24, 30, *34*
questionnaires 50–51, 180

radiologists 63
reactive learning 8, 43
readiness to learn 163
reasoned action (Fishbein & Ajzen) 173
reception work 144
recognition 22
reflection: cyclical model 6; and feedback 26; innovation processes 85; innovative work behaviour study 90–92; learning 43, 82–83; meta-cognition 67–68, 76; opportunity exploration 94; problem

solving strategies 59; terms for 5; as thoughtful consideration 84–85
"reflection-in-action" (Schön) 3, 103
"reflection-on-action" (Schön) 103, 173
Reichbron, A. N. 165
reliability coefficients 95
reluctance to participate 22
resources 29
"resources caravans" 29–30
restrictive learning environments 115
rewarding learning 21–22
Richter, D. 19
Roffe, I. 2
Rooney, D.: employee safety 179; everyday working life 162, 173, 174; future research 180; informal learning as a contested term 159; informal meetings 148; inhibiting factors 183; *Neighbourhood Centre* study 144
Rosen, M. A. 63
Ruiz Ben, E. 49
rural societies 1

safety practices 143
salaries 21, 22
Salas, E. 63
Sambrook, S. 24, 25, 164
Schatzki, T. 134–135, 137, 148
Schollaert, E. 76
Schön, D. A. 3, 4, 103
school context (coding) 128
schools, expansive/restrictive practices 126
Schwarzer, R. 53
scientific knowledge 156
Scotland 101–102, 182
Scottish Teachers for a New Era (STNE) 100–129; antecedents to learning 110; coding glossary 128–129; contributions to knowledge 127; interview analysis 106–107, 108–110; interview design 105–106; methodology 103–105; responses 107–108
secondary analysis of quantitative data 138–140
Segers, M. 4
Seibert, S. E. 122
self-efficacy 20, 43, 58 *see also* personal characteristics
self-report measures 94
Senker, P. 182
settings 44
sex 19
Sfard, A. 137
Shanks, R. 181, 182

Shanteau, J. 65, 69, 74–75
sharing knowledge 23
site walks 146
situated learning theory (Lave & Wenger) 3, 102, 125
size of organisation 21
skill variety 48–49
Skinner, B. F. 2
Skruber, R. 115
Skule, S. 18, 21–22, 24, 27, 165
"social-cognitive learning activities" 54
social learning activities 44, 49, 53, 56, 57
social network analysis (SNA) 94–95
"social-physical learning activities" 54
social profit organisations 156–157
social support 24–26
Soderquist, K. E. 2
software developers: cross-sectional study 42, 49–51; developing expertise 44; experience-based knowledge 48; learning activities 57; teams 40
Solomon, N. 148
Sonnentag, S. 75
Soulliere, D. 172
specification of context factors 166, *168–169*
"specifying the problem" learning activities 56, 58–59
spontaneous collaboration 118
spontaneous learning 13, 43, 161
sports 64
staff characteristics *169*, 177
Standard for Full Registration (GTCS) 102
Statistical Package for Social Sciences (SPSS, Kinnear and Gray) 106
Sterck, G. 156, 158
Stewart, J. 24, 25
stimuli for learning 7, 58
Stowe, S. 18, 24
Strategic Leverage through Learning© 180
student-centred learning 100
sub-tasks 47 *see also* complexity of work tasks
supervisors 24–25, 84
Supina, J. 171
support 114, 124 *see also* antecedents to learning; mentors

talking and learning 46–47, 146
task experience 67, 73–75
Teacher Induction Scheme (Scotland 2002) 102

teaching: classroom experience 101, 119; workshops 22 *see also* new teacher learning
team players 20
teams 40
temporary roles 144
tenure 18
Tesch-Römer, C. 4, 63–64, 66, 75
theoretical frameworks 3–6, 155, 163–165, 171, 172
theories 4–6
theory-of-action analysis 180
theory-of-change evaluation 180
theory of learning and change 172
theory of learning (Skinner) 2
Tikkanen, T. 24
time as an inhibitor 27
time (coding) 129
Toms, E. G. 48
trade union members 19
Training and Development 1–2
training centres 154
"transfer" metaphor 138
transformational learning theory (Mezirow) 3
trial-and-error learning 25
triggers for learning 9; contextual factors 181; disturbances 46, 173; errors 41; feedback 76; and learning activities 44–46; learning at work 162, 163; learning dispositions 20, 120, 123; supervisors' activities 25; teachers' induction year *124*; teaching 116–122; "what would you do" question *55–56*; work tasks 41
Tynjälä, P. 14, 81, 173

UNESCO 158–159
unintended informal learning 13
universal theoretical framework *see* comprehensive theoretical frameworks
University of Aberdeen 103
"unplanned" learning 161 *see also* spontaneous learning
unstructured learning 13
Unwin, L. 122

validation 7
valid/invalid information 64

validity of environments 65–66
Van Bree, L. 158
Van der Heijden, B. 19, 27
Van Valckenborgh, K. 173
Van Woerkom, M. 18, 19, 21, 26, 27
variables, and factors 172–177, 180–182
Vignette Technique 50–53, 58, 180
vocational education 85
Volpe, M. 6, 66, 67, 162, 171
VTO policy 182

Walker, D. 3
"war for talent" 154
Waterhouse, J. 48
Watkins, K. E.: everyday encounters 83; informal learning characteristics 162; informal learning definition 13; informal learning model 6, 45, 46, 175; learning climate 67, 70
Watts, G. 66
Wenger, E. 3, 102, 114, 123, 127, 136
Wilcoxon Signed Rank Test 56
Willemsen, M. 69
work areas 23
work-embedded activities 174–175
work engagement 20
worker safety 143
working and learning, relationship 173
"working while learning" 154
workplace, defining 157, 159
"Workplace Informal Learning Matrix" (CEW) 165
workplace learning: activities as learning opportunities 13, 42; apprenticeships 1; defining 3, 159–161; factors affecting 126; organisational environment 21–29; start and end points 162; use of terminology 30 *see also* learning at work
work-related learning 3, 5
workshops 22
workspaces 24
work task characteristics 41, 46, 47, 48 *see also* complexity of work tasks

young people 18–19

Zapf, D. 41, 45, 46